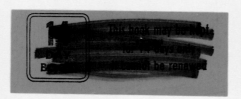

THE GLORIOUS FAILURE

Black Congressman
Robert Brown Elliott
and the Reconstruction
in South Carolina

PEGGY LAMSON

W · W · NORTON & COMPANY · INC ·
NEW YORK

COPYRIGHT © 1973 BY PEGGY LAMSON

First Edition

Library of Congress Cataloging in Publication Data

Lamson, Peggy.
  The glorious failure.

  Bibliography: p.
    1. Reconstruction—South Carolina. 2. South
Carolina—Politics and government—1865–1950.
3. Elliott, Robert Brown, 1842–1844.   I. Title.
F274.L3   1973   975.7'04   75–152665
ISBN 0–393–05451–9

To Constance Baker Motley
with thanks for starting me on this path

Contents

Preface

THERE ARE countless people in the United States who know a great deal about the Civil War, but few who are very keenly aware of the period which followed—that gray era known as the Reconstruction when four million Negroes ceased to be property and became citizens. The years from 1868 to 1877 are a historical vacuum, forgotten or misunderstood by a surprisingly large number of Americans. Until four years ago, I myself fell into the category of those who knew nothing whatsoever about this epoch.

I recall that when Edward W. Brooke was elected to the Senate from my own state in 1966, various newspapers referred to him as the first black senator since Reconstruction. But somehow the significance of that statement never registered. It was not until I heard Judge Constance Baker Motley discussing the black legislators who were in the United States Congress during the Reconstruction era that I made the startling "discovery" that between 1869 and 1877 sixteen Negroes—all from Southern states—served in Washington, two in the Senate and fourteen in the House of Representatives. Equally stunning to me was the revelation that in two of the eleven ex-Confederate states—South Carolina and Mississippi—the newly enfranchised blacks constituted a majority of the voting population and held undisputed control of their state legislatures.

Here indeed seemed fruitful material to pursue. Three ques-

9

tions at once suggested themselves. First, what was the train of events which moved the blacks in the three short years after Appomattox from degradation to supremacy? Second, what ultimately ended their dominance in the Southern states? And third, why is the story of their nine years in power of interest today? It is my hope that the first two questions have been answered fully in the pages which follow, and that the third—the relevancy of that decade for today's readers—will be painfully implicit. Still, a brief setting of the scene seems in order here.

In 1865, at the close of the Civil War, the defeated Southern states were under the jurisdiction of provisional governments appointed by President Andrew Johnson, who was following Lincoln's "with malice toward none and charity for all" plan of reconstruction. These provisional governments were made up entirely of Confederate leaders who accepted the inevitability of emancipating the slaves but, nonetheless, adopted a series of Black Codes designed to subordinate the freedmen and, in the view of many modern historians, to push them "a giant step backward toward slavery." The repressive actions of the Southern states infuriated and stiffened the backs of the Radical Republicans in Congress, who reacted by repudiating Johnson's mild reconstruction policy and by refusing to seat the Southern senators and representatives elected by the white provisional governments.

Spurred by the Radical Republicans (in this book the reader must accustom himself to thinking in general of the Republicans as liberals and the Democrats as conservatives), the Congress in 1866 proposed the Fourteenth Amendment to give the Negroes full citizenship, which, of course, meant the vote. In the same year the Radicals' hand was much strengthened by the severe reverses that all of the pro-Johnson candidates throughout the country suffered in the fall elections. Shortly thereafter Congress passed the first of its Reconstruction acts designed to protect the political rights of Negroes; a temporary military occupation of the South marked the beginning of the Radical Reconstruction.

In late 1867 and early 1868, blacks in the eleven Southern states, voting for the first time, elected delegates to the constitutional conventions which were being convened throughout the South to draw up new constitutions embodying universal manhood suffrage and other civil reforms, and to elect new legislatures. It was at this point in history, during a period of cataclysmic change and turmoil, that Negroes began to play significant roles in shaping their own destiny.

The era ended in 1877 when the so-called Redeemers, through the Democratic party, regained political control of the South and white supremacy again prevailed. From that time on, the blacks lost their rightful political power, and gradually most of them were in effect disenfranchised by literacy tests and other restrictive election practices which defied the entire intent of the Fourteenth and Fifteenth amendments. Only six blacks served in Congress during the remaining years of the nineteenth century. From 1901 until 1929 no blacks from any section of the country were elected to either the House or the Senate. Thus far in this century only one black from any of the eleven Southern states has stood in the halls of Congress—Andrew Young of Georgia, elected in 1972.

The brief period of the Radical or Black Reconstruction was almost invariably regarded by late-nineteenth- and early-twentieth-century historians as a disaster. The titles of their books alone— *The Tragic Era, The Dreadful Decade, The Age of Hate*—reflect a prevalent view that those years represented, as one historian put it, "the nadir of national disgrace." Black legislators were regularly dismissed as ignorant or corrupt or both, and linked, always in pejorative terms, with carpetbaggers and scalawags, the opportunists and collaborationists of the day.

In the 1930s, however, this one-dimensional view of Reconstruction was subjected to new scrutiny by a group of revisionists spearheaded by W. E. B. DuBois, the first black scholar to write extensively on the epoch. Today most historians, while conceding some of the shoddy aspects of the era, have increasingly come to recognize the many positive and innovative accomplishments which took place during this brief and poignant chapter in the history of our country.

Reconstruction was a time of great promise for blacks. After the dark years of slavery, when the Negro counted as only three-fifths of a man, he was, with the passage of the Fourteenth Amendment, at last accorded the full privileges of citizenship. He could no longer be deprived of his life, liberty, or property without due process of law. There were reasonable men (then as now) who believed that the blacks were ill prepared to accept their manifest rights in one fell swoop, that they should have been indoctrinated slowly into the ways of freedom. But those who argued thus failed to appreciate, among other things, the tremendous power and skill which emerging black statesmen exercised to help their race progress with equanimity and understanding from emancipation to enfranchisement and toward equality. The sixteen men who served in the federal Congress during Reconstruction—two senators and one representative from Mississippi, six representatives from South Carolina, three from Alabama, and one each from Georgia, North Carolina, Florida, and Louisiana—were the apotheosis of such leadership.

It had been my intention to write this book about eight of these legislators, but I soon found that I had a growing partiality toward one of them, that it was always the name of Robert Brown Elliott of South Carolina that I looked up first in library catalogues, in archives, and in indexes. The more I learned about Elliott, the more drawn I was to him, at first by the intriguing mystery of his origins, but then increasingly, as I came to know him, by the clarity of his mind, by his vision, his compassion, his eloquence, his fiery spirit, and his anger. Others among the sixteen men had some of these qualities; none, I believe, demonstrated them so compellingly. So, inevitably, I gave in to Robert Brown Elliott. Furthermore, since South Carolina had sent the largest delegation of representatives to Washington and was also one of the two states which had a black majority, it seemed eminently suitable to set the story of Reconstruction there and to tell it from the point of view of the man who, more than any other statesman on the scene, tried to grasp the historical imperative of his own time.

Elliott's enemies—and he had many—always referred to him as the "ablest colored man in South Carolina" and cited his great and, they thought, dangerous influence over the blacks. His friends, of whom he also had many, knew that Robert Brown Elliott would use this influence to the last drop of his prodigious energy to fight for binding civil rights legislation (a phrase that was as prominent in the 1870s as it has been in the 1960s and 1970s) to insure lasting equality for his race.

Reconstruction has been termed a "glorious failure"—glorious because it was a beginning, a noble experiment which encouraged Negroes to look forward to the day when race would no longer

be a factor in judging men and their capabilities; a failure because in the end it only served to sharpen, perhaps irrevocably,
the subtle antagonisms which divided whites and blacks. Robert
Brown Elliott's dedicated efforts mirrored these hopes and dis-
appointments.

PEGGY LAMSON

Cambridge, Massachusetts
September 1972

Acknowledgments

I AM HAPPY to acknowledge the kindness and cooperation of at least some of the many people who helped me in the preparation of this book. My first thanks must necessarily go to the staffs of the various libraries where I did my research for their generous guidance in leading me through unfamiliar labyrinths and onto proper paths. In South Carolina the Department of Archives and History yielded my most valuable source material; from that institution I should like especially to thank archivists Nicholas Olsberg and Wylma Wates for their interest and for their many imaginative suggestions. Both the South Caroliniana Library at the University of South Carolina and the Charleston Library Society were important treasurehouses for me. I am grateful to Mrs. Clara May Jacobs of the South Caroliniana Library for her assistance in the manuscript division, to Mr. E. L. Innabinet for his generosity in providing me with interlibrary loans, and to Miss Virginia Rugheimer of the Charleston Library Society for her many attentions.

I am fortunate to live near and have access to the Harvard College Library, with its magnificent collection of books and manuscripts (many dealing directly with South Carolina during Reconstruction), and the Boston Athenaeum, which has an outstanding number of Republican newspapers of the Reconstruction —a rarity in South Carolina itself. The staffs of both these libraries have been exceedingly forebearing and have cheerfully granted my many requests. For special favors I should like to thank Judith Harding and Hilda Conlon.

Without the riches of the Library of Congress and the National Archives, this book could not have been written. Mrs. Mary C. Lethbridge of the Library of Congress and Mr. William Lind of the National Archives greatly facilitated my work at these institutions. I am also indebted to the staffs of the Duke University Library, the Moorland Collection at Howard University, the Beaufort (South Carolina) Township Library, the Schomburg Collection of the New York Public Library, the Massachusetts Historical Society, the American Antiquarian Society, the Boston Public Library, and the Boston University Library.

Of the four important books which deal directly with the Negro in South Carolina during Reconstruction, the oldest, John S. Reynolds's *Reconstruction in South Carolina, 1865–1877,* while expressing a viewpoint quite opposite from my own, has nonetheless been a valuable source of hard facts. Alrutheus A. Taylor's pioneer revisionist work of 1924 has also been very useful. I have borrowed most heavily from Francis B. Simkins's and Robert H. Woody's classic *South Carolina During Reconstruction* and from both authors' numerous scholarly articles on this subject, and have also had the pleasure of meeting and receiving encouragement from Mr. Woody himself. The most recent book, Joel Williamson's *After Slavery: The Negro in South Carolina During Reconstruction, 1861–1877,* has been for me an invaluable interpretive study; furthermore Dr. Williamson has, from the moment of my first letter to him, been generous in sharing with me his knowledge and understanding of the period and staunchly supportive of my efforts to untangle its complexities.

I have been greatly assisted (and rarely impeded) by numerous friends and relatives. The law firm of Hamilton and Lamson has helped me to penetrate some of the legal and constitutional problems posed by this book, as has Eliza McCormack Feld, who is both a lawyer and a novelist of note. Betty Fladeland, a distinguished American historian, kindly read my manuscript in its early stages and in doing so forestalled numerous blunders. Even more importantly, she helped by her lucid comments to enlighten me on many aspects of nineteenth-century American history. Professor Hallett Smith took time from his own researches at the Huntington Library to find an important Elliott letter about which

I would otherwise not have known. Dr. Laurence Bryant of South Carolina State College has been unfailingly kind and cooperative in putting his materials at my disposal.

For the literally hundreds of people who answered my letters of inquiry with helpful suggestions I must content myself with a blanket expression of appreciation which I hope each will accept in lieu of a personal thanks.

There is no way in which I can properly express my gratitude and affection for the two persons most closely connected with this project. Maxine Terner has worked with me from the outset as research assistant and typist and has performed both these functions with high intelligence and skill; she has, furthermore, constantly encouraged me by her own commitment to the idea and substance of this book. Carol Hulsizer has contributed her talents, her patience, and her understanding toward bringing about a wide range of improvements in the manuscript. I owe her warmest thanks for helping me to clarify my thoughts and the manner in which I expressed them.

Finally my thanks go, as always, to my husband, Roy Lamson, himself no stranger to the world of scholarly research, who has during the past four years listened with equal tolerance to my complaints and my boasts and tactfully persuaded me that neither were justified.

THE GLORIOUS FAILURE

Black Congressman Robert Brown Elliott
and the Reconstruction in South Carolina

1

A Man of Mystery

I N M A R C H of 1867 Robert Brown Elliott, an intense, articulate young Negro from the North, became associate editor of
the *South Carolina Leader,* a position somewhat less impressive
than its title indicates, for the *Leader* was a Republican newspaper in a state where there were few Republicans who could
read. The war between the states had been over for barely two
years; virtually no whites, from the Bourbon aristocrats to the
sand-hill crackers, could stomach the Republican party—the party
of Abraham Lincoln. In the second-floor office of the *Leader* at
430 King Street in Charleston, however, Elliott and Richard Cain,
the editor of the paper, were concerned not with how few white
Republicans there were in South Carolina, but rather with how
many black Republicans they hoped there soon would be.

In Washington the Radical wing of the Republican party, in
opposition to President Andrew Johnson, had just that month
passed two Reconstruction acts which were to give blacks political
equality. In a short time the Negro would, for the first time in history, register to vote. The vast majority of the emancipated freedmen were illiterate, but they had already shown a keen interest in
exercising the rights which their new citizenship would confer
upon them. And the question which the two Negro editors
pondered was whether members of their race would, from long
habit, follow their former white masters or whether they would

cast their lot with the Republicans who had won these new rights for them.

The *South Carolina Leader,* with its limited circulation, was to have only a brief life; but as one of the first newspapers in the South to be published and edited primarily by blacks, it was an influential voice in the newly emerging social order.

Antebellum Charleston, the most important metropolis of the Palmetto State, had been a city infatuated with its own prosperity as a busy port and commercial center, proud of its glorious history. Its charming street life flourished and an air of grace radiated from its white-pillared, balconied homes. Postwar Charleston was a city cruelly devastated; what the shelling of the Union Army had not destroyed, the military occupation had. After Appomattox its banking capital and private resources were depleted, its railroad and shipping lines were out of commission; but still Charleston retained its indomitable pride. Weary, bitter, yet determined, the people began to rebuild. Damage was repaired, new construction undertaken along the city's labyrinthine streets. Trade revived at a promising pace and the pulse of Charleston quickened. However, by 1867, its traditional power structure was threatened by a new reality. Of the city's nearly fifty thousand residents, half were blacks who now demanded a role in the destiny of their city, their state, and their nation.

When the twenty-five-year-old Elliott became associate editor of the *South Carolina Leader,* a change appeared on its masthead for which he must have been, at least in part, responsible. Since 1865, when the *Leader* first started publication, the slogan had been a quotation from Paul, "First the blade, then the ear, after that the full corn in the ear." But Robert Brown Elliott was not a gradualist. Under his editorship the slogan became simply "Equality and Union."

Elliott was a full-blooded black of medium height with close-cropped hair and a neatly trimmed mustache. Buoyant, graceful, vigorous, he was described by one of his contemporaries as having a "countenance stamped with soul and intelligence" and by another friend as "commanding in appearance, yet by his easy manner and his kind words inspiring love, confidence and respect." [1]

A longtime associate who was a printer at the *Leader* recalled his first sight of the new young editor. Elliott had just returned from a mass meeting, one of many he must have addressed during that spring of 1867, exhorting the blacks to vote, and vote Republican. He came bounding up the stairs to the office, in high spirits, and stopped before going into his office to say a few words about the meeting. He was full of enthusiasm. "I thundered," he said, "and by golly they cheered." [2]

So he began his career in South Carolina, a career which would see him become a moving force within the Republican party, a powerful legislator in the state, a proud and respected leader of the freedmen whom he represented in the federal Congress, and an eloquent spokesman for his race everywhere.

Robert Brown Elliott had first appeared in South Carolina sometime after the war. Gradually an elaborate tale of his antecedents began to unfold—a tale which was accepted by his contemporaries and which has persisted to the present day.

He was born in Boston of West Indian parents, so the story goes, on August 11, 1842. He was educated in private schools in that city before being sent to Jamaica (to a rich uncle, according to one source) for more schooling. [3] In 1853 he went to England and attended High Holborn (sometimes referred to as High Hollow) Academy; in 1855 he entered England's celebrated Eton College, from which he graduated with honors in 1859. Subsequently he read law with Sergeant FitzHerbert before returning to the United States in 1861.

Accounts vary concerning his activities during the next few years. While Elliott himself implied that he served in the Union Army, a contemporary story says he was in the Union Navy; it also mentions a wound which left him with a slight limp and speaks of his voyages to Ireland, Scotland, South America, and the West Indies. [4] Most biographical notes simply pass over the period of the war altogether and suggest that he went to South Carolina some time after the fall of Richmond as a printer and then became editor of the *Leader*.

The only portion of the account of Robert Brown Elliott that is incontestable is that, as of March 23, 1867, he was associate editor of the *South Carolina Leader*. There is no record of his birth in Boston in 1842, or in any other year. This in itself is not definitive, since birth records, particularly of "people of colour," were notoriously sparse in the nineteenth century. However, there is no mention of Elliott in any accounts of prominent Negroes who had lived in Boston prior to the Civil War, which casts suspicion on Elliott's claim that he was born there.[5]

Of some significance is the fact that Elliott's death certificate states that he was a native of South Carolina and that the records of St. Louis Cemetery in New Orleans,[6] where he is buried, say that both he and his parents were born in South Carolina.* It is possible that Elliott's wife, who survived him, was so stricken with grief at his untimely death that she could not put her mind on the formalities; therefore, the New Orleans doctor, I. T. Newman, who attended Elliott in his last illness, knowing that his patient had been a congressman from South Carolina, may simply have assumed that he was born there (and his parents before him) and so entered it on the death and cemetery certificates.

More blatant discrepancies in Elliott's accepted biography concern his education in England. In the first place, there is no evidence that a High Holborn Academy ever existed, though it is difficult—and in this case quite impossible—to prove that such an institution did not exist, for there were many short-lived, unregistered schools in England during the nineteenth century.

But as to Elliott's alleged education at Eton College, the authorities there categorically state that no Robert Brown Elliott ever attended Eton, nor is it possible that he enrolled under a different name, for there was no one who could have fit his description at the school during the years 1853 to 1859.[7]

In the second place, there is every reason to view his study of law with Sergeant FitzHerbert in London with skepticism. Sergeant is neither a name nor a military designation, but a legal title which at that time was given to the highest rank of barrister in England and Ireland. The title is extinct today, the order having been dissolved in 1877. Yet students of law familiar with practices in England at the time point out that traditionally a young man who read law nearly always did so with a so-called junior, almost never with a king's counsel and certainly not with one of the rare and lofty sergeants. Furthermore, the yearly Law Lists

* There is another reference to the South Carolina origin of Elliott's parents in a sketch of him written by the Negro historian, John W. Cromwell, in which the author opens with the conventional account, but challenges it in a footnote stating, "A very high authority who knew Elliott intimately says he was born of South Carolinian not West Indian parentage" (*The Negro in American History*, p. 179).

in which were printed the names of the relatively few members of the Order of Sergeants did not include the name FitzHerbert for the relevant years.

Finally, there is no mention of Elliott in lists of Negroes in the Union Navy, nor in any of the rosters of black regiments in the Union Army.[8] In sum, his name does not seem to appear in any accounts of any sort until 1867.

If then one accepts the conclusion that vital portions of Robert Brown Elliott's accepted biography are false, one is left with the puzzling and intriguing question of just what the truth is about the early life of this man of mystery.

If he did not go to Eton, where then was he educated? For educated he certainly was, and brilliantly so. If he did not read law with Sergeant FitzHerbert, could his legal preparation have been limited, as John Cromwell suggests, to a "six months close study of the South Carolina Code," after which he passed a rigid examination and was admitted to the bar? *

And if he was born, not in Boston, but in South Carolina, was he then born of slave parents and could they have come North on the Underground Railroad sometime after their son's birth? If so, it would have been quite logical for them (and later on their son) to have lied to protect those who helped them to freedom. This would have been particularly likely after 1850 when the Fugitive Slave Law made rescue or concealment of a slave punishable by six months' imprisonment and a $2,000 fine. However, if his parents had been runaway slaves, one would think that Elliott, with his intense pride of race and his flair for the dramatic, would have boasted in every speech he ever made of his hair-raising escape from the South and the cruel treatment which necessitated it.

Contemporary newspaper references to Elliott's antecedents tended to confirm first one theory, then another; all, unfortunately, within the realm of pure speculation. For example, the *New York Herald* of October 17, 1874, refers to Elliott at the height of his career as "the only important negro † in South Carolina who

* Cromwell's footnote gives as his source for the statement about Elliott's legal training the Honorable T. McCants Stewart, who was Elliott's law partner and who years later wrote Elliott's obituary for the *New York Globe.*

† Capitalization of the word *Negro* was first introduced during the Reconstruction period, but in actual practice was rarely used at that time.

cordially resents the white man's former mastery, having family reasons anterior to emancipation to hate the white race." This story could reinforce the hypothesis of Elliott as the son of runaway slave parents.

Quite different conjectures spring to mind when one considers an earlier reference to Elliott in the *New York Times* of January 23, 1868, which characterizes him as "very black, very well spoken and bitter as gall," then goes on to say that "he received an education abroad at the expense of a Southern gentleman." Could that Southern gentleman have been one of the many South Carolina Elliotts (all of whom spelled their name with two *l*'s and two *t*'s) from whom Robert might have derived his name? Could the boy have been brought up on one of the Elliott plantations and might he have attracted the interest of a benevolent master who decided to give him the education which he was denied by law in South Carolina? But what then of the rich West Indian uncle who paid for his nephew's early schooling in Jamaica?

One of the fullest, and at the same time the most absurdly contradictory, accounts of Elliott's early years appeared in the April 12, 1874, *St. Louis Globe* and was reprinted four days later in the *National Republican*. The full-page story, headed "The Colored Congressman. How the Enfranchised Race is Represented in Washington," was written by Marie LeBaron and placed Robert Elliott first among the seven Negroes then serving in the Forty-third Congress. After a lengthy and complimentary physical description of her subject ("teeth perfect and white in strong contrast with surrounding color, . . . deep in chest, broad in the shoulders, shapely in limb"), Miss LeBaron went on to say that he was "born free in New England, and from childhood was remarkable for exhibitions of mental power that, notwithstanding a weight of color and poverty, would not 'down.' "

To illustrate the brilliance of her favorite "sable legislator" the writer recounted a story. In a small town in New York state young Elliott appeared one day, "a boy of sixteen, a ragged negro, to deliver an anti-slavery lecture. . . . The members of the little village lyceum were so impressed with the boy's ability," the story continues, "that they cordially invited him to remain and take part in a debate, the question for discussion being the feasibility of immediate abolition of slavery. Among the members of the lyceum were several who have since proven their mental caliber in Congress and in various official positions." Apparently Elliott, "in his ragged dress and with a modest and unassuming manner," demolished his opponents and thrilled his supporters in words that were "electrical with a strange eloquence." [9]

Having told this story, Miss LeBaron then picked up an entirely different skein and with fine disregard for consistency went on in the next paragraph to repeat the standard biography of her subject, gleaned probably from the Congressional Directory (which Elliott himself must have written), mentioning that he entered High Holborn Academy in London in 1853 (at the age of eleven), went on to Eton at the age of fourteen, graduated with honors at seventeen. In other words, at the precise moment when he was a ragged boy astounding and confounding his elders in a little town in New York state, he was also marching around a little town in England in a high silk hat, short black jacket, and stiff white collar doing honors work as a student at Eton College.

The most significant newspaper reference to Elliott apparently passed unnoticed, or at least unchallenged when it was printed in the *Charleston Daily News* on February 25, 1871, and has never, it seems, been considered by later historians.

This account was reprinted from a New England newspaper, the *Charlestown* (Massachusetts) *Chronicle,* where it first appeared on February 18, 1871, in a column headed "Brief Locals." Elliott had just been elected to Congress and was in Washington preparing to take his seat; the *Chronicle* noted that three years ago Congressman-elect Elliott had been a typesetter in Boston. At that time, they said, he had lived in the West End of the city and had, during the few months he was there, established quite a popularity and had been a prominent member of the colored literary society. He had also during his stay in Boston married a handsome and intelligent mulatto girl.

"Mr. Elliott," the story continued, "was born and educated in Liverpool, England,* where he also learned the printers trade.[10] He has travelled considerably, and has served in the English Navy. His education is quite complete, he possessing a good knowledge

---

* Neither the county archivist in the Lancashire Record Office nor the superintendent registrar of Liverpool has been able to find any record of Elliott's birth in that city. However, there were many blacks in Liverpool in the nineteenth century, since this port was a stopping place for slave ships bound from Africa to America, and some fortunate souls managed to escape.

of classical literature, and speaking and writing the English, Latin, French and Spanish languages. He has the reputation of being the ablest colored man in the South."

The "Brief Local" ended by saying that Elliott had left Boston to go to Charleston, South Carolina, where he became one of the editors of a Republican paper published by colored men.

Given the many disparate facts, half-truths, contradictions, and outright lies surrounding Elliott's background, this little item offers by all odds the most plausible explanation. Although unfortunately none of the details can be proved, it still provides the basis for a strong presumption about Elliott's early years.

First, it answers satisfactorily the question of Elliott's obviously superior education as demonstrated by his elegant Spencerian script, the graceful turn of his written phrases, the eloquence and the wealth of literary and historical references in his speeches. It would have been very difficult indeed for a Negro boy growing up before the Civil War to have received a classical education anywhere in the United States. In the South, of course, an education of any sort was impossible; but, even in Boston, home of the abolitionists and enlightened social thinkers of the period, Negroes were admitted only to segregated public schools until 1855, and even then there were no public high schools which accepted blacks.

But in England, where because there were so few Negroes there was virtually no race problem, a little black boy could have attended a borough or parish school along with the white boys. A second reason to believe that Elliott was an Englishman was his Eton College fable. Had he been an American boy educated somehow in one of the small private schools that were started in the North for Negro children, would he ever have heard of Eton College, let alone known enough about it to invent the improbable story of having studied there and graduated with honors? By the same token a British upbringing would much more readily explain his figment of Sergeant FitzHerbert. Surely only a few Americans had the remotest knowledge of the Order of Sergeants, and probably even the average Briton was unaware of this recondite legal society. But a British schoolboy who had set the law as his ultimate goal in life could certainly have been familiar with the entire structure of the English bar.

A further point favoring his British origin is that it credibly explains why there were no traces of Elliott's antecedents or endeavors anywhere in the United States until he was twenty-five years old. In the case of all other Negroes who were prominent during the Reconstruction, there was solid documentation concerning birth, education (if any), employment, and service during the Civil War. For Robert Brown Elliott there was only a vacuum, one which might now be filled by the story of his Liverpool birthplace, his apprenticeship as a printer, his service in the British Navy, and his extensive travels.

Still, the Liverpool saga leaves a crucial question unresolved. If Elliott had indeed been born in England, why did he not say so? What possible reason would he have had for fabricating a Boston birthplace?

Here one can only construct a scenario which could be a speculation far off the mark but which has much to recommend it as a logical and even a probable truth: Suppose that Robert Brown Elliott, a seaman in the British Navy, had put in at the port of Boston in the year 1866 or 1867 and decided to remain, either jumping ship or legally signing off. As a trained printer he would not have had difficulty finding work as a typesetter. Certainly the West End was a part of the city where he might well have lived; his popularity and his involvement with the intellectual Negroes of Boston were entirely consistent.

Suppose that one of his friends, perhaps another printer or a member of the Negro literary society, knew of the *South Carolina Leader* (a distinct possibility since the *Leader* carried many advertisements of Boston companies) and suggested to Elliott that a black man of his ability might move more rapidly from typesetter to editor in South Carolina than in Massachusetts. Suppose that Elliott went south primarily because a better opportunity beckoned, although a concern for the status of the freedmen could certainly have also been a factor.

Suppose, finally, that during his few months in Boston he had not yet begun the process—had perhaps not yet even considered the possibility—of becoming an American citizen. It is known that, on his arrival in South Carolina, Elliott was at once drawn into the vortex of a new political life in which his race was for the first time playing a vital role. Negroes and whites alike were soon to elect delegates to a constitutional convention. Elliott, with a handful of other educated blacks, was a natural candidate. Given the fast-moving pressure of events, he had no time to wait for citizenship papers. He had either to renounce elective office entirely until he became naturalized, or simply to confer American citizenship upon himself.

It is reasonable to assume that Elliott would have had no qualms in choosing the latter course. No one knew better than he how few qualified Negroes there were in South Carolina and how desperately the freedmen needed forceful, intelligent, thoughtful leadership. He did not suffer from false modesty. He must have known he had much to contribute and, convinced of that, he might easily have justified the invention of his Boston birthplace as a small and quite unimportant expedient.

Merely inventing Boston was not enough, however. There was that vacuum to be filled and Elliott must have decided to fill it with a flourish. Eton College was his boldest conceit; audaciously he placed himself as a student in one of the oldest, most eminent, and, from his point of view, most unlikely institutions of learning in the world; and he got away with it throughout his lifetime and beyond.

Why no one, publicly at least, ever questioned his antecedents is indeed puzzling. The story from the *Charlestown* (Massachusetts) *Chronicle* was after all reprinted in the *Charleston* (South Carolina) *Daily News,* where any of Elliott's political enemies among the white Democrats could have read it. Some of them certainly must have seen it, for the story, though brief and inconspicuous, appeared on the front page of the paper. And anyone reading it must have wondered: Born and educated in Liverpool? This black carpetbagger from Massachusetts, this Eton man? Yet apparently no one challenged him.

If Elliott himself saw the piece in the *News,* he must also have decided to ignore it in order not to call further attention to the discrepancies in his, by then, "official" biography. For, once elected a delegate to the South Carolina Constitutional Convention, the die was cast for him. It would have been too late—and too dangerous—for him to go off quietly and start the process of taking out citizenship papers. He was committed irrevocably to his alleged Boston birthplace.

If this hypothesis is true, it then follows that Robert Brown Elliott never became an American citizen, in which case he was, and will doubtless remain, the only British subject ever to be a member of the House of Representatives of the United States of America.

There were nearly as many conflicting stories about Elliott's wife as there were about his own origins and early years. The reality, however, was that, at least from 1870—and probably earlier— until his death in 1884 Robert Brown Elliott was married to Grace Lee Elliott. This fact is attested to by the numerous land deeds dating from 1870 to 1879, and also by a letter which Elliott wrote to Grace L. Elliott in 1871 which began "my dear wife" and which years later she probated as his will.

It will be remembered that the *Charlestown* (Massachusetts) *Chronicle* referred to his having married a handsome and intelligent mulatto girl during his stay in Boston.* In South Carolina the first mention of Elliott's wife was made by the venerable, though hardly objective, *Charleston Mercury*. In an 1868 thumbnail sketch of Elliott they wrote, "In the Zenith of his importance and glory he took unto himself a wife in the person of an abandoned mulatto woman of notorious habits and character, repudiated even by the negroes." This hardly sounds like a handsome, intelligent mulatto girl from Boston, but doubtless even so wide a discrepancy can be attributed to the *Mercury's* rabid anti-Republicanism.

More in line with the *Chronicle* story from Massachusetts was the view expressed by Marie LeBaron in her *St. Louis Globe* report. Observing Mrs. Elliott as she sat in the visitor's gallery of the House of Representatives listening to her young husband deliver his famous civil rights speech in January of 1873, the effusive Miss LeBaron described her as a "quadroon with the complexion of the creamy hue of Southern magnolia, just tinted with the suggestion of primroses on cheeks and lips." Her eyes, gushed Miss LeBaron, were large, brown, and expressive, and under their long lashes she had the "sweetest brightest expression and manner in the world. She was, in sum, one of the most beautiful and intelligent of women."

Total confusion on the subject of Elliott's wife stems from a story printed in 1874 in the *New York Herald* on the South Carolina "Beggars on Horseback." The paragraph on Elliott, headed "The King Congo" described his pretty white-trellised and mansarded cottage in "the best quarter of town," his yard filled with magnolia and mock orange, his fine stable of horses. Then the story went on to say, "He is in debt and the cottage is held

* No record of this union can be found in Boston's Registry Division.

in his wife's name. She used to flourish in Columbia as a pretty rose-tinted light mulatto under the name of Nancy Fat. Removed from the loose foundations of slavery she has been a very fair mistress of her own home, barring a little mutual jealousy here and there." [11]

The change in names could conceivably have been a misprint (except that Nancy Fat sounds very little like Grace Lee). Even more specious is the "cottage held in his wife's name," for, although both of Elliott's Columbia houses were indeed held in his wife's name, the deeds indicate indisputably that that name was Grace L. Elliott.[12]

However, another account bears out the *New York Herald* story. It is contained in a book called *Recollections of a Rebel Reefer* written by a Southern gentleman named James Morris Morgan in 1917. The paragraph about Nancy Fat, which is full of lively exaggeration and heedless inaccuracy, was used by the author to illustrate his conviction that the Negroes had not only been quite content with the ways of slavery but that in fact they often looked back quite wistfully on the good old days:

> The speaker of the House was a very highly educated and able man, as black as a highly polished boot; some said that he was a Jamaica negro who had been to school in England and others insisted that he was a product of Harvard University. Be that as it may, he certainly was one of the most brilliant orators I ever heard speak. His name was Eliot [sic], and he evidently had a susceptible heart, for in the midst of his meteoric career of loot and pillage he fell desperately in love with Nancy, the most beautiful mulatto girl in Columbia. Nancy was the nurse-maid for Mrs. Heyward's little children, and although the Heywards, like all other aristocrats, had been impoverished by the war, and Nancy was then free, not even the high wages offered by the carpetbaggers could tempt her to leave those little children of whom she was so fond. But Eliot offered marriage, and the girl was dazzled by the high position to which he proposed to raise her, and tearfully she left the Heyward home to become the proud wife of the wealthy speaker. Nancy had been brought up among aristocrats and she knew how to do things. She was no sooner married than she set up a handsome establishment, and she could be seen in full ball toilet, in the middle of the day, with her neck and arms covered with jewels, driving down Main Street. But besides the love of finery Nancy had another side to

her character. Nothing could have induced her to stop in front of Mrs. Heyward's house in that costume or in her carriage, but in the cool of the afternoon, Nancy, arrayed in the neat cap and apron of a nursemaid, would stop her carriage around the corner from her former mistress's home, and alighting would walk to the house and beg to be allowed to take the children out. The people who had seen her in gala attire in the middle of the day would behold the strange spectacle of the same Nancy, as demure as a novice, seated on the front seat of her own landau, with the children occupying the back seat. Everybody liked Nancy and her promenades with the children were among the strange features of that strange time. Nancy attended one of the inauguration balls in Washington and was said to have been one of the most beautifully gowned women of the occasion.[13]

There is much about Mr. Morgan's little narrative that rings false. Certainly if Nancy Fat had been Robert Elliott's wife and had ever gone so far as to step out of her "full ball toilet" and into "the neat cap and apron of a nursemaid" in order to "beg" her former mistress to take the little Heyward children out for a drive, she would have done so only once. It is hard to imagine any action which would have been more infuriating to Elliott, who looked on any form of servility toward whites as nothing short of perfidious.

Still, it is difficult to dismiss entirely such widely separate sources as the *New York Herald* and Morgan's *Recollections.* Who then was Nancy Fat? Might that name have belonged to Mrs. Elliott as a young (and plump) girl in the days of slavery and been changed after the war to the more dignified Grace Lee? Or—and this seems more likely—was Nancy Fat a separate person who perhaps never became Nancy F. Elliott, but who was at some time the mistress of the hotheaded Elliott and the recipient of his extravagant favors? A sympathetic obituary speaks of the mistakes he made in his private life. Nancy Fat may well have been one of them.

But this, of course, is speculation. More significant than Robert Elliott's probable transgressions were his positive achievements. And these began as a matter of record on March 23, 1867, the day his name first appeared on the masthead of the *South Carolina Leader.*

2

All Colors and Conditions

ELLIOTT'S superior, who had been editor and publisher of the *Leader* since 1866, was forty-two-year-old Richard Harvey Cain. A clergyman, Cain had been sent south from Brooklyn, New York, by the African Methodist Episcopal Church to stimulate religious activity among the freedmen. His principal mission was to reorganize and rebuild the Emmanuel Church in Charleston, which had been closed since 1832 when Denmark Vesey was found to have laid plans for his famous insurrection within the sanctuary of the church.

Cain was a man of great energy and outstanding ability as an organizer. He must have had a great influence on his young assistant Elliott, for he was a shrewd character, intelligent and dedicated to the interests of the freedmen. Elliott, no less dedicated, was idealistic and hotheaded, while Cain achieved his purposes by more carefully calculated tactical moves.

Shortly after his arrival in the state, Cain spoke at the Colored People's Convention held in the Zion Church in Charleston in November 1865. The convention, which marked the first concerted action by the new Negro leadership in the state, was called primarily to protest the all-white state Constitutional Convention which had been convened two months earlier in Columbia by Provisional Governor Benjamin F. Perry.

The white Constitutional Convention (and the subsequent white legislature) accorded with President Andrew Johnson's attempt

34

to fulfill Lincoln's mild plan for Reconstruction. It was dominated by ex-Confederate leaders described by Governor Perry as the "ablest, wisest, most distinguished men of South Carolina," as in many instances they indeed were.

After nullifying the Ordinance of Secession, the Constitutional Convention voted 98 to 8 that "the slaves of South Carolina having been emancipated by the action of the United States authorities, neither slavery nor involuntary servitude . . . shall ever be reestablished in this state." [1]

With this acceptance of the inevitable, much of the wisdom ended. Members of the Constitutional Convention of 1865 would not listen to any suggestion of Negro suffrage, insisting over the objections of a prescient few that "the matter be ignored in toto." [2] Their failure to face a question that was central to the rights of the newly emancipated freedmen would have bitter repercussions for the whites within the next few years.

Even more dire consequences for the whites were to flow from the enactment, during the special legislature which immediately followed the Constitutional Convention, of the famous Black Code. Intended to clarify the position of the freedmen, the code, more than any other instrument, illustrated the attitude of the responsible Southern white ruling class toward the free black man. These Bourbons were well aware that they could not hold the Negro liable for all that plantation America had lost in the war; the planters were disposed by custom to deal with their former slaves kindly, paternalistically, and, by their lights, generously.

Their Black Code decreed, for example, that Negroes could acquire property, could sue and be sued, could enter into marriage contracts—children were to be given legitimate status—and could receive the protection of the law in person and property. All these rights were granted the blacks for the first time. On the other hand, the white man's basic view of the Negro as an inferior caste led to restrictions that treated the freedman oppressively.

No person of color could be employed in any capacity except "husbandry" or domestic service without a license that required him to prove his fitness for a trade or business and for which he was obliged to pay a fee of from $10 to $100. Servants must work from sunup to sundown; masters were given the right to "whip moderately" servants under eighteen.

For crimes "not infamous," which did not demand the death

sentence, colored persons could be confined at hard labor, whipped, enclosed in treadmills or stocks; but punishment no more degrading than imprisonment was to be imposed on white persons who committed the same crimes.[3]

Negroes were not permitted to join the state militia nor to keep a firearm, sword, or other military weapon except in the case of a farmer who was allowed a fowling piece. Nor could a black man be owner "in whole or in any part of any distillery where spiritous liquors of any kinds were made." [4] Vagrancy and idleness were punishable by imprisonment at hard labor not exceeding twelve months; the definition of a vagrant ranged from a person who did not have a fixed place of abode to one who hunted game of any description or fished on the land of others.

A Negro child could be apprenticed to a white master who was required to teach the apprentice a trade, furnish wholesome food, and, if there was a convenient school, to send the child there for six weeks each year. The apprentice was to receive up to $60 at the end of his service. The master was authorized to chastise the servant and to capture him in case of flight.

Throughout the Black Code the repeated use of the terms *master* and *servant,* the severity of the punishments, the many restrictions, and the obviously inferior status to which the Negro was assigned led to widespread fear among Negro leaders in the South and liberals in the North that the whites were attempting to keep the Negroes in a position of serfdom.

The Colored People's Convention assembled at the Zion Church in Charleston in November 1865 took up the cry against the Black Code and against the entire Constitutional Convention from which they had been excluded. In a sternly worded "memorial" they asked the Congress of the United States to place "the strong arm of the law over the entire population of the state," to grant equal suffrage, and to abolish the Black Code.[5]

Similar codes, some milder, some harsher than South Carolina's, were adopted by the other Confederate states in the fall of 1865. Their effect was to set off a reaction in Congress against President Johnson's conciliatory plan of Reconstruction, marking the beginning of a long tug of war between the legislative and the executive branches of the federal government. Johnson had initially appointed the provisional governors, who had convened the all-white constitutional conventions, which had in turn elected state legislatures, which then elected the first reunion representatives to Congress.

Congress responded—moved in large part by their dissatisfaction with the Black Codes—by refusing to seat the members-elect from South Carolina and the other Southern states.

Few South Carolinians of either color would have believed during that critical fall of 1865 that the men who would eventually represent them in the United States Congress would be drawn, not from the convention of "wise, able and distinguished men" convened by Governor Perry at the Baptist Church in Columbia, but from the Colored People's Convention which met at the Zion Church in Charleston.

South Carolina would soon send six Negroes to the House of Representatives during the Reconstruction, the largest number by far from any Southern state; four of these six had attended the Colored People's Convention. The other two had not: Elliott apparently had not arrived in the state at the time, and Robert Smalls, a naval war hero from Beaufort, had not yet entered the political arena. The other four were Richard H. Cain, Robert C. De Large, Alonzo J. Ransier, and Joseph H. Rainey. De Large, a light mulatto whose father was a Charleston tailor and whose mother a mantua, or cloakmaker, was himself a journeyman tailor by trade. By inclination, De Large was a politician; he attended every conceivable assemblage and talked continually at all of them. The phrase "on motion of R. C. De Large" appears again and again, sometimes two or three times on a page of proceedings of various meetings. Still, he was an able if slightly tricky parliamentarian who had considerable influence among the Charleston freedmen.

A more modest and straightforward man, Alonzo J. Ransier had been born free in Charleston. Destined to become the first black lieutenant governor of the state and then a congressman, Ransier was a typical compromise candidate, a reliable party workhorse, if not a great moving spirit. He was prominent at the Zion Church meeting as the man chosen to present the convention's petition to the federal Congress.

Joseph H. Rainey was the first Negro ever to sit in the United States House of Representatives and was to serve there for four terms. He was born of slave parents in Georgetown, South Carolina, but his father managed to purchase his family's freedom.

Rainey was a barber in Charleston at the beginning of the war; when drafted to work on the fortifications in Charleston, he escaped to the West Indies. Although largely uneducated, he had native wisdom and good judgment which won him respect, even among whites. As was true of many of the delegates, Rainey's appearance at the Zion Church marked his debut into public life; with Ransier he was chosen a vice-chairman of the convention.

Whitelaw Reid described one of the sessions of the Colored People's Convention in his book, *A Southern Tour, May 1, 1865 to May 1, 1866*. At the time Reid was a correspondent of Horace Greeley's *New York Tribune,* a liberal journal sympathetic to the freedmen; later he was to become its most celebrated managing editor. The meeting in Zion Church afforded Reid his first opportunity to observe large masses of Negroes assembled together. He found the audience "a study." On one side of the church sat the men, "a group of the blackest faces with the flattest noses and the wooliest heads, I ever saw." The freedmen represented "a range of all colors and conditions." Some were dressed like farm laborers, others in the garb of city workers—"in broadcloth, scarfs and gaudy pins"—and a few were decked out in full military regalia, including one with "an enormous regulation hat . . . of flowing plume, gild cord and knots." On the other side of the church where the women sat it was a "motley but brilliant array of bright colored turbans . . . tawdry bandanas, and hats of all shapes that have prevailed within the memory of this generation from bonnets to coquettish little bits of lace and flowers." Some wore kid gloves and a few, "barring the questionable complexion, had the air and bearing of ladies."

Reid was struck by the intelligent enthusiasm of the audience as they listened to an address by Salmon P. Chase, former secretary of the Treasury under Lincoln, who was at that time chief justice of the Supreme Court and one of the first Republicans openly to woo the Southern Negroes.

Although the chief justice's "single stump speech" drew patronizing comments from Reid, Chase's words contained both soothing balm and inspiration for his black listeners. He was not reticent about giving credit where he thought it was due. He pointed out that it was he, Chase, who had been the first to recognize that the colored people of the South were the natural allies of all the nation (prolonged cheers), that it was he, Chase, who had prevailed upon President Lincoln to "summon black soldiers to battle." Now he told his audience that he believed the ballot, "the freedman's weapon in peace," should replace the bayonet, "the freedman's weapon in war."

Then, in what Reid characterized as "Chase's usual avuncular attitude toward the 'helpless Negroes,' he reminded them that with the sudden emancipation of their great race numbering four millions of souls, people are waiting to see if the baleful predictions would prove true about their incompetence to live as freedmen.

"The answer to that question, men and women of color, is with you. Your enemies say that you will be disorderly, improvident; lazy; that wages will not tempt you to work; . . . that you will become drones and vagabonds. . . . It remains with you whether these [predictions] shall be fulfilled or not." Industry, morality, education, and religion would have their reward. And patience. "Show by your acts that you deserve to be entrusted with suffrage . . . and you will not have to wait very long." [6] They had exactly two years to wait, not only for suffrage but for the opportunity to become masters of their own fate.

Meanwhile, Negroes had to throw off their long habit of servility, which they managed with greater ease than was anticipated. As a modern historian has put it, "Most Negroes, to the dismay of their former masters, joyfully accepted their freedom; and for a time many of them took special pleasure in making use of one of its chief prerogatives: the right to move from place to place without the consent of any white man. . . . They wanted to see new things; they looked for relatives from whom they had been separated in slavery days; they went to cities in search of work or to find schools for their children. . . . There was, after all, only one way that the Negroes could learn to live as free men, and that was for them to *start* living as free men—to make mistakes and to profit from them." [7]

As they experimented and faltered and learned and progressed, the ultimate fate of the freedmen vacillated, depending largely upon who was ahead in the struggle between President Johnson and the Congress.

Essentially the controversy between the executive and the legislature involved, on the one hand, finding just terms to impose on the defeated white Southerners and, on the other, determining exactly how the free Negro would fit into the fabric of American life.

To this enormously complex question Andrew Johnson brought

two overriding personal prejudices, stemming from his origins as a poor white in Tennessee and which dominated his actions during the four years of his presidency: He passionately hated the Southern aristocracy and he was totally unable to regard the Negro as the equal of the white man.

The Fortieth Congress, the other antagonist, composed of many men with many ideologies and predilections, was more difficult to characterize. But the majority of the Radical Republicans who finally prevailed over the conservative and moderate Republicans and fragmented Democrats were consistent in their belief that the Southern Negro must have complete political equality—in other words, the vote.* The motivation behind their conviction, however, was open to a variety of interpretations.

The freeing of four million blacks created a curious backlash for Northern liberals in Congress. As a slave the Negro had counted in apportionment of congressional districts only as three-fifths of a man, but as a freedman he counted as a whole man, thereby increasing the number of representatives from Southern states by at least fifteen, an irony which gave the South more power in the federal Congress after reunion than it had had before secession.

Obviously to be feared by all Republicans was a coalition of this increased number of Southern Democrats and the Western agrarians, which would give the Democrats (or Conservatives) a majority in the House of Representatives.

The Radical Republicans contended that the proper power play to block such a fusion of Southerners and Northern "copperheads" † was to enfranchise the Negro and then insure that he voted Republican. The latter should not be difficult, they believed, considering how much the Negro owed the Republicans who had first pressed for his emancipation, who had fought to arm him during the war, and who were fighting even then for his civil and political rights.

Although all realistic Republicans were conscious of the political gain to their party in Negro suffrage, many of them were sincerely motivated as well by their deep concern for the welfare of the black race. Two names have traditionally symbolized

---

* Few Radical Republicans, however, were willing to give Negroes the vote in their own Northern states. Only in New England (except Connecticut) were blacks enfranchised by 1867.

† Northerners who sympathized with the South during the Civil War.

Radical Republicanism in Congress: Charles Sumner of Massachusetts in the Senate and Thaddeus Stevens of Pennsylvania in the House. Both these men, by their long friendship toward and understanding of the Negro, showed a devotion to the cause of racial equality which far exceeded purely political considerations.

The seesaw battle between Johnson and the Radicals intensified in February of 1866. Congress proposed a measure to extend the life of the Freedman's Bureau, an agency created early in the Civil War to assist and guide the Negroes. Johnson vetoed the measure; his veto was subsequently overridden.

Johnson had made no objections to the Black Codes as passed earlier by the Southern states; but to the Radicals and moderates in Congress the codes signaled a need for some legislation to protect the rights of Negroes by forbidding the states to discriminate against them. Sumner and Stevens were leaders in framing and pushing through the first Civil Rights Act of 1866. Originally drafted by Lyman Trumbull of Illinois, the bill, which President Johnson also vetoed, was also passed over his veto.

To insure the legality and permanence of the Civil Rights Act, Radicals felt that a constitutional amendment was desirable. The result was the Fourteenth Amendment, which explicitly declared Negroes to be citizens of the United States and then decreed that "no state shall make or enforce a law which shall abridge the privileges or immunities of citizens of the United States; nor shall any state deprive any person of life, liberty or property without due process of law; nor deny to any person within its jurisdiction, the equal protection of the laws."

The amendment did not require a presidential signature, but Johnson publicly denounced it and urged the Southern states to reject it. All but Tennessee followed his advice. Predictably, reaction to the president's vetoes and denunciations of Radical measures was glowingly favorable in the South. South Carolina hailed him as "the man who will eventually work out to a happy ending the vexed problems of social and political rights." [8]

The rest of the country was apparently less convinced. After a noisy, brawling campaign in which Johnson accused the Radicals of cowardice and treachery and the Radicals responded by "waving the bloody shirt" and matching the president's uncontrolled demagoguery, anti-Johnson forces won a stunning victory at the polls in 1866. In so doing they gained control of every

Northern state legislature, every statehouse in which there was a contest, as well the United States Senate and the House of Representatives.

The Radical Republicans in Congress read their triumph as a mandate to try their own plan of reconstruction in the South. They began in March of 1867 with two Reconstruction acts, the first of which threw out all the Southern state legislatures which had refused to ratify the Fourteenth Amendment.* In their stead, Congress divided the South into five military districts, each under a federally appointed general who was empowered to declare martial law.

At the earliest possible date the district commander was to convene constitutional conventions, delegates to which were to be chosen by universal male suffrage. The conventions were to be charged with the duty both of writing new state constitutions, which specified political and civil rights for freedmen, and of creating new state governments embodying the principles of the new constitutions. State legislatures, in turn, were required to ratify the Fourteenth Amendment as a condition of their return to the Union and to their representation in the federal Congress.

With the scene thus set for Radical Reconstruction, the task of registering the Negro to vote loomed as the first step on his long—no one in 1867 could have imagined just how long—road to full equality.

It was no mean task to prepare the South Carolina blacks to exercise their tenuously won franchise—to explain that they must first register before they would be permitted to vote, to insure that when they did vote they would vote Republican. The few early Negro activists who assumed this responsibility joined with two other groups—carpetbaggers and scalawags—in providing political leadership while offering guidance to the blacks.

Carpetbaggers made their appearance "at the South" † toward the end of and directly after the war. Through the years, the term *carpetbagger* has come to have only a pejorative meaning, calling forth an evil picture of a reprobate playing on the feelings

---

* Tennessee was excepted, as it did ratify the amendment in July of 1866, after which its senators and representatives were promptly seated.

† This phraseology is invariably used rather than "in the South" in contemporary writing.

of ignorant Negroes; seizing power from the hands of the helpless, defeated whites; and swindling both to gratify his desire for self-aggrandizement.

In some instances this image was all too true, but in many cases it was either greatly exaggerated or totally false. Numerous carpetbaggers had come south as agents of the Freedman's Bureau; their mission was to promote the physical, mental, and moral well-being of the newly emancipated slaves. Some were teachers, ministers, or farmers with the most high-minded ideals and little inclination to engage in politics. Many, of course, were drawn into public life as the Negroes, turning from force of habit to the white man for protection, looked to them for leadership.

To the vast majority of white Southerners, the scalawag was an even more heinous figure than the carpetbagger, for he was a native white whose entire upbringing and culture had taught him to look on Negroes as an inferior race. But scalawags betrayed their heritage, joined the Republican ranks, and, while cynically encouraging the Negroes in feelings of racial equality, thought always in terms of purely personal profit. There were, of course, many notable exceptions to this rascally picture.

Carpetbaggers and scalawags combined—or competed—with those Negro leaders who had some political understanding and who, as one observer has put it, "infused into their work the zeal of the missionary and adopted innovations designed especially to charm the ex-slave." [9] Chief among the innovations was the introduction of the Union Leagues. Although generally, and probably erroneously,* considered to have stemmed from the Northern Union Leagues, the Southern leagues, being secret, oathbound, and ritualistic, were of a quite different nature.

In elaborate initiation ceremonies amid mysterious hocus-pocus, candidates were surrounded by the faithful and addressed by the president, " 'Worthy sons of America! We bid you welcome. This circle of freedom and equal rights now encircling you

* Maxwell Whiteman, librarian of the Union League of Philadelphia, in a letter to the author, March 23, 1970, writes, "The Union Leagues of the South during the early years of Reconstruction have been repeatedly identified with the Union Leagues of the North. I have been unable to find evidence that would positively establish a connection between the two, although the name used was identical. It is true that most twentieth century historians, including the most discerning of the revisionists, have endorsed, supported and upheld this view. None of them, so far as I know, has documented such a connection."

must never be broken by treachery.' . . . Then all circled around
the 'fire of liberty' and swore to elect only true Union men to
office. . . . The ceremonies were closed by a communication of
the secret signs of the order. They were the four L's, Liberty,
Lincoln, Loyal and League, the utterances of each was to be
accompanied by special movements of the arms." [10]

Still, neither imaginative leadership nor the exciting ritualism
of the Union Leagues would have been enough to bind the blacks
so solidly to the Republican party had the white planters made
any attempt to win the political support of their former slaves.
But such an effort, demanding as it did an acceptance of the ex-
slave as an equal, worthy to be won, was impossible for most of
plantation America.

Instead, in the months following the first and second congressional Reconstruction acts, the South Carolina whites adopted
what they called their policy of "masterly inaction." With some
justification, many of the former ruling class in South Carolina
and elsewhere felt that they had no alternative to inaction, for
the Congress in its first Reconstruction Act had specifically disenfranchised "all persons who had held state or federal office and
then subsequently engaged in insurrection or rebellion against the
United States, *or* given aid and comfort to the enemies thereof."
The last phrase of this Iron Clad Oath made it difficult for state or
federal officers who had not even been in the war to, in good conscience, take the qualifying oath required to register.*

On the other hand, as the *Charleston Mercury* reminded its
readers, the "aid and comfort" stricture did not apply to the rank
and file who had not held state or federal office before or during
the war, which meant that, unfair as the disenfranchisement
doubtless was to many highly placed Southerners of good will, the
great mass of whites was unaffected and could still vote—and in
most states could outvote the Negroes. Not so, however, in South
Carolina, which was one of two Southern states (the other was
Mississippi) in which the majority of males over twenty-one was
black—84,393 blacks as opposed to 65,610 whites.[11]

When registration in South Carolina began in late August 1867,
the blacks responded eagerly. By the end of September an as-
tonishing 78,982—approximately 94 percent—had registered. Of

---

* Actually only about nine thousand persons were disenfranchised in
South Carolina.

thirty-one districts in the state, twenty-one had Negro majorities. The foundations of the white man's government shook ominously. That the Union Leagues had done their work of education well was unquestionable; but still, among the vast body of unlettered Negroes, there were obviously many who had only the vaguest idea of the significance of the momentous step they were taking.

A correspondent for the *New York Herald* filed this story on September 24, 1867: "Many of our new found brethren, in fact nearly all of them, had no idea what registering meant, and as a natural consequence the most ludicrous scenes transpired. Quite a number brought along bags and baskets 'to put it in,' and in nearly every instance there was a great rush for fear we would not have registration 'enough to go round.' Some thought it was something to eat, others thought it was something to wear; and quite a number thought it was the distribution of confiscated lands under a new name."

At the actual election, which was held on November 19 and 20, 1869, citizens of the state voted either for or against the Constitutional Convention; all those who voted for it voted simultaneously for delegates to the convention from their districts. Of the blacks who had registered, 87 percent voted, and all 68,875 of them voted for the convention. The total white vote was only 2,221, less than 5 percent of those registered. Of this number, 130 persons—scalawags who must have represented the entire white Republican party in the state—voted in favor of the convention.[12] The whites apparently just stood by in grim despair, clinging to the vain hope that, as long as they did nothing, the Radical Republicans could do nothing to them. Appalled at the collapse of their own power, they simply abdicated, effectively turning the reins of state over to the carpetbaggers, the scalawags, and the Negroes, all of whom they abhorred. They evidently could not bring themselves to work with these new elements of the population, or to meet them on equal terms.

Their attitude, understandable as it may have been, was unfortunate and shortsighted. Because the blacks had been accustomed to accepting the authority of their masters, these planters could have been instrumental in helping their former slaves find their way in freedom and in seeing that the state made proper preparations to receive them into the economic and social system. The rejection of this responsibility by the ruling class at this critical time—their weary laissez-faire attitude—was the first of many missed opportunities which might have changed the course of history.

Thus the Negro himself had to be alert to any compromise of his precariously won rights. One of the first to realize that his race could not merely sit back and enjoy the fruits of its liberty was Robert B. Elliott: "Behind us lie two hundred and forty-three years of suffering, anguish, and degradation," he said in one of his orations. "Before us lies our mighty future, with all its hopes and its aspirations. . . . That future is ours to shape. . . . Let us realize that upon each of us rest duties commensurate with our rights." [18]

3

The Great Doctrine of Manhood Suffrage

T H E R E had never before been an assemblage like it in South Carolina; there has never been one since. Officially it was called the Convention of the People of South Carolina; its purpose was to write a new constitution which would restore the state to the federal Union. On this momentous occasion in 1868 complete manhood suffrage was invoked to convene a body which would write the fundamental law for all citizens. Of the 124 delegates who filed into Charleston's Club House on January 14, forty-eight were white and seventy-six were black.

"Yesterday the great ringed-streaked-striped convention called together to provide a new constitution for the once great state of South Carolina, assembled in, and thereby desecrated the Charleston Club House, a building erected by a society of Charleston gentlemen for the pleasure of each others' company in the pursuit of that pleasure."

Thus wrote the powerful *Charleston Mercury* on January 15, and thus during the fifty-three days it took to write the constitution did they refer unfailingly to the "ringed-streaked-striped convention." Other newspapers alluded equally offensively to the "Black and Tan," the "Great Unlawful," or the "Congo Convention." The choice of the once hallowed Charleston Club did indeed seem to be rubbing salt in the wound, even though the Charleston Club itself had been disbanded in 1866 and the building sold to J. P. M. Epping, the United States marshal for the

47

district, who rented it to the military authorities for the convention.

The "sentimental grievance" of using the Club House for this purpose seemed to have been the "worst aggravation of the whole proceedings," wrote Carl Benson in the *New York Times* on January 27, 1868. "A stranger . . . might suppose that the choice of locality was expressedly intended to humiliate the quondam 'swells.' It is hardly necessary to say there was no such design," Benson concluded. Perhaps not, but it is still hard to believe that some degree of malice did not dictate the choice, especially since the handsome building with its beautiful grounds and luxurious shrubbery was not ideally suited to accommodate the convention. It had no gallery, for instance, so that railings had to be built to separate the delegates, who sat in the middle in arm chairs, from the spectators, who sat on either side on wooden benches. A platform was built for the president's desk and on either side of this the press, who had come from all over the country to see this show, set facing the delegates. The spectators who crowded behind the railings on the first day were almost entirely black. "These colored people were dressed in the fragmentary style of the Charleston negroes but were perfectly orderly and spat [sic] around as naturally as any white," wrote Benson.

As to the delegates themselves, both the Southern and Northern press acknowledged that many of the Negroes looked intelligent and were suitably dressed, although some could not sign their names and none owned property or paid taxes. Actually the local papers seemed to direct most of their initial vituperation toward the white delegates rather than the blacks, who, according to the *Charleston Mercury,* presented a decidedly more respectable appearance than the whites, "for the simple reason that they represented the highest type of their race while the white men represented the lowest type of theirs." [1]

As the meetings got underway at twelve noon on Tuesday, January 14, the forty-eight white delegates instinctively took the front seats, while the seventy-six blacks ranged behind them. At a given moment an attendant "pushed forward an earthenware spittoon weighing perhaps a quarter of a ton. The production of this national institution seemed to be the signal for coming to order." [2]

The convention was more formally opened by its temporary

chairman, Thomas J. Robertson, a wealthy businessman and graduate the University of South Carolina, who briefly reminded the gentlemen of the convention that they were assembled to frame a "just and liberal constitution" which would guarantee equal rights for all, "regardless of race, color or previous condition."

"I trust there will be no class legislation here," Robertson said. "I hope we will act harmoniously, promptly, judiciously and in such a manner as will reflect credit on ourselves, and secure the confidence of the people of the State whom we represent." [3]

The roll was then called. One hundred and twenty-four delegates answered present. For twenty-six-year-old Robert Brown Elliott, responding to the call of his name as a delegate from Edgefield, it was surely a heady moment. Citizen in fact or in fancy, he was on his way, ready to take his place in a new society in which his opportunity was as great as that of the white men sitting in front of him.

Unlike his colleague De Large, who was the first delegate on his feet calling for a point of order, Elliott remained silent and made no particular impression during the first few days of the convention, although his name was mentioned in the *New York Times* of January 21—as a delegate who lived in Charleston, but represented Edgefield County, some 150 miles to the northwest. The *Charleston Mercury* in its largely inaccurate "thumbnail sketches" of the delegates wrote that Elliott was commissioned by the Republican party to organize clubs in the "district which he honors by misrepresenting" and that while "swaggering insolently" he created a furor among the Edgefield County Negroes by the "boldness of his declamation, the splendor of his eloquence and the extravagances of his promises and assumptions." For the first sixteen days in the Club House, however, the splendor of Elliott's eloquence was confined to one or two routine motions.

The convention organized itself efficiently, elected Dr. A. G. Mackey, the generally respected collector of the Port of Charleston, as permanent president, and promptly settled down to work. From the very beginning it appeared that there would be no division along color lines and that the blacks, far from banding together, felt perfectly free to disagree with each other, often quite vehemently. On the third day, for example, J. J. Wright, a black lawyer, offered a resolution to ban the reporter of the *Charleston Mercury* from the hall because of the burlesque fashion in which the newspaper had reported the proceedings. Wright's motion that "we go as far as becomes gentlemen to cause the *Mercury* to 'evaporate' " was greeted by cries to "second the motion" from all over the hall.

At once William J. Whipper, a black lawyer educated in the North, was on his feet protesting that the convention had higher aims than to seek to control the columns of a newspaper. He was joined by several other black delegates, including Francis L. Cardozo, a clergyman and teacher originally sent South by the American Missionary Society, who said that any attempt to bar the *Mercury* reporter would only be to exhibit a "smallness and a pettiness of spite unworthy of our character."

Wright's motion did not carry, and the *Mercury* continued unchecked in its raucous reporting of proceedings and its sarcastic portrayal of delegates. A characteristic sample read, "S. A. Swails is a very light mulatto with scarcely any of the features characteristic of the negro race. He sports a thick black moustache and when sober would make a good looking bandit." [4]

Of De Large the *Mercury* wrote, "The Hon. Robert might have lived and died without having his name in print except in an advertisement if it had not been for the great social revolution which like boiling water has thrown scum on the surface." [5]

Francis L. Cardozo, educated at the University of Glasgow and generally considered, along with Elliott, to be the most intelligent of the black leaders, was characterized as a pompous man who had "neither abilities nor accomplishments that would distinguish him among white men, yet he appears to great advantage among the more ignorant people of his own race." [6]

In the same manner Richard H. Cain, "although black, ugly and shabby, or perhaps because of these exceptional qualities, enjoys considerable influence among the darkies." [7]

Joseph H. Rainey fared somewhat better than his other black colleagues as "a barber who had officiated at the Mills House in a manner acceptable to the proprietor and patrons." [8] And Whipper, in what was perhaps the highest accolade of all, would "in the days of slavery have been esteemed a likely fellow for a house servant or coachman." [9]

Probably the most illustrious and dashing of the black delegates was Robert Smalls of Beaufort. A genuine war hero, Smalls, at the outbreak of the war, had been a pilot aboard the steamer *Planter* which was taken over as a Confederate transport. On May 12,

1862, the ship was moored in Charleston harbor loaded with a cargo of guns and ammunition. In the evening when the white officers went ashore, Smalls and the other Negro seamen who had families living in Charleston rowed them out to the ship; in the early morning, with Smalls at the helm, they weighed anchor and steamed out of the harbor, giving the Confederate salute on the ship's whistle as they passed under the guns of Fort Sumter. At daybreak Smalls broke into the captain's wardrobe, put on his dress uniform, and strutted back and forth on the bridge imitating the captain's distinctive walk. He headed the ship for Beaufort via the inland waterway. Inside St. Helena Sound and in sight of the Union blockade fleet, the Negro crew hauled down the Confederate ensign, ran up the Stars and Stripes and turned themselves and their sixty thousand dollar vessel over to the Union Army.

The *Mercury* referred to Smalls's betrayal of trust in stealing the boat as an exploit which led to "great notoriety for Robert and much caress by his new allies." Smalls was permitted to retain command of the *Planter* for a while after the war. However, the *Mercury* concluded, since that time "Robert has been gradually subsiding to his proper level which he has at last attained in the mongrel convention." [10]

The more responsible local press was considerably less sensational but equally outraged by the Club House proceedings. The *Charleston News* bemoaned that "the demagogue is to rule the mass, and vice and ignorance control the vast interests at stake." [11] And ex-Governor Perry, quoted in the *Charleston Courier*, expressed what the prevailing view was among the newspaper's readers when he wrote, "I have for sometime thought that when the negro government went into operation it would be impossible to preserve the peace of the country. A war of races must ensue and it will be the most terrific war of extermination that ever desolated the face of the earth in any age or country." [12]

Meanwhile the convention moved determinedly forward. On the fifth day, assignments were made to the eleven standing committees, each one of which was charged with the writing of a different section of the new constitution.* As this work proceeded

---

* Elliott was on the Committee on the Bill of Rights, as was A. J. Ransier. De Large was on the Committee on Franchise and Elections, Cardozo on Education, Rainey on the Committee on the Executive Part of the Constitution, Whipper, the Legislative Part of the Constitution. Cain was on

in committee, many searching questions arising out of the totally unprecedented situation were raised on the floor of the convention. Some of these issues had little to do with the writing of a new constitution and belonged more properly before a duly elected legislature. But, since no such body existed as yet, the convention in some instances simply acted in a legislative capacity.

There was, for instance, an ordinance calling for the nullification of all debts contracted for the purchase and sale of slaves, which brought Elliott to his feet for his first real address to the convention. The implicit point at issue was that to recognize a debt contracted for the purchase of a slave seemed, in effect, to be recognizing the right of slavery.

Elliott began his speech with what was for him a routine, falsely modest opening note, "The importance of the subject overcomes my reluctance to obtrude my feeble opinion." But his words were anything but reticent as he went on to call for the unanimous passage of the ordinance invalidating the slave contracts in order that the convention might put its "stamp of condemnation upon this remnant of an abominable institution . . . this bastard of iniquity." He hit at the crux of the matter when he said, "I contend there never was, nor never can be any claim to property in man. . . . A few years ago the popular verdict of this country was passed upon the slave seller and the slave buyer and both were found guilty of the enormous crime of slavery. The buyer of the slave received his sentence, which was the loss of the slave, and we are now to pass sentence upon the seller. We propose that he shall be punished by the loss of his money." [13]

Cardozo was the only black to take issue with Elliott, a difference that was but the first of many. As opposed to Elliott's frankly vindictive aggressiveness, Cardozo was inclined to take a longer, more moderate view, but tended to pontificate slightly about his conciliatory approach. The true key to the ordinance, he contended, was the desire on the part of Elliott and other black delegates to make the slave seller suffer. And why, he asked, should they go out of their way to punish anyone, and more importantly why should they touch on a matter which could affect only that very small minority—the slave sellers? Surely this was "class legislation," and as such to be avoided. "I hope my tongue may cleave

the Committee on Miscellaneous Provisions of the Constitution and Smalls on Finance.

to the roof of my mouth, my right hand be paralyzed before I urge the oppression of any. . . . But I hope we shall have no class legislation." [14] He would vote against the ordinance, Cardozo said, and hoped that his colored friends would have the wisdom to do so also, "notwithstanding the unfounded and inflammatory appeals made by the opposition."

Here Whipper gave his objection that, if there were no invalidating legislation, the courts would have to settle these arguments between slave buyer and seller, and he was not willing that they should be thus used for the purpose of "wringing the bone from the two dogs."

"On what principle do you decide which dog is the meanest?" Cardozo interrupted.

"The dog that went and stole the bone first in Africa or elsewhere is the meanest," Whipper shot back, "and that is the dog the gentleman proposes to pay." [15]

The arguments of Elliott, Whipper, De Large, and Ransier easily prevailed; the ordinance invalidating debts owed to slave sellers passed by a vote of 95 to 19, with the blacks joined in their aye vote by most of the convention's prominent whites, many of whom were later to hold high elective offices in the state. With only one or two exceptions, all the men of both races who were to be elected to South Carolina's top posts in the next nine years began their public service as delegates to the 1868 Constitutional Convention.

Two future governors, Franklin J. Moses and Daniel H. Chamberlain, played important roles in the convention proceedings. Moses, a scalawag, son of a distinguished and universally respected judge, was always credited with having been the man who hauled down the Stars and Stripes from Fort Sumter as the Civil War began. Partly because he had been such a "shouting rebel," his shift to the Radical side caused him to be one of the most hated white natives in the state.*

Daniel H. Chamberlain was an atypical carpetbagger. A grad-

---

* Just after the convention closed, Moses and T. J. Robertson (who had been temporary chairman of the convention) were expelled from the honorary Euphradian Society of the University of South Carolina for having "lowered their dignity and station as true gentlemen of South Carolina." No longer could they be considered "an ornament to or a jewel in the honorary role of this society, but [are] two black stains upon the otherwise unblemished role of brothers true and faithful to their vows."

uate of Yale, he attended Harvard Law School for one year before joining the Union Army, where he served in the Fifth Massachusetts Cavalry, a regiment of Negro volunteers. As a result of this experience he had a good rapport with the South Carolina blacks.

Another white delegate, Charles P. Leslie, an aging, erratic carpetbagger from New York, was sardonic, sharp-witted, and patronizing toward his Negro colleagues. He and Elliott tangled at an early session of the convention over a triviality concerning the relocation of the county courthouse in Leslie's district, Barnwell, which was adjacent to Elliott's district, Edgefield. Leslie accused Elliott of stubborn unreasonableness and Elliott intimated that Leslie was logrolling.[16]

A few weeks later they again crossed swords when a resolution on voting qualifications was read and referred to the Committee on Franchise and Elections. Among numerous qualifications, one of the obvious ones was that no person who was *non compos mentis* should be qualified to vote. Elliott rose to say he thought that they should strike out the *non compos mentis* qualification so as not to disenfranchise one of the members of the Committee on Franchise and Elections.[17] Since Leslie was a prominent member of the committee, Elliott's meaning was clear to everyone, including, of course, Leslie, who bided his time for a few days until he found an opportunity to remind the convention, by implication, that Elliott and other Charleston politicians had a few months earlier foisted themselves upon the Barnwell and Edgefield districts as delegates to the convention because the Charleston slate had been full. "I tried to resist," said Leslie piously, "but they came there too strong for me and I was overwhelmed by them." [18] Indeed, for all Leslie's sanctimoniousness, it does seem quite plausible that some such stratagem facilitated Elliott's start in public life.

Leslie's scorn was by no means confined to Elliott alone. Richard H. Cain, Elliott's onetime editor on the *South Carolina Leader*,* was also the target of it in a controversy of genuine substance which occupied the convention for several days. Cain had offered a resolution asking that they petition Congress to appropriate $1 million for the purchase of land in the state as a measure of relief for the freedmen, whose need was desperate. By

* On April 17, 1868, the *South Carolina Leader* became the *Missionary Record*.

the end of the war, freedom to the Negroes meant land. The popular slogan "40 acres and a mule" symbolized their passionate desire to "own the land which for so long owned them." [19] In fact, W. E. B. DuBois, the pioneer Negro historian, wrote in 1918 that "to give the Negro only the ballot without the land as an economic underpinning was to end a civil war by beginning a race feud." [20] Obviously one of the overriding obligations of this first Radical Reconstruction assemblage was to try to find a viable means of securing land for the freedmen. "The abolition of slavery has thrown these people upon their own resources," said Cain. "How are they to live? I know the philosopher of the *New York Tribune* says root hog or die. . . . My proposition is simply to give the hog some place to root." [21]

Leslie considered Cain's proposal "humbug," a grandstand play designed by Cain to dupe the Negroes into thinking he was working for their interests when, in fact, he knew very well that the Congress was certainly not going to give the state of South Carolina $ 1 million out of the nearly empty federal treasury.

Cain replied that a crafty, cunning politician like Leslie was so far removed from the interests of the poor, the needy, and the oppressed that he could feel nothing for them. Furthermore, Cain made clear that the money was not to be an outright gift, but a loan drawn from the $7 million surplus still remaining in the Freedman's Bureau fund, which would be paid back by the Negroes who bought the land within five years' time. The measure passed by a vote of 101 to 5. Among the five nays were Robert Smalls (who so far had taken virtually no part in the proceedings) and William Whipper, who voted against the resolution on the grounds that it would "raise the hopes of the entire poor people of the country . . . three-fourths of whom will be compelled to go away with shattered hopes." [22]

When news of Cain's proposal reached Washington, Senator Henry Wilson of Massachusetts sent a telegram advising the convention to drop the resolution because Congress would never appropriate the money.[23] The delegates thereupon worked out a far more realistic substitute measure which provided for the creation of a state land commission with authority to "purchase at public sale, improved and unimproved real estate" which was to be sold in "suitable tracts" on the condition that one-half the land "shall be placed under cultivation." [24] Title to the land was to remain with the state until the purchase price, in a maximum of eight years, was fully paid. It was an enlightened plan, unfortunately far less successful in execution than in conception. Ironically, the man first chosen to head the Land Commission, when it was finally activated in March 1869, was none other than Charles P. Leslie.

On a par with the freedmen's hunger for land was their intense desire for education. As early as 1865 the delegates to the Zion Church Colored People's Convention had passed a resolution solemnly urging, "by the sad recollection of our forced ignorance and degradation in the past and by the bright inspiring hopes of the future," that schools be established in every neighborhood and that children be "kept in regular attendance at same." [25]

At the Constitutional Convention, however, the section of the report of the Committee on Education which called for compulsory attendance for all children between the ages of six and sixteen at either public or private schools provoked lively debate.

For some blacks the very word *compulsory,* even in the most benign context, was an anathema. To Robert De Large the word was "contrary to the spirit and principles of republicanism." Furthermore, De Large contended that a proviso compelling attendance at school was unenforceable: "It is just as impossible to put such a section in practical operation, as it would be for a man to fly to the moon," he said.[26]

Rather surprisingly, Cain agreed with De Large about the insertion of "the obnoxious word." A. J. Ransier differed, pointing out that "to be free is not to enjoy unlimited license."

Elliott, continuing his rather irritating habit of saying, every time he rose to make a speech, that he was not rising to do so, was vigorously in favor of compulsory attendance: "Some gentlemen have said it is anti-republican. I deny it. It is in conformity with the ideas of republicanism to punish crime. If you give a man the privilege of remaining in ignorance, it is anti-republicanism to punish him. You must compel them to learn. It is republicanism to reward virtue. It is republicanism to educate people without discrimination. . . . The question is not white or black united or divided, but whether children shall be sent to school or kept at home." [27]

Underlying the ideological question of republicanism (which today we call democracy) were racial implications. The Constitu-

tional Convention was framing a fundamental law which applied
to all citizens, raising for the first time the "ugly specter" of white
and black children going to school together: "The white man may
prefer that his child shall be ignorant rather than debased and
corrupted by negro association," wrote the *Charleston Mercury*.[28]

Capitalizing on the obvious revulsion of South Carolina whites
toward biracial education, C. P. Leslie tried to threaten the black
delegates into removing the compulsory-school clause on the
grounds that, if they did not, the constitution would be defeated
when it went before the people to be voted. This method of
persuasion had been tried several times before by white delegates
and, on this occasion, it was F. L. Cardozo who responded: "The
gentleman from Barnwell has made an appeal to the fear of the
colored delegates on this floor, by holding up before them the
bugbear of the defeat of our Constitution. I would simply say,
that I do not think there is a colored delegate but what knows that
we have carried the convention against the white people of this
State, and will carry the Constitution also." [29]

On the other hand, Cardozo put into words the sense of urgency
which must have been shared by most of the thoughtful delegates.
In matters concerning the particular interests of his race, Cardozo
urged his colleagues to use the present opportunity to their best
advantage, since they might never have a more propitious time:
"We know that when the old aristocracy and ruling power of this
State get into power, as they undoubtedly will, because intelligence
and wealth will win in the long run, they will never pass such a
law as this. . . . They will take precious good care that the
colored people shall never be enlightened." [30]

As was characteristic throughout the convention, protagonists
and antagonists often shifted from issue to issue. When the matter
of how to pay for public education was debated, Elliott and
Cardozo, who had stood together on compulsory attendance, were
at loggerheads. As soon as Section 5 was read, calling for, in addition to property tax, an annual poll tax of $1.00 to be applied
solely to educational purposes, Elliott demanded, "What is the
penalty to be attached for non-payment?"

"We did not provide for that," said Cardozo, referring to the
Committee on Education on which he was chairman, "because we
knew it would never occur."

"It is not often that I rise to take part in debate," Elliott began, but there were no false disclaimers in what he had to say about the proposed poll tax. "While we may secure the education of our children by adopting the clause as it stands we run the risk of depriving many of the parents of the right of suffrage," he warned.

"Do we say in this report that it shall prevent the right to vote?" asked Cardozo.

"That is exactly what I am getting at," Elliott replied. "If an educational tax is to be levied it should be distinctly laid down that the non-payment of that tax should not deprive the parent of this privilege."

"As we expect the services of the eloquent gentleman from Edgefield in the Legislature," Cardozo responded silkily, "we hope he will make this matter all right there."

But Elliott was not satisfied to leave the question to the mercies of future legislatures which might be made up of the former ruling class. He was determined that it be covered in the constitution and, accordingly, offered an amendment providing that "no person shall ever be deprived of the right of suffrage for non-payment of said tax." [31]

His opponents contended that other states—notably Massachusetts, which was always held up as the model of enlightenment—had, from long experience, been forced to adopt a poll tax. Moreover, they argued, if a citizen knew he would not lose his vote, he would have little incentive to pay the poll tax, in which case the revenue, estimated at $150,000, might be cut by as much as a third, to the serious detriment of the public school program.

Said B. F. Whittemore, a white schoolteacher from Massachusetts who was to become a powerful vote getter among the Negroes, "It appears to me that we would have but a poor opinion of the energies of the people of South Carolina, if we could not believe that they would put forth an extra effort to raise an extra dollar to become electors." [32]

Whittemore's argument, and similar ones offered by black delegates Wright and Rainey, failed to touch the essence of the argument, Elliott insisted. The real issue was the perversion of the ballot box. Even in Massachusetts, men unable to pay their taxes had been "drummed up by the opposite parties, their poll taxes paid for them, and their votes thus secured." And if the privilege of denying a man his vote was given to the legislature,

Elliott doubted whether in two years hence the Republicans would still control the state of South Carolina.[33]

Gradually Elliott began to swing the convention his way. De Large added his prophetic warning that someday the poll tax might "be used against us for partisan purposes and to our injury." [34] Franklin Moses asked dramatically how the delegates would feel, if, for the pitiful sum of $1.00, they took the elective franchise "from the men to whom it has just been given by the blood of thousands of loyal men." [35]

Finally, Cardozo graciously acknowledged that, when the Committee on Education had provided for the poll tax, they had perhaps not sufficiently reflected on the wisdom of the contention of the gentleman from Edgefield. Ultimately, with even C. P. Leslie switching to vote aye, the amendment passed by a vote of 81 to 21 and became part of the new constitution.

With this success Elliott began his political ascent. Single-handedly he had fought and triumphed on a substantive issue. Evidence of his improved status was the shift in tone of Francis L. Cardozo, whose amused condescension toward an upstart changed to grudging respect for a colleague.

If Elliott had prevented the poll tax from being used to disenfranchise any citizen, he still had an enormous battle to wage in the convention on the all-important question of universal suffrage, as opposed to suffrage qualified by a literacy test.

Six days before adjournment, this urgent and far-reaching question of qualified versus universal male suffrage was still to be settled. On March 9 when the section on Election and Franchise was read, it included a clause providing that any person who could not read or write by the year 1875 would not be allowed to vote.

Robert Elliott was the first to protest, as he offered an amendment to strike the literacy clause entirely from the section. Compromise measures were proposed, changing the year 1875 to 1890, in order to give the public school system more time to become established. But Elliott would have none of it. He said that even if the literacy clause were not to be in effect for thirty or forty years hence, he would still be unalterably opposed to it: "I claim that this Convention has met for the purpose of laying down a basis of universal suffrage. The Reconstruction Act declares that all male citizens of the State shall possess the right to vote. . . . Here we, who have met together under that very act, under that very authority, propose to say to Congress, you are wrong; you had no right to give any such privileges to the people, and therefore we will restrict the privilege. How could you face your constituents?" [36]

Once again Elliott prevailed. Strongly backed by forceful arguments from Whipper (who also put in a good word for women's suffrage), Cardozo, Cain, Ransier, and De Large (although the latter was chairman of the Committee on Election and Franchise which wrote the qualified suffrage section), the amendment won overwhelmingly.

Considering that he was treading on totally unfamiliar ground and facing situations with no precedent to guide him, Elliott seemed to have had an extraordinary ability to predict the future. In rejecting both the poll tax and the literacy tests, he correctly sensed the means that would eventually be used to disenfranchise many of his race.

In conformity with the federal House of Representatives procedures, each section of the constitution had to be read and voted upon three times before it was finally adopted, meaning that many points, large and small, were still being argued in the final days before adjournment. On March 14, however, the arduous labors of fifty-three days finished, the Honorable A. G. Mackey bid an eloquent farewell to the gentlemen of the convention. He looked back with much self-congratulation upon the time they had spent together, said the president of the convention. He had no unpleasant recollections of "acrimonious bickerings." Disagreements, while "boldly expressed and sturdily maintained," had never been characterized by the "petulance of personal retort," Mackey claimed, obviously moved by the solemnity of the occasion to overlook a few exceptions.

The result—the constitution which they were about to present to their constituents for ratification—was worthy of much commendation for the improvements made in the organic law, Mackey told the delegates. In it, for the first time in the state's history, the "great doctrine of manhood suffrage was distinctly recognized and all the rights secured to every citizen. . . . Here have we stricken every vestige of serfdom from out situations," said Mackey, "and that too in so emphatic and unambiguous a way that no doubt can ever be entertained of our determination that this relic of barbarism shall never again in any form pollute our soil. . . . Here we have made every needful arrangement for the free education of our people. . . . Here too we have obliterated from our political system that most pernicious heresy of State sovereignty. . . . We do not claim for ourselves a pre-eminence of wisdom or virtue, but we do claim that we have followed in the progressive advancement of the age; that we have been bold enough and honest and wise enough to trample unworthy prejudice underfoot." [37]

There was very little hyperbole in Mackey's closing words; for, indeed, the instrument that blacks and whites, working together as equals for the first time, had forged was a sound one. The creation of an entire public school system remains perhaps the convention's most noteworthy achievement. Not to be ignored, however, were the acts that protected homesteads of a certain value against the procession of creditors, the extension of women's property rights, and the adoption of the state's first divorce law. The new constitution also devised an entirely new county system, providing for the direct election of the governor and other state officers, who had formerly been chosen by the legislature. Most importantly, the document never deviated from the recognition of the equal civil and political rights of all men.

Although written at a time of almost cataclysmic change, the constitution itself was not particularly innovative in form, borrowing heavily, particularly in the Bill of Rights section, from the federal Constitution. Perhaps this was just as well, for in the final analysis South Carolina's 1868 constitution stood the test of time. Even when the state was "redeemed" by the white supremacists and a new constitution was written in 1895, it retained a large part of the 1868 constitution, although, of course, eliminating the vital universal male suffrage provision.

Before adjournment, a committee of the delegates fixed the date on which the constitution would go to the people for ratification and on which the senators and representatives to the General Assembly would be elected. The date they chose was April 14, which was the anniversary of the assassination of President Lincoln, the anniversary of the hauling down of the flag at Fort Sumter, and the anniversary of replacing the flag over Fort Sumter. Said E. W. M. Mackey, chairman of the committee and son of the convention's president, "It was deemed by your committee a most glorious time for holding the election." [38]

4

God Save the State
of South Carolina

DURING the weeks that the Constitutional Convention was in session, and while the newspapers ceaselessly poked fun at the proceedings, the white citizens of South Carolina continued to tell themselves that nothing consequential was really happening at the Club House assemblage in Charleston. But when finally the new constitution, a concrete document which decreed a complete change in their way of life, was presented to them, the whites were forced to confront the realization that they no longer enjoyed any particular rights that the Negroes were compelled to respect. The blacks were claiming absolute equality with their former masters and owners and, because there were more blacks than whites in the state, they were claiming what amounted to supremacy.

To the whites this was an all but inconceivable state of affairs. Besides all that they had lost—their sons in battle, their plantations, their wealth, their slaves, much of their cotton (the chief source of their revenue), their position of leadership, and, in many instances, their franchise—they were now being asked to accept the dominance of "the inferior race."

Next to stunned disbelief, the emotions most prevalent were revulsion and fear—fear that the "semibarbarians," intoxicated with liberty, wholly unfit for freedom, would perpetrate "dire deeds of riot, rape, robbery, incendiarism and bloodshed" against helpless white victims.[1] (Ironically, when these frightful consequences did not occur, the whites credited the "peculiar institution" of slavery, which they claimed had humanized and civilized the Africans' "savage ferocity.")

Some thoughtful members of the former ruling class took a more rational view. They earnestly believed themselves to be kindly disposed toward the Negro; they felt they cared more sincerely for his welfare than did the carpetbaggers from the North, who were exploiting him for selfish or partisan purposes. They also remembered that during the dark days of the war when Southern men were at the battlefronts it was the Negro slave who tilled the field, kept watch over unprotected dwellings, and guarded wives and children. ("Nobly suppressing the manhood that burned within him, he learned to labor and to wait," said Robert Brown Elliott of the slave during the Civil War.) But even the most enlightened of the white leaders also felt that the Negro, with his "credulous nature" and his "weak moral and intellectual capacities," could hardly be regarded as an adult. To invest him with leadership was intolerable.

As for the new constitution itself, South Carolina's whites universally considered it an abomination. It was "bogus," "monstrous," "unjust," a "subversion of the American republic." The most horrendous feature was that part of the document which called for a system of public education open to whites and blacks alike. "The grand purpose of the negro constitution is to set up and establish negro rule in South Carolina," wrote the *Charleston Mercury*. "And to support this policy the white people, by this constitution, are to be taxed, made to support the schools at which negro children are to be educated and be compelled to send their children to these schools. The white man may prefer that his children shall be ignorant rather than be debased and corrupted by negro association. Yet he is to be *punished* and *forced* to send his children *male and female* to the negro school whether he wills it or not." [2]

Clearly the time for "masterly inaction" had passed. Faced with what were, by their lights, dreadful alternatives, at least some whites were moved to act, and to organize. "Fellow citizens of Sumter," cried one Democratic appeal, "Arouse from your lethargy! Think of your wives and children. Let the love of them stimulate you to action." [3]

Soon Democratic clubs were created in various counties; these clubs joined together to hold a convention in Columbia on April 2,

1868, and issued a series of papers—resolutions, appeals, remonstrances and memorials to Congress.

One of the remonstrances spelled out twelve objections to the proposed constitution. "We object to the instrument itself," ran Article 4. "As we repudiate the parent we denounce the progeny. It is a patchwork of contradictions . . . abstracted from constitutions of other states having different conditions and habits of thought from ourselves."

And Article 5: "We object to it because, professing to be a constitution it is full of mere legislation. . . . The ordinances which were passed indicated that the delegates were of the opinion that wisdom would die with themselves and that it was necessary to settle beyond a possibility of change, every question under the sun." [4]

There was considerable truth in that statement; in fact, Robert Elliott might almost have written the last part of it himself. For, as he demonstrated frequently during the convention, he did indeed feel it necessary to settle beyond the possibility of change all questions of political and civil equality which confronted his race. He knew that, while wisdom might not die with him and the other black leaders, the opportunity for effective accomplishment might. Therefore all actions had to be swift, sure, and irreversible.

The whites knew it too. They were counting on the fact that sooner or later the white man would regain control of the government. Meanwhile, in the understandable hope that it would be sooner, the Democrats tried to appeal to the masses of blacks, whom they believed to be more gullible than their leaders: "Your present power must surely pass from you," began "An Address to the Colored People of South Carolina," another of the papers issued by the Democratic convention. "It is therefore a most dangerous tool that you are handling. Beware of the use you make of your temporary power. Remember that your race has nothing to gain and everything to lose if you invoke that prejudice which since the world was made has ever driven the weaker tribe to the wall. Forsake then the wicked and stupid men who would involve you in this folly and make yourselves friends and not enemies of the white citizens of South Carolina." [5]

The Negroes were then exhorted to join with the Democrats in voting against the constitution. In urging this upon the blacks, the whites were caught in a dilemma that was peculiar to their time and even more so to their state: There were not enough white votes in South Carolina to defeat the constitution. Therefore, even though they deplored universal male suffrage, the whites appealed to the Negro to cast his vote to negate the instrument which had granted him that suffrage in the first place. In other words, what they seemed to be saying to the Negro was, *Just this once, use the vote you should not have and do not legally possess to assure that you will not have an opportunity to use it again.*

The blacks were unmoved; they voted solidly and in strength for the constitution. The recorded vote was 70,758 for ratification, 27,288 against.[6] *

In a last-ditch stand, the State Central Executive Committee of the Democratic party presented a formal remonstrance to the Congress of the United States, begging it not to adopt the constitution of South Carolina and warning, "A superior race—a portion, Senators and Representatives, of the same proud race to which it is your pride to belong—is put under the rule of an inferior race; the abject slaves of yesterday, the flushed freedmen of today. . . . We do not mean to threaten resistance by arms, but the people of our State will never quietly submit to negro rule. . . . By every peaceful means left to us, we will keep up this contest until we have regained the political control handed down to us by an honored ancestry. . . . This is a duty we owe to the land that is ours, to the graves that it contains . . . to the proud Caucasian race, whose sovereignty on earth God has ordained." [7]

On a less emotional and more dollars-and-cents basis the whites sent a pamphlet entitled an "Appeal to the Honorable Senate of the United States" [8] (the House of Representatives having already given its approval to the South Carolina constitution). The main thrust of the argument here was that the Conservatives (Democrats) were threatened with "taxation without representation" since a certain number of their leaders suffered from political disabilities and therefore could not vote, although they continued to pay taxes. At the same time the majority of those serving in the

---

* There were, however, 35,551 registered voters (almost certainly whites) who did not go to the polls at all. Had they done so the result would have been far closer (although still about 8,000 short of defeating the constitution), and certainly a greater proportion of Democrats would have been elected to the General Assembly.

state legislature paid taxes minimally if at all, and yet they all voted—thus, "representation without taxation."

"Exhibits" attached to the appeal showed that the Negroes in the combined Senate and House paid a total of only $143.74,* with one black (William McKinlay of Charleston) paying $83.35 of that amount, and that the whites paid a total of only $761.62, with one white (a Democrat, of course) paying $505.85 of that amount. Yet these were the legislators, the appeal continued, who had increased the burdens of taxation under the new constitution to $2,230,950, thus raising the tax on real estate from an alleged .05 percent of an estimated 3 percent.

These figures, the appeal stated, truthfully demonstrated to the honorable Senate the "character of the men" and all that they did not represent in the state of South Carolina: they represented neither its wealth, its commercial, agricultural, or industrial interests, nor its intelligence (though exactly how the size of their tax bill proved the latter is somewhat obscure).

Another "exhibit" indicated that the largest proposed expenditure was for education. To build literally from scratch an entire public school system in the state, the budget called for "1 school house to each 16 square miles of territory making 1800 schoolhouses in the State, at $200 each"—a total of $360,000. The 1,800 teachers for the new schoolhouses at salaries of $300 per annum each were to cost the taxpayers $540,000.

These and other similar figures were doubtless what caused Pennsylvania's Representative Thaddeus Stevens to comment, "What the protest claimed as grievances . . . [we regard] as virtues." [9]

The last resort of the Conservatives failed to move the Senate; the Congress promptly accepted South Carolina's new constitution, along with those of Alabama, Florida, Georgia, North Carolina, and Louisiana, and, on June 25, 1868, passed an omnibus bill over the veto of President Andrew Johnson † declaring

---

* Elliott was one of only two men in the legislature to pay the capitation tax of $1.00 which all persons who had no assessed property were asked to pay. Obviously they had to do so voluntarily, since there was no way to check up on persons living in the state with no property to identify them. Elliott was also one of the few who paid a tax—also of $1.00—on his dog.

† President Johnson had just the month before survived an attempt to remove him from office. Having been impeached by the House, he escaped conviction by one vote in the Senate.

these states eligible for representation in the federal Congress as soon as their newly constituted legislatures ratified the Fourteenth Amendment.

South Carolina's new legislature had been elected on April 14, at the same time that her citizens had voted either for or against the constitution; all who voted *for* it had had the right to vote for state officers and for representatives and senators to the General Assembly. Nominations for these posts had been made while the Constitutional Convention was still in progress, the Republicans taking advantage of the hours when the convention was not in session to do party business.

The arrangement to hold caucuses right at the Charleston Club House was eminently practical, since almost all the Republican candidates for office at every level were members of the convention. There was one notable exception: General Robert K. Scott, the assistant commissioner of the Freedman's Bureau, one of the two leading contenders for governor, was not a convention delegate. The other nominee was scalawag T. J. Robertson. Scott was a white native Pennsylvanian. He migrated to Ohio, then to California, and then back to Ohio to raise a regiment of volunteers. He entered Charleston as a prisoner of war, was later brevetted from colonel to major general, and remained in South Carolina after the war to work, generally very effectively, with the Freedman's Bureau.

On March 12, after Robertson retired from the race, the Republicans nominated Scott for governor and immediately moved on to the selection of the lieutenant governor. Here the blacks made their first bid—somewhat tentatively as it turned out—for fair representation in state offices. Robert Brown Elliott had obviously been busy politicking for both himself and his race, for he was one of three black contenders for the office. When he saw that he did not have the votes to win, he yielded to another black whose chances looked better—Jasper J. Wright, a lawyer who was to become a member of the state Supreme Court. But a white man, Lemuel Boozer, eventually won, partly because William J. Whipper, also a hopeful, withdrew in his favor, thereby enraging Elliott.

The office of secretary of state went to Francis L. Cardozo, whose posture as a Negro during the maneuvering for offices was somewhat questionable. A *New York Times* dispatch from South

Carolina on May 1, 1868, reported that Cardozo had been fiercely opposed to the idea of a black man occupying the lieutenant governor's seat, considering it "a surrender to the enemy by going beyond the limits of true victory." According to the *Times*, the Radical element, in an attempt to persuade Cardozo, even offered the position to him, but he indignantly refused and carefully sought to "prevent any of his brethren from falling into such a well planned trap." The brethren, "with the exception of a few Northern importations, stood with him and escaped the snare."

One wonders exactly how Cardozo, having prevented the blacks from demanding the office of lieutenant governor, could then, without scruple, have accepted the next constitutional office down the ladder, that of secretary of state. Elliott, clearly one of the "Northern importations," must also have had his doubts, and he expressed them vociferously. In fact, everything about Cardozo's cautious, calculated actions probably infuriated Elliott, for he was certainly not a man given to compromise or halfway measures.

The new Radical Reconstruction legislature began its first session on July 6, 1868, eleven days after the United States Congress had pronounced South Carolina qualified for readmission to the Union. In the state Senate were twenty whites (of whom six were democrats) and ten blacks. But in the House of Representatives there were only forty-six whites (fourteen Democrats) to seventy-eight blacks, making a majority of twenty-nine blacks in the two houses which constituted the General Assembly. Negro supremacy was thus an uncontested fact. Among the Negro leadership, two of the six future black federal congressmen were now in the state Senate: Richard H. Cain—now almost invariably referred to as "Daddy" Cain, always to his annoyance—and the solid, steady Joseph H. Rainey. In the new House were Robert C. De Large, Alonzo J. Ransier, Robert Smalls, and Robert Brown Elliott.

The Carolina district military commander, General E. R. Canby, in his General Order No. 120 of June 30, ordered that incumbent lameduck Governor James L. Orr and his lieutenant governor be removed from office and that Governor Robert K. Scott and his lieutenant governor take over when the General Assembly convened. On that date "all authority conferred upon and heretofore exercised by the commander of the second military

district" was to be remitted to the civil authorities. The shift from
military to civil control also meant that the center of power
changed from Charleston to the capital at Columbia.

Since the state capitol was still without a roof, the new legislature was obliged to hold their first session in Jainey Hall on the
campus of the University of South Carolina. As they began to
assemble, William J. Whipper, who had had some idea of making
a try for the speakership of the House, decided (or was persuaded)
to throw his support behind Elliott for that contest. His espousal of
Elliott for speaker represented a change in position from his
previous backing of white Lemuel Boozer for lieutenant governor.
Clearly he and Elliott had had a meeting of minds in the meantime; his strong speech in favor of Elliott on the opening day of
the legislature was reasoned in such a way as to suggest that
Elliott himself had had a hand in writing it.

It was high time, Whipper said, that colored men should have
places of honor and trust. They had been excluded under the
pretext that it was impolitic to put black men in office, and he,
Whipper, was therefore determined to make an issue of it. If the
Republican party could not afford to be led except by whites,
many of them inferior intellectually and socially to the blacks,
then the party should fall to the ground. The speech, reported the
Charleston Daily Courier, made a deep impression and "is thought
to foreshadow the intention of the colored men to insist hereafter
on good offices to the exclusion of many of the white Radicals." [10] * Nevertheless Franklin J. Moses, Jr., was elected speaker
of the House on the first ballot with 62 votes to Elliott's 32.

Because South Carolina and Mississippi were the only two of
the eleven Confederate states to have black majorities in their
Reconstruction legislatures, much national interest was focused,
and much rich, scornful prose expended, on descriptions of their
general assemblies. Prominent among journalists visiting the South
was James S. Pike of the Republican *New York Tribune.* Pike's
subsequent book, *The Prostrate State,* was for many years and in

---

* Massachusetts Senator Charles Sumner at this time put in a strongly
worded plea that the Southern states "seize this golden opportunity" to elect
a Negro to the Congress of the United States. To this the *New York World*
responded that people would be more inclined to believe in Sumner's sincerity if he made a similar plea to the Massachusetts legislature, urging
them to elect a Negro to the Senate to replace Charles Sumner, whose term
expired in 1869.

many quarters regarded as the definitive account of South Carolina during her years of black supremacy. Since Pike had been a leading abolitionist, his assessment was naturally considered to be objective and thus significant. ("In view of his long and enthusiastic service in the antislavery cause, [he] can hardly be accused of color prejudice." [11]) What his many admirers did not at the time appreciate was that James Pike operated under a dichotomy not unusual in the latter half of the nineteenth century; he was both abolitionist and a Negrophobe. Thus he, who had looked upon the "peculiar institution" of slavery with utter repugnance, could with impunity refer in his writings to the Negro as "Sambo."

No matter what the subject for discussion was in the legislature, Sambo could chatter about it, Pike observed. "There is no end to his gush and babble. . . . His misuse of language in his imitations is at times ludicrous beyond measure . . . . [He] will burst into a broad guffaw on the smallest provocation. He breaks out in an incoherent harangue on the floor just as easily, . . . he will go on repeating himself, dancing as it were to the music of his own voice forever." [12]

However, Pike did concede that the Negroes had a "wonderful aptness at legislative proceedings." They were "quick as lightning" at detecting points of order. Furthermore, they had an "earnest purpose born of a conviction that their position and condition are not fully assured, which lends a sort of dignity to their proceedings." [13]

Pike's twentieth-century disciple, Claude G. Bowers, added his own fanciful embellishments to Pike's eyewitness account, in his book *The Tragic Era*. Describing the first South Carolina Radical legislature as if he had been there, he wrote:

> We enter the House, where Moses, the Speaker looks down upon members mostly black or brown or mahogany, some of the type seldom seen outside the Congo. . . . Moses is hammering for order, members are shouting to one another, ridiculing the man speaking, asking silly questions. Ordered to their seats, the disturbers flop down with uproarious laughter, their feet upon their desks. Then, like a jack-in-the-box, up again. It is a lark, a camp-meeting. . . .
> Meanwhile, amid the cracking of peanuts, the shouting, laughing, stamping, members are seen leaving and returning in a strange state of exaltation—they come and go in streams. Let

us follow the trail to the room adjoining the office of the clerk of the Senate. We learn that it is open from eight in the morning till two or four the next morning, and now, as we push in, it is crowded. A bar-room! Here gallons of wine and whiskey are consumed daily. Members enter blear-eyed in the early morning for an eye-opener or a nightcap—some are too drunk to leave at 4 A.M. Champagne? Wine? Whiskey? Gin? Porter? Ale?— and the member orders to his taste.

Since even "good men and true" could not live on wine alone, the State was taxed to supply the refreshment-room with West-phalia hams, bacon, cheese, smoked beef, buffalo tongue, nuts, lemons, oranges, cherries, peaches. . . . "The State has no right to be a State unless she can afford to take care of her statesmen," said Senator C. P. Leslie. Yes, and their wives and sweethearts too. Thus much of the taxpayers' money went into tapestries, rugs, table linen, imported chignons, ladies' hoods, ribbons, hooks and eyes, extra long stockings, bustles, rich toilet sets; and white and dusky sirens found the Golden Age.[14]

Bowers's use of the present tense and of the royal "we" lent a note of accuracy to a description which was purely an exercise in wild hyperbole.

The city bells rang out in Columbia at twelve noon on Thursday, July 9, 1868, to honor the inauguration of Robert Kingston Scott as governor of the state. (The use of such a celebratory symbol to mark such a "depressing" occasion brought forth a vigorous letter of protest from a group of white citizens to the mayor of the city.) Jainey Hall was crowded with onlookers, mostly black, as Dr. A. G. Mackey, who had been president of the Constitutional Convention, stepped forward to administer the oath, concluding his invocation with "God save the State of South Carolina."

As Governor Scott repeated the words, the blacks jumped to their feet and began to take up the cry—"God save the State of South Carolina"—accompanying their rhythmic chant with much clapping of hands, stamping of feet, and waving of hats and handkerchiefs. Their spontaneous reaction, so joyous, so naïve— such a poignant expression by a people who had never before been citizens and had never had a state they could glorify—was infectious to all who witnessed the scene. Many spectators and white members of the Assembly joined in, "with some exceptions not necessary to specify," reported the conservative *Columbia Phoenix*,[15] which found the whole scene "painfully suggestive, to say the most of it."

Governor Scott's inauguration address, however, contained several ounces of soothing balm for those whose feelings had been bruised by ringing bells and ritualistic chants, and for the many more thoughtful white citizens who believed that the tensions and passions of the moment called for measures of moderation and compromise. In four specific areas Scott appealed directly to that "influential minority," the former ruling class.

First, he earnestly recommended that the legislature memorialize Congress to relieve every citizen of South Carolina of all political disabilities; second, he directed that, since the state was rapidly resuming all civil functions, the Freedman's Bureau be promptly phased out. Third, he called the continued presence in South Carolina of the federal troops a "reproach to a republican state," and recommended that their services be dispensed with. Fourth— and this more than any other aspect of his first message must have reassured the whites—Scott unequivocally called upon the legislature to provide for the establishment of "at least two (2) schools in each district," one to be designated for white children and one for colored children.

To justify his recommendation, which ran quite contrary to the intent of the new constitution, Scott added this rather wry note: "While the moralist and the philanthropist cheerfully recognizes the fact that 'God hath made of one blood all nations of men,' yet the statesman, in legislating for . . . two distinct, and, in some measure, antagonistic races, . . . must, as far as the law of equal rights will permit, take cognizance of existing prejudices among both. . . . Let us therefore recognize facts as they are," he concluded, "and rely upon time, and the elevating influence of popular education to dispel any unjust prejudices that may exist among the two races of our fellow citizens." *

Scott was a decent, if somewhat weak man; had he been as prescient as some of the black leaders, he might have stood firmly by the constitution and resisted giving the first impetus to a doctrine of separatism which, rather than having been dispelled by "elevating influences," would be sanctioned at the end of the

---

* This point of view would ultimately be espoused by Booker T. Washington at the famous Atlanta Compromise of 1895.

century by the Supreme Court of the United States in their Plessy versus Ferguson opinion.

The first business to come before the General Assembly when it convened on July 6, 1868, was the ratification of the Fourteenth Amendment, which was speedily accomplished with only the Democrats (all twenty of them) in both houses voting no.

Elliott was much in evidence in the House. Undeterred by his failure to win the speakership, he threw himself with apparent zest into his role as legislator, offering numerous bills, resolutions, and motions. Some of these proposals were trivial; some were politically expedient; some were pay-offs or maneuvers to collect future IOUs. Some of his proposals, however, were quite progressive, such as his bill to "prevent and punish the offense of carrying concealed deadly weapons." Another—an early attempt to define eminent domain—was a bill "to declare the manner by which lands, or the right of way over the lands of persons or corporations may be taken for the construction and uses of railways and other works of internal improvements."

In debate Elliott was establishing himself as a confident, articulate, and stubborn spokesman for his race. "Men listened to Robert Brown Elliott, idol of the negroes, who did much to inflame their ambitions and cupidity with disturbing speeches on social equality," wrote Claude Bowers.[16] A case in point was Elliott's strong advocacy of a bill offered early in the first Radical legislature by the blacks to prevent discrimination because of race, color, or previous condition by persons carrying on businesses which were under license—in other words, hotels, restaurants, and transportation—thus beginning the battle for public accommodation which was to continue for a hundred years.

In the state House of Representatives opponents and proponents of the bill divided without exception along color lines. The gist of the white argument was expressed by H. H. Jervis of Sumter, who began with an appeal to black pride: "I do not think there are very many persons of color who are in favor of voting themselves into hotels or into a body of society where they are not wanted." This was followed by a threat: "You will array race against race and furnish the best argument the Democratic party can use." Jervis ended with an appeal to reason: "Why should South Carolina go in advance of Massachusetts? Here we have universal suffrage.

There an educational qualification is required. Here you propose to allow the colored man privileges which there he never has asserted or claimed." [17]

Elliott's answer to Jervis began with one of his usual disclaimers: "I had doubted the expediency of bring forward this bill at the present time, but after listening to the gentleman from Sumter, I should be recreant to my identity if I remained in my seat." [18] He then took up the challenge of the Massachusetts situation and spoke like an Englishman as he began. It was the Irish, he proclaimed, who were responsible for the fact that Massachusetts had changed from universal to qualified suffrage. Not until the men from the swamps and bogs had begun to be imported from Ireland had the great state of Massachusetts ("which I, thank God, am able to claim as the place of my nativity") been obliged to pass a law that no one should be allowed to vote unless he could read or write. Having thus turned the tables on his opponent Jervis, an Irishman, Elliott addressed himself to the larger issue: "The gentleman says it is we who are arraying race against race. I deny it. The bill contemplates nothing of the kind. It treats only public carriers or persons engaged in public business requiring license and I ask the gentleman from Sumter if we could do less as legislators than to provide that no distinction should be made against us? Would it not be bad taste for us to debar ourselves from the enjoyment of privileges we create for others?" He concluded by asking every man who claimed to be a Republican to vote for the bill, not because he was white or black, but because the measure was "right and proper and in accord with the principles involved in the whole scheme of reconstruction." [19]

The bill did pass by a vote of 61 to 37; but, of course, the gap between legislating nondiscrimination and actually putting it into practice, was (and is) infinite.

On September 12, 1868, the *Charleston News,* assessing the Radical legislature, wrote that there were eight men who really held control of the government: four whites—Scott, Chamberlain, Corbin, and Whittemore—and four blacks—Cain, Elliott, Whipper, and De Large. Cardozo was put into a lower echelon, which could hardly have pleased him. Describing each man briefly, the *News* said that Elliott ("a real kinky-headed Negro from Massachusetts") was a good speaker with more personal influence than any other man in the House. "He has a violent temper which he doesn't hesitate to display and always handles his opponents without gloves." Of De Large, the *News* wrote that, "while ignorant," he deserved credit for having opposed some of the most scandalous measures with all of his powers. The *News* quite obviously had in mind a scene which had occurred on the floor of the House a few days earlier when De Large had made highly disparaging remarks about Whipper over some inconsequential issue.

Elliott, quick to spring to Whipper's defense, rose in all his wrath and demolished De Large. He was a "pigmy who was trying to play the part of a giant." He was ignoble, contemptible, he had sold out, he was playing into the hands of the Democrats, he was talking for the benefit of the Charleston press and "elocutionizing himself into a perspiration which stood out upon his skin like warts." The speaker was obliged to call Elliott to order on account of his violence.

Elliott's legislative activities were not confined to the floor of the House chamber; in addition to his often showy but generally effective performance there, he was chairman of one key standing committee, the Committee on Railroads, and a member of another, the Committee on Privileges and Elections. He also served on several ad hoc committees, including one charged with auditing all accounts contracted for by the General Assembly—a tall order had it been conscientiously carried out. There is no evidence that it was.

Outside the General Assembly, Elliott held another elective post as one of five—and the only Negro—county commissioners of Barnwell County. In addition, all during this period, he was engaged in a further endeavor which would have been demanding enough to occupy the full time and attention of most men: preparing for admission to the bar and for the interrogation he had to undergo before an examining board of eminent white lawyers. If, as his friend T. McCants Stewart allegedly suggested, the extent of his legal training was a six months' close study of the South Carolina code, he must have been hard pressed between April and September 23, 1868, when he was formally admitted, along with all the other Negro and carpetbagger lawyers, to practice law in the state.

The first of at least three law firms with which he was connected was Whipper, Elliott, and Allen, with offices at 91 Broad Street in Charleston. W. J. Whipper, described by one conservative white as "a black, bestial, dissolute carpetbagger" [20] and by another as "the ablest colored man I ever met," [21] was reared in Michigan. He came south with a regiment of volunteers, and ultimately settled in Beaufort, some sixty miles south of Charleston. He and Elliott were fellow delegates to the Constitutional Convention and became close friends. They had a strongly symbiotic relationship; one always seemed to be battling for the other for some office or position. And Elliott wrote to his wife in 1871, "If anything happens to me, send for Whipper."

The name of Macon B. Allen, the third partner, should by all rights have been first instead of the last in the firm. Allen was a considerably older man who came from Massachusetts, where he had passed his examination on May 3, 1845 (when Elliott was only three years old), to become the first Negro in the United States ever to be officially admitted to the bar.

Little remains to illuminate Elliott's early career as a lawyer. Few vital documents during Reconstruction, including records of law cases, particularly in the lower courts, were preserved. (One often wonders if all reminders of the "Tragic Era" were not deliberately destroyed when the white supremacists again prevailed in the South.) However, when Negro lawyers first began to plead cases, their presence in the courtrooms excited enough interest (or afforded enough opportunity for derision) that reporters from the conservative press often dropped in to see the show.

In one such instance, at the Court of General Sessions at Barnwell, Elliott was appointed to defend a man named Nelson Sanders, accused of murder. After six challenges by Elliott, the jury was finally empaneled; the case was tried; and, on August 23, 1869, the prisoner was found not guilty.[22] A reporter from the *Charleston News* was on hand for the proceedings, which were newsworthy for several reasons: The court had convened for the first time in the little town of Blackville and was holding its session in the Baptist Church; the judge, newly elected Radical, Zabaniah Platt, presiding from the pulpit. More importantly, this particular court session gave the press and the "legal brethren" an opportunity to judge the mental character of the defense attorneys, Elliott and Whipper. Wrote the *News* reporter, "Although the stomach of your correspondent may not be as thoroughly reconstructioned as those of others upon whom he might place his finger, and becomes a little nauseated at taking these black Radical appeals, it must be admitted that the easy politeness and general good bearing of these 'gentlemen' of color has impressed the community with no feelings other than those of good will and, we may say, respect." [23]

Elliott's ambition during his first year in public life was endless, as was the breadth of his activities. By no stretch of the imagination, for example, could he be said to belong to the laboring class. Yet later during the summer of 1869 when there was a growing agitation on the part of laborers for some kind of organization which would strengthen their nebulous position and combat their exploitation, Elliott was to champion their cause. A state labor convention was called in Columbia on November 25, 1869, and he was elected president.

The meetings were attended by three hundred delegates both black and white, the blacks for the most part being agrarian laborers. The whites represented various trade unions, painters, masons, wheelwrights, blacksmiths, and other skilled occupations in which only a handful of free Negroes had engaged before the war and in which only a comparatively few former slaves were engaged in 1869.

The proceedings commenced in what Elliott later described as a "turbulent and confused fashion." Some of the delegates—obviously primarily the whites—balked at a slate of officers loaded with black Radical politicians. At their insistence, De Large, proposed as vice-president, yielded to T. F. Clark, head of the longshoremen's union, and Ransier gave way to the head of the painters' union. Elliott, on the other hand, was accepted with considerable enthusiasm by all elements and was said to have been elected president in a "most complimentary manner." There is no way of knowing whether the widespread approval of him came as a result of his intelligent, progressive views, his skills as a politician, or both.

Primarily the convention focused on the problems of Negroes who had become farm laborers. All delegates were given a questionnaire which asked, What is the monthly wage paid in your county and what ought planters to pay? What share crops are given? What share should be given? How do planters in your county treat the laborers? Do they pay wages as agreed? Do they divide the crops fairly? If not, in what way do they defraud the laborers? What can and ought to be done to prevent these wrongs? What do the planters in your county say about the convention? Will they agree to a fair system if proposed by this convention?

The answers to these questions pointed up the need for a memorial to the General Assembly spelling out the grievances of the agricultural laborers and suggesting some remedies. Elliott appointed the committee on the memorial and worked with it to produce a document that was temperate, judicious, and a model of enlightened self-interest; its objective was to "confer upon the laborer a greater power of self-protection than he now possesses." [24]

The labor convention produced results both bad and good. Many white planters felt even more threatened than they had before by the convention's demand that sharecroppers receive one-half instead of one-third of the crop or that straight laborers be paid a daily wage of one dollar.[25] Some planters even tried to turn away altogether from Negro workers by importing Northern or foreign labor: "Let your old niggs know that you can do without them," wrote a physician son to his landowning father in urging him to "try some foreigners," as his neighbors were doing.[26] On the other hand, since free Negro laborers and white planters did in the long run succeed in making a sort of marriage of convenience, it is possible that the creative efforts of the convention had some salutory effects.

As for Elliott himself, his role as a labor activist was short-lived. When delegates to the forthcoming National Labor Conference were elected he, as president of the state convention, was automatically chosen. He declined this honor in favor of his white colleague T. J. Mackey, whom he called eminently fitted for service as a national delegate. His gesture was so uncharacteristic that it gives rise to the suspicion that Elliott was acting from some enlightened self-interest of his own. Apparently he feared becoming identified too exclusively with the problems of labor. The paths of glory that he intended to follow were wider.

There were many straws in the wind during that first year of the Radical Reconstruction. While men like Robert Elliott jockeyed for positions of personal or racial power, both in and out of the General Assembly, others saw in the disorder that inevitably accompanies a great social upheaval an opportunity for quick financial gain. In committees, barrooms, and parlors, legislators—some perhaps unwittingly, others quite deliberately—began sowing the seeds of peculation and corruption which would one day be used to oust them from office.

Beyond the legislative halls the white aristocracy, instead of taking an affirmative, effective step forward, continued to look back to an older South Carolina of Rutledges, Heywards, and Pinckneys—a South Carolina that was dead. But if these former leaders remained paralyzed, the poorer whites did not. To them, especially the rednecks from up country, the Negro had always been not merely inferior but actually subservient. After all, a black man had been obliged to step off the pavement of a city street just as fast to make room for country crackers as for the grandest plantation aristocrat. Now these "preening, strutting niggers" were looking at themselves not merely as the white man's equal, but sometimes even as his superior. It was insupportable. If the planter class would take no forcible action, then the ordinary yeoman class would have to.

The Ku Klux Klan, first heard of in South Carolina in the spring of 1868, soon became a force which inflamed an already dangerous state of affairs. By the end of the summer the volatile situation began to erupt; the violence which was to dominate the state for the next nine years had its first serious manifestation.

5

Their Murderous Work

O N   M A R C H   25, 1869, two years and two days after his name had first appeared on the masthead of the *South Carolina Leader,* Robert B. Elliott was named assistant adjutant general of the state, a position which gave him tremendous power, since it involved him in the formation of a state militia.

For months there had been an urgent demand in South Carolina and other Southern states for an armed force to maintain the law and the authority of the government. But positive action was impeded by the fact that the federal Reconstruction Act of 1867 explicitly forbade the states "lately in rebellion" to organize state militias. However, as the Radicals in Congress became more concerned about the unstable situation in the South, they urged the repeal of that part of the 1867 act. There was strong opposition in the Congress to arming militias in the Southern states, and, in a sense, crucial issues of reconstruction policy had to be thrashed out all over again in the debate that ensued in the Senate chamber.

Radicals who, during the early conflicts over reconstruction, had insisted upon disarming rebel militias made up of "unrepentant and unwashed traitors," now argued that, unless United States Army troops were substantially increased, there were no powers in the Southern states adequate to suppress the outrages being perpetrated on the loyal (Republican) people.[1]

Democrats and some Republicans held that the law, not military strength, should be counted on to preserve the peace; that the dangerous situation in the South was the result of the Radical's attempt to "reverse the American doctrine" and put all power in the hands of the minority.[2]

But Francis Sawyer, the recently elected Republican senator from South Carolina, reminded his colleagues that, even though a large part of the population of his and other Southern states was not "well affected" toward them, the governments of their states were realities, elected by a clear majority of the people. Why then should there be any objection to putting these states on the same basis as Massachusetts or Indiana, for example, and allowing them the same powers of self-protection? Furthermore, Sawyer pointed out, "Those of us who represent the loyal sentiments of the State of South Carolina are an unarmed people, while those who are opposed are an armed people, and have used their arms without stint." [3]

Even allowing for some exaggeration on Sawyer's part, it is important to remember that attacks by whites against blacks were carried out by the Ku Klux Klan *before* the militia was armed in South Carolina. Nineteenth- and early twentieth-century historians have traditionally put this matter in the reverse and held that it was the arming of the Negro militia which gave birth to the Klan and spurred the formation of the many rifle clubs which sprang up all over the state.

But, regardless of which element—and basically it boiled down to black versus white—was responsible for initiating the violence, one cannot fail to empathize, though perhaps in varying degree, with both sides. To the white Democrats the very thought of giving arms to the Negroes who had so recently been their slaves seemed an indignity and a menace surpassing any they had had to bear since the end of the war. To both the black and white Republicans a state militia seemed the only way to preserve order, civil rights, and the power of the Republican party. In Washington it was this point of view which prevailed and won the day for the Radicals. On January 13, 1869, the stricture on militias in the rebel states was lifted.

However, many Southern states had not waited for congressional action to agitate for the establishment of militias. As early as July 10, 1868, before the matter had even been reported out of committee in Washington, Governor Scott was urging members of the South Carolina General Assembly, in his first message to them, to take prompt action to organize a state militia. Moreover, he blithely assured them that the quota of arms to which the state was entitled would be "promptly furnished" by the War Department.

At that time there had already been one political assassination in the state; sporadic harassment of Negroes and white Republicans was occurring, and the name Ku Klux Klan had begun to appear occasionally in the press. As the general election of November 3, 1868, approached and the Negroes prepared to vote for the first time for a president of the United States, terrorist activities increased markedly.

In the state's Third Congressional District alone, at least four Negro politicians were murdered during September and October, and widespread rumors of outrages, threats, and intimidations led the General Assembly to appoint an investigative committee to look into the facts. Elliott was a member of this committee, along with two other blacks, Robert Smalls and J. J. Wright. The other Republican was Joseph Crews; George T. McIntyre and J. Bryant were the two Democrats. The chairman of the committee was Crews, a rough, crude, powerful, and much-feared Radical. The investigation occupied four and a half months, from May 3 to September 28, 1869, and was said to have cost the state $68,000 (of which $7,500 was allegedly pocketed by Chairman Crews).[4]

The hearings were conducted first in Newberry County, where a black named Johnson Stuart had been murdered in September as he came with his mother and brother from a political (Republican) meeting. A few weeks later in the same town a black named Lee Nance, president of the local Union League, was killed. It was believed that Stuart and Nance were shot by the same man, identified by Nance in his dying statement as William Fitzgerald, who came from Tennessee and was reported to belong to a "scouting group of bushwackers." Fitzgerald and his associate Samuel Murtishaw escaped with the obvious assistance of some locals who were alleged to have planned the murders of Nance and Stuart and to have been members of the Ku Klux Klan.

Much of the questioning by members of the Third Congressional District investigating committee concerned the activities of the Klan. A typical exchange between Elliott and a white man named W. P. Harris, acting constable at the time of the crimes, follows:

Q. (by Mr. Elliott): Do you know of any outrages committed by this organization?

A.: Well, they went around whipping and scaring people. I don't know who did the killing; there have been forty men killed in this County, and those parties must have done it. There have been five or six killed around here. I don't know how many are on the Coroner's book, for he would not give me the report, when I asked for it. I asked for it when I was in office.

Q.: What was the cause of the outrages, which were committed against so many persons?

A.: Because they were Radicals. They swore in the public streets that a Radical should not live in this County.

Q.: Do you know of any means of violence or intimidation used to prevent persons from voting?

A.: They told them if they voted they would not hire them, and they should not have houses to live in, &c. . . . On the day of election Republican votes were only given at three boxes [polling places]. There were eleven boxes in this County. Republican tickets were not allowed to be carried there. I could not get a Constable to go to the polls. I appointed thirteen Constables, but not one would serve.

Q.: What was the cause of those men not being willing to serve?

A.: They were afraid to serve.

Q.: Whom and what were they afraid of?

A.: Afraid of violence from the Democrats. That is what they told me.[5]

In other interviews a Negro named Nelson Roof testified that, as he sat by the fire in his house one evening, shots rang out, six or seven bullets going "clean through the house." Terrified, he peeked through a crack in the door and saw a group of men who "had on false faces and long white sheets." Another black, William Carter, was waylaid at three o'clock in the morning by men "all in white with big gowns." "I was very much scared," Carter reported. "I was drunk and was scared sober." [6]

In Abbeville County the investigation centered around the assassinations of two members of the General Assembly, James Martin and B. F. Randolph. Martin, a white Radical, member-elect of the lower chamber, described as an industrious, unobtrusive man of good character, was killed early in October at a spot four miles from the town of Abbeville Court House. According to the testimony of numerous persons, the coroner had the briefest possible inquest at which, after a perfunctory examination of a few wit-

nesses, the jury decided that Martin had been killed by persons unknown. When Sheriff H. S. Cason (Democrat) was asked by Elliott
what steps had been taken to apprehend Martin's murderer, he
answered, "I don't know that any steps were taken at all." And
when asked what had been the conclusion of the coroner's inquest,
Cason responded, "I don't remember that I ever heard their report." [7]

B. F. Randolph, a black Northern preacher and a state senator,
was shot in broad daylight on a railroad platform as he was depart-
ing from a Republican electioneering meeting. His three assailants
were seen by many witnesses, but were allegedly not recognized
and made their escape.

Information subsequently gleaned by the Third District investigating committee from sympathetic eyewitnesses revealed that the
probable murderers were William K. Talbert, John Wesley Talbert,
and Joshua Logan. William Talbert later confessed to a United
States House of Representatives investigating committee that he
was a member of the Ku Klux Klan, that nearly all the Democrats
he knew also belonged to the Klan, and that their objective was to
"kill out the leaders of the Republican party, and drive them from
the state." [8]

The evidence thus points indisputably to the fact that the KKK
was not only in existence in 1868, but that its members perpetrated
many of the atrocities which occurred in the state during the November elections.

There was at that time no state militia, Negro or otherwise, in
South Carolina. In fact, shortly after the murders of Randolph and
Martin, Governor Scott issued a proclamation in which he warned
that if the rights of citizens, white or colored, were further frustrated by "turbulent and lawless men resisting executive authority," he would be compelled, however reluctantly, to "arm and
organize a sufficient force of loyal citizens to overcome the resistance." Consequences of such a step, however disastrous, would
rest upon the heads of those who provoked it.[9]

Given this clear juxtaposition of events, it is difficult to see how
a historian as responsible, albeit strongly conservative, as John S.
Reynolds could write two decades later in his *Reconstruction in
South Carolina,* "Whatever the hostility of the whites to the negro
government, whatever the acts which made that government at
once a disgrace to its agents and a menace to the white race in

South Carolina, it is safe to say that the Ku Klux would have remained inactive but for the arming of the negroes and the conduct
of the State militia into which they were enrolled."

When the General Assembly reconvened on November 25, 1868,
for its first regular session (following the special session which
had run from July to October) one of the first orders of business
was the passing of resolutions memorializing the two fallen members, Randolph in the Senate and Martin in the House. Many of the
prominent members took the floor for brief speeches; Elliott, Whipper, and De Large all managed, along with their florid rhetoric, to
inject a partisan note into their eulogies. Said Whipper, "Could
the shades of the departed Martin and Randolph stalk forth from
their bloody tombs, they would point their gory fingers at the
Democracy and say, 'you are the cause!' "

Elliott in his remarks dwelled dramatically—even melodramati-
cally—upon the pall of apprehension under which members of the
Radical legislature must have lived during that summer and fall.
"We all felt," he said, "that there were persons in this State who
were waiting to do their murderous work. We asked ourselves,
will it be I? Will it be I? and each wondered whether he should be
the first martyr to the cause of truth, justice and liberty." Then,
although claiming he did not intend to inspire feelings of revenge,
he concluded, "I will add to the testimony submitted by the gentleman from Beaufort [Whipper] by saying that the intelligent portion
of the people of this State are, at least indirectly, responsible for
these diabolical deeds. We have suffered much and may suffer
more. . . . Let us not be driven from our position by any
threats." [10]

On December 17, 1868, a joint House and Senate resolution
provided for a temporary organization of a hundred men (more if
needed), "properly officered and controlled," whose function, at
the call of the governor, was to keep the peace, quell disturbances,
and arrest guilty persons. They were to remain in force until such
time as the militia was officially formed. On this note in the legislature, the year 1868 came to a close.

A "bill to organize and govern the militia of the State of South
Carolina" occupied much legislative time in the first weeks of the
new year, especially in the Senate, where the bill originated. On
March 16, 1869, Governor Scott signed the militia bill into law,

along with enabling legislation which permitted him to purchase "two thousand stands of arms of the most approved pattern with the usual complement of ammunition." [11]

Section 15 of the militia bill provided that an assistant adjutant general could be appointed by the governor with the advice and consent of the Senate. When Elliott was named to that post, he set to work at once, and almost singlehandedly as it turned out, to organize the National Guard Service South Carolina (NGSSC), as it was officially called.

All males between the ages of eighteen and forty-five, white and black, were eligible to enroll in the militia. Virtually no whites took advantage of this "opportunity" to serve with, or in some instances under, Negroes; nor were they encouraged to do so by the blacks, who looked on any white who attempted to join as a potential spy. Thus, to all intents and purposes, the militia was almost exclusively black. Some whites did try to form militia companies of their own, but Governor Scott, reacting no doubt to Negro pressure, refused to commission them. His failure to do so may have been a mistake, for it gave the whites an excuse to form their own rifle clubs, which were far more dangerous than a white company under the Republican controlled militia would have been.

One of the most famous of these organizations was the Carolina Rifle Club, established in Charleston in July 1869 at the same time that the Negro militia was being formed. A history of the club written by its first vice-president and ultimate president, C. Irvine Walker,[12] states, under the heading "Why the Club was formed," "The conquerers of our 'Prostrate State' with diabolical spite, let loose upon a defenceless [sic] community the scum of an inferior race. . . . During this period of negro rule, the white men, of course, were determined to protect their women and children from danger and insult and their property from incendiarism. How to organize to secure this was the qustion. We tried a modified form of the famous Klu [sic] Klux Klan which proved too cumbersome and liable to be abused." Eventually the founders, recalling the German rifle clubs that had been popular before the Civil War, settled on that format. Since the militia law forbade any organization except the militia itself to be armed, the constitution of the Carolina Rifle Club proclaimed it to be a purely social body enjoying picnics, dinners, and an occasional shooting match. However, the weapon adopted by the club was not a sporting or target rifle, but a sixteen-shooter Winchester. Still, Walker's history indicates that, despite its militant objective, the club staunchly maintained a select and exclusive membership. Even in the face of suggestions by some members that, considering their real purpose, they might expand their base, it was deemed essential by the majority that "thorough congeniality should exist" and that only members "prominent in the social, professional and business life of Charleston should be included." All were "South Carolina gentlemen of the olden time." *

While numerous such illegal "defensive organizations" were being established and while the Ku Klux Klan was growing more widespread and menacing, Elliott was faced with the formidable task of enrolling blacks into the militia and shaping the organization into some sort of manageable size. Although figures vary widely as to how many Negroes actually were involved, the number is usually put at 95,000, which is obviously a gross exaggeration, since the 1870 census showed that there were only 85,475 Negro males over twenty-one in the entire state. Although youths of eighteen were eligible for service in the militia, males over forty-five were not. A more accurate count, based on the number of weapons issued, would be no more than 14,000 armed men and perhaps again that number of unarmed members.

To accomplish the enrollment as speedily as possible, Elliott took advantage of the fact that the 1870 census was in process and had the governor order all the census takers (most of whom were black patronage appointees) to act as enlistment officers as well. On June 2, 1869, letters to this effect went out to the census takers in the twenty-four Republican counties of South Carolina—those in the six Democratic counties were ignored—each letter including two types of enrollment forms, one to enlist citizens between the ages of eighteen and thirty and one to enlist those between thirty and forty-five. Pay for each day of active duty in the militia was fixed at $1.50.

Many of the census takers did their work in a rather slapdash fashion, which clearly irritated Elliott, as illustrated by his letters preserved in the Adjutant General's Letterbook, 1869–70: [13] "Sir,

---

* Eventually there were ten similar (if slightly less select) clubs in Charleston alone that banded together under one commander in 1876 and organized as a regiment of infantry with artillery and cavalry support to help defeat the Republicans and bring about the end of Reconstruction.

you will please send to the Department *legible* copies of the militia rolls sometime ago returned to you, as soon as possible," he wrote to R. R. Purvis, enrolling officer of Lexington County. And to T. J. Eichelberger of Edgefield County, who must have been particularly recalcitrant, "Sir, you will please send to the Department immediately the remaining rolls of militia for your county or compulsory steps will be taken to make you do so."

In addition to prodding his subordinates to obtain up-to-date rosters, Elliott had to concern himself with finding suitable halls where the militiamen could drill and with ordering provisions for the men. A daily ration consisted of 1¼ pounds of salt pork or "in lieu thereof" 1 pound of fresh beef; 1 pound of flour or cornmeal, 2⅖ ounces of beans or peas, $12^{8}/_{100}$ ounces of coffee (based on 8 pounds per hundred men), 2⅖ ounces of sugar or molasses, ⅕ ounces of "adamantine" [hard] candies. Most importantly, Elliott was responsible for the safe shipment of arms and ammunition to the various units, although the actual securing of arms and the choice of their distribution remained largely in the hands of Governor Scott himself.

All this cost money; the militia was supported by a loosely defined Armed Service Fund, which soon became one of the principal breeding grounds for fraud and corruption. Directly before Elliott's eyes was the example of his superior, Franklin J. Moses, Jr., the white adjutant general, whose first action in connection with the militia was to write a contract with two gun companies to change ten thousand muskets owned by the state into breach loaders. The arrangement provided for a kickback (euphemistically referred to as a royalty) to Moses of one dollar per weapon.

Moses's preoccupation with graft, along with his natural predilection for leaving the hard work to others, meant that most of the organizational and operational tasks fell to his assistant adjutant general. Thus Elliott faced considerable conflict between his sincere belief in the importance and validity of his job and his growing awareness of the potential monetary benefits which it contained for him. He was not ingenuous or guileless, nor did he stand above the questionable dealings going on all around him. He was extravagant, ambitious, and poor. Perhaps a share of the boodle found its way into his pockets, but he was not a man to bother with the constant, almost daily, petty theivery practiced by many of his colleagues.

One of the principal sources of information about the militia and, in fact, about the entire question of malfeasance during Reconstruction is the *Report on Public Frauds, 1868–1877.* When South Carolina was "redeemed" by the whites in 1877, the new Democratic legislature at once initiated an exhaustive investigation into the frauds and corruptions perpetrated by the Radical Republicans during their nine years in public office. The voluminous findings of the investigating committee, while extremely biased and sanctimonious, are filled with irrefutable documentation and with statements made under oath by most of the principal Republican politicians.

Taken with suitable grains of salt, the *Report on Public Frauds* offers an important insight into the period. It has much to say about the militia and a certain amount about Elliott's activities in connection with it, but no concrete evidence was presented to show that he was ever involved with the routine pay-offs, kickbacks, and bribes. There was reason to believe that he liked large schemes, especially those which permitted him to charge excessive legal fees. Invariably, however, he was dismissed in the *Report on Public Frauds* as a corruptionist and, perhaps, with graft so prevalent, it was hardly to be expected that the Democrats would look further for an interpretation of his behavior. It is regrettable that they could not or would not see that, like so many of his race, Robert Elliott was motivated far less by venality than by his own intense pride and his fierce determination that his dignity as a man not be denied because of his color. Certainly at the beginning of his term as assistant adjutant general, he appeared far more concerned with the function of his office than with the spoils of it. He performed his duties as colonel (later general) in a straight-arrow fashion.

His orders were peremptory and had a strongly military flavor, deriving perhaps from his training in the British Navy. Clerks in the adjutant general's office were expected to "conform cheerfully" to his order prohibiting "loud and boisterous talking during office hours." "You will promptly take proper steps in order to have your company enrolled, drilled and ready to act," he wrote to his fellow state representative Prince Rivers in Edgefield. "You will exercise great care in the selection of your men and use great energy in the enforcement of discipline." And again to an officer in Hamburg, "You will in no case act on the aggressive, neither will you permit any of your command to do so, but be at all times vigilant and prompt to assume the defensive." [14]

Many of his communications stress Elliott's determination to maintain the image of a peace-keeping rather than an offensive militia. "Should any of your men commit any act of violence or perpetrate any outrage, or be guilty of any unbecoming act of insubordination, you will immediately cause such offendants to be placed under arrest and report your action together with the cause to these headquarters without delay." [15]

The need to be alert against retaliation by whites was constant. Elliott's very first letter in the adjutant general's book (Moses was adjutant general but nine-tenths of the letters in the book were written by Elliott) was written to various members of the General Assembly, requesting each man to confer at once with his delegation and with other reliable Republicans in his district and to "speedily transmit" to the adjutant general's office all rumors of resistance against the militia.

Although the whites were invariably and quite understandably disturbed by the existence of the militia, they only reacted with force against those units which were armed, as at least half of the companies and perhaps more were not. To many Negroes the pay and the opportunity to cut a dashing figure were far more important lures to the militia than were its peace-keeping aspects, so most of them did not even care if they were armed. There was drilling in public squares to the roll of drums, there were uniforms, some even with ribbons and plumes, and there was particular élan connected with the various companies named for prominent Radicals—for example, the Elliott Guards—whose duties were almost entirely ceremonial. Because these quasi-military units appeared to relish their chance to rather harmlessly "play soldier," they came to have a sort of *opera bouffe* aspect to many. Looking back on the militia, today's revisionists tend to describe its activities, in the words of one historian, as "little more than a series of playful pranks committed by a troupe of benevolent comics." [16]

If the militia was not quite as innocuous as all that, it also bore little relationship to the lethal, incendiary organization cited as justification for the Klan and for the rifle clubs created by whites to guard their women and children and their right to life and liberty. The era was grossly distorted by D. W. Griffith in his celebrated epic, *The Birth of a Nation,* which depicts savage blacks, intoxicated with power, emboldened by guns, roaming the countryside, breaking down doors, raping white women, and slaughtering

the brave men who stood in their defense. This portrayal is a perversion of truth equaled only by that grotesque film's rendition of
the hero—the Little Colonel—who conceived the entire idea for
the Ku Klux Klan while watching two small children play hide
and seek beneath a white sheet.

The truth about the militia (like most truths) lay somewhere in
between the two extremes of interpretation. Obviously its effectiveness depended largely on the number of men under arms: as
of 1869, there were comparatively few weapons available for
militia use. Given this fact, Governor Scott had to concentrate his
strength in communities where he believed the white forces were
strong enough to jeopardize either Negro rights or the Republican
party or both. By the summer of 1870, with an election looming
and Scott a candidate to succeed himself as governor, he used the
militia more and more as a political instrument to further his own
ends, a practice which brought him into growing controversy and
ultimate rupture with Elliott.

Another organization which Scott employed virtually exclusively
for personal political purposes was the state constabulary, a special
force consisting of five hundred deputy constables who could, on a
moment's notice and for $3.00 a day, be dispatched to any loca-
tion where the Republican managers deemed their presence valuable. The chief constable was a Northern import named John B.
Hubbard who was appointed in August 1868 by the governor, soon
becoming one of his most faithful lackeys and a thorn in Elliott's
side. It rankled Elliott that, as assistant adjutant general, he did not
take precedence over Hubbard and that he was carefully reminded
of that fact by the chief of the constabulary. A case in point concerned horses: Captain Hubbard's constabulary force of five hundred included some twenty mounted men whose function the
governor apparently considered superfluous. Accordingly Elliott,
acting on Scott's orders, wrote to Hubbard on March 17, 1870, requesting him to transfer to the Adjutant General's Department the
horses and saddles belonging to the state, together with a full report about the purchase of the animals and the expenses incurred
in caring for them.

Hubbard forwarded the list of horses and their accoutrements
but refused to transfer the animals themselves without specific instructions from Governor Scott, who happened to be in Washington at the time. Elliott then dispatched John B. Dennis, his white

assistant ordnance officer, to demand the horses; Hubbard again refused. Hubbard then telegraphed the governor for instructions. Scott answered, "You will *turn over the horses on paper,* but retain control of them until I return." [17]

Elliott was furious, and the *Report on Public Frauds* automatically attributed his anger to the fact that he had hoped by "cunning means" to acquire the horses in order to sell them and pocket the cash but was thwarted in this attempt by Governor Scott, who "came in and swept the proceeds." As reflected in his lengthy and bellicose letter to Scott on the subject, however, Elliott's resentment stemmed from an entirely different source. Hubbard, a subsidiary officer, had questioned his authority as assistant adjutant general of the state and the governor had in effect backed up the lower-ranking captain of the constabulary. "I desire to know if I am a menial or an officer of this state," Elliott wrote the governor on April 1, 1870. "If my position is one of responsibility and respectability . . . I will demand now and at all times from every individual the amount of respect attached to it. . . . If [I am] a mere nomenclature . . . I desire that it be understood by each and every individual that I will not so far forget my manhood as to cling to any such position." [18]

The horses were eventually sold, bringing a total of $2,375, most of which was split between Scott and Hubbard.[19] Elliott received none of the take, and, if the governor ever replied to Elliott's letter, the answer has not been preservd. However, it is easy to trace the deterioration in Elliott's relationship to Scott from that point on.

Elliott was often described as being a man generous and loyal to his friends, but he had a quixotic pattern in dealing with his associates, particularly with the three governors under whom he served, of shifting from loyalty to antagonism and back and sometimes back once again. Parenthetically, such a turnabout had also been true in his dealings with Chief Constable Hubbard. His enemy in the horse-transfer affair had been his ally in an episode which had taken place six months earlier.

"A Negro from Massachusetts Cowhides a White Carpetbagger," ran a headline in the *Charleston Daily News* of Saturday, October 25, 1869. On Friday morning, the story went on, Elliott had accosted James D. Kavannah, an assistant private secretary to Governor Scott, in front of the state executive building in Columbia and given him a severe horsewhipping. The incident grew out of some "domestic entanglement" which, as was later revealed, involved Kavannah's having written a letter of assignation to Elliott's wife Grace. Kavannah's friends, the *News* reported, were looking for Elliott and were determined to shoot on sight, but Elliott, apparently unmoved, was said to have "stood his ground."

The next evening Kavannah encountered Constable John Hubbard in the barroom of the Columbia Hotel and "assailed him with abusive language," charging him with having countenanced, even encouraged, Elliott in the cowhiding. Ultimately Kavannah, who was reported as having "served freely at the shrine of Bacchus," began assaulting Hubbard with blows. The chief constable finally terminated the ruckus by clapping the governor's secretary in the guard house for the night. As a result of this second fracas, the *News* remarked that the hapless Kavannah seemed "no more successful in the service of Mars than in that of Venus." While threats against Elliott continued "loud and sanguinary," the *News* still obviously felt he had come off the better of the two: "The logic of the carpetbagger politicians has been that a Negro is as good as a white man, but the logic of Elliott goes to prove that a Negro is superior to a white man at least when the latter is a carpetbagger. This latter logic is good in this community *viz* Elliott. God speed in the application of all such syllogisms." [20]

Elliott's battle with the governor's assistant private secretary received wider press coverage than did most of his contretemps with the governor himself. To trace and to understand the ambivalent relations between Elliott and Scott is an often baffling exercise. Of the two men, Elliott was beyond question the more intelligent and probably the better-educated. He was also the stronger; Scott was reputed to have had a fondness both for women and alcohol; no account of Elliott ever mentioned any penchant on his part for drink, and his relations with women do not appear to have influenced his public life.

Still, though he may have been weak, Scott was the governor of the state and at first Elliott was inclined to treat him with due deference: "Hoping that I have not in the least transcended my duty and that I have not trespassed too much on your Excellency's attention, I ask to remain very respectfully your Excellency's Most Obedient Servant" was the way he concluded a letter in September 1869.

Gradually, however, although he remained perfectly correct in his dealings with Scott, Elliott began in various subtle ways to manipulate the governor for his own purposes. During most of 1870 Scott cooperated in furthering Elliott's ends, partly because he doubtless thought them consonant with his own and partly because he may have been somewhat intimidated by this rising young black politician, who, as a result of statewide exposure in forming the militia, was becoming more and more important around the statehouse, in the legislature, and in Republican party councils. Furthermore, Elliott's personal attributes—his intelligence and acumen, his energy and resoluteness, his imagination and courage (and perhaps also his temper)—made him a man to reckon with. By late 1869 it was apparent that his political ambitions had begun to crystallize.

Barnwell County, which Elliott represented in the General Assembly, was in the Third Congressional District. Although this district had only a slight black majority, the Negroes were much better attuned to political affairs by 1870 and were going to be a far larger factor in congressional elections that they had been in 1868.* Elliott therefore began to focus his attention on moving upward to the Congress of the United States, and he needed assistance from Governor Scott. He also needed to establish his residence in the district.† On November 27, 1869, Elliott bought, for $1,500 his first property—a parcel "together with all buildings and other appurtenances situated thereon"—on Sumter Street in the town of Aiken, which was then still in Barnwell County although later it was to become part of Aiken County.

The Elliotts obviously did not occupy the Sumter Street property for very long, if at all, because three months later, in February 1870, Elliott bought another parcel in Aiken (without selling the first one) on Richland Street, also for $1,500. Meanwhile, it is probable that he did not want to live in Aiken in any case, but rather in Columbia, where all the drama of the time was being

---

* The four congressmen elected in 1868, all white and all Republicans, were B. F. Whittemore, C. C. Bowen, S. L. Hoge, and A. S. Wallace.

† This need had not arisen for Elliott as a member of the General Assembly, where residence requirements were extremely lax.

enacted and where all the really important Radicals had their residences. Therefore, in March 1870, only one month after his second Aiken purchase, he bought still another house and lot which cost him the large sum of $4,800,[21] this time on Taylor Street in the capital city. Here too he needed assistance from Governor Scott.

At that time Elliott was earning $600 as a state representative, $1,500 as assistant adjutant general, and whatever else he could pick up from his new and struggling law practice. His total income would hardly seem to justify the $7,800 spent in real estate over a four-month period. But he was known to be profligate in his tastes—contemporary reports all spoke of his fine library, some also of his excellent stable—and to pay for his extravagant overexpansion, he persuaded Scott to take a first mortgage (perhaps with some of the money from the sale of the horses) on the Taylor Street house.*

Having solved his personal financial problems, at least temporarily, Elliott then turned to Scott for funds to run his campaign to win the nomination for Congress from S. L. Hoge, a white lawyer who was the other leading Republican candidate in the Third District. Once more the governor obliged. Sometime in May or June of 1870 he sent for his chief constable, John Hubbard, and, according to Hubbard's later testimony in the *Report on Public Frauds,* said to him, "Hubbard, I want De Large and Elliott nominated for Congress, and you must use all the influence you can bring about to prevent Hoge and Bowen from being nominated. When the time comes I will want you to appoint as many constables as De Large and his friends may ask, for Bowen must be defeated, no matter what it costs." [22] †

* Scott's involvement is presumed, because six years later, in 1876, a claim for foreclosure was filed against the Elliotts and Scott, and, the following year, in what must have been the nadir of their association, Scott filed his own complaint against Grace Elliott, as the titular owner of the property, "praying for a decree of foreclosure and sale of the premises" (as recorded in the Aiken County and Richland County Deed Books).

† Scott's greater concern over De Large was doubtless based on the fact that De Large's opponent, C. C. Bowen was one of the most reprehensible characters in the Republican party. (Among other things he was a bigamist.) To win the nomination from him, De Large depended heavily on having enough of his friends appointed to the constabulary to push for him in key districts. De Large was also land commissioner by then and was able to "divert" some funds from that source to finance his campaign.

In executing Scott's order to get Elliott nominated, Hubbard said, "I used money (or, at least, I drew it and turned it over to R. B. Elliott) raised on fraudulent accounts approved by R. B. Elliott, Acting Adjutant and Inspector General, and R. K. Scott as Governor. . . . I agreed to make out an account for alleged services, which was to be approved as hereinbefore mentioned. The following account marked 'RE,' . . . was made out July 25th, 1870. It is in my handwriting. Elliott said I must not trust my clerk to make it out." [23] The account was certified as correct by Elliott, according to the *Report on Public Frauds*. Hubbard drew the total and delivered it to Elliott. The Third District convention met on July 30, 1870, and nominated R. B. Elliott as their candidate for Congress.

Elliott, realizing he would need further money to finance his election campaign, told Hubbard—and by this time he seemed to be riding high enough to give the chief of the constabulary orders—to "make out another account for $1500 and see Governor Scott at once concerning it." But this time Scott was far from acquiescent; in fact, he "became very much enraged and cursed Elliott, the Convention and almost everything he could think of; swore that damn nigger cost more than he was worth but finally said 'I'll approve this account for the damned rascal but tell him it shall be the last.' " [24]

The most likely reason for Scott's change of attitude toward Elliott was that the two men were coming into constant conflict over Scott's increasing use of the militia for political purposes. As Franklin Moses was to testify later, "By appointing the local leaders in various Counties as officers and keeping them on full pay, Governor Scott was enabled to secure to himself friends and supporters in almost every County in the State. Not one-fourth of the persons whose names appear on the payrolls rendered any service except of a political nature." [25] Although Elliott's objectives were the same as the governor's as far as Republicanism was concerned, he still felt that Scott was undermining the discipline and effectiveness of the militia, and he protested strenuously. He especially resented it when his own authority was challenged or his office bypassed.

On this issue Elliott and Scott remained at swords' point until December 3, 1870, when Elliott finally resigned as assistant adjutant general. Outwardly, however, Elliott maintained an *entente cordiale* with Scott through most of 1870. During the campaign, as will be seen, he worked ceaselessly for the governor's renomination and re-election, thereby repaying his political debt to him.

But underneath he must have been seething, as suggested by his bitterly accusing letter of resignation: "I am constrained to this act by reasons well known to Your Excellency." [26] His primary objection, he stated in his elegant prose, was that the governor was paying persons for services which they had never rendered— in other words, using the adjutant general's office as a sort of political pork barrel while at the same time refusing compensation due those who had faithfully performed their duties in the office. "Therefore I feel called upon," Elliott concluded, "to sever my connection with a Department which has for its basis so unjust a discrimination, so unfair a controlling favoritism."

Scott's version of the resignation, according to his testimony in the *Report on Public Frauds,* was quite different: "Elliott was Assistant Adjutant General under F. J. Moses," Scott stated, "and had been instrumental in organizing the militia throughout the state, and had a number of attachees and presented their bills, which I disapproved. Elliott then tendered his resignation which I accepted. He and Moses subsequently begged that I would recall my acceptance which I did." [27]

In evaluating the truth of the incidents described in the *Report on Public Frauds* it is important to bear in mind a peculiarity of that 1877 document. All the witnesses summoned by the Democrats after the Reconstruction to illustrate the corruption of that period were themselves Radical Republicans who had been involved in the affairs of state. These men, now completely out of power and hoping probably for some favor from the ruling Democrats, were called upon to bear witness against each other. Thus, individuals as characterized by the carefully selected testimony of their peers or partners in crime were made to appear totally reprehensible, under no circumstances to be trusted. But, when these same men were witnesses and gave testimony against other individuals' misdeeds, their word was regarded as gospel.

In the case of Scott's affidavit concerning Elliott, there is no evidence to indicate that the governor ever recalled his resignation or that Elliott ever resumed his duties as assistant adjutant general. Indeed, on the face of it, it is inconceivable that he would have continued in that office after his resignation, for by December 1870 he had been elected to Congress and was due to leave for Washington early in the next year. One further point casts doubt on Scott's testimony: Robert Elliott had by that time shown his political mettle; he was widely recognized as the spearhead of the Republican state party. It is difficult to imagine him ever "begging" for anything.

6

Republicanism First, Foremost, and Always

THE FIRST concerted political action to combat the car-
petbagger-Negro government was initiated by the Conservative
(or Democratic *) press which called a meeting of all its editors
in Columbia on March 16, 1870. After two days of deliberations,
the assemblage, which came to be referred to as the Press Conference, adopted a resolution recognizing the legal rights of all
citizens, "irrespective of color or previous condition," to vote and
to hold public office "subject only to personal qualifications and
fitness." This was a landmark—the first time a body composed
entirely of whites had publicly acknowledged the political equality
of the Negro in the state of South Carolina.

Even in this rather obvious acceptance of a *fait accompli* there
was not unanimity. Objections to the resolution were raised by a
group of editors in a privately printed minority report. The dis-
senters argued against the resolution on the grounds that, while
it was perhaps necessary to tolerate the situation temporarily,
surely when the blacks were finally swept from office it would
no longer be necessary to accept their political equality. To recognize their right to suffrage and office was but to "rivet the chain
with which our hands and feet are now bound." The minority re-

---

* Throughout the nine years of the Reconstruction, the Democrats preferred to call themselves Conservatives. It was not until 1876, with "redemption" of the state in sight, that the Straightouters finally insisted on
calling a Democrat a Democrat.

port also raised an ugly specter: Would not political equality lead to some form of social equality? "We cannot consent to a social mixture of races." And then, inevitably, "There is no dividing line between social equality and miscegenation." [1]

Although many of the editors may well have shared this fear, they were also realists. The blacks had a voting majority of thirty thousand in the state; the time had come to try to woo them to the Conservative side if the state was ever to be "redeemed." Furthermore, the editors must have been aware that if they did not quickly and publicly admit the political equality of their "black brethren," they would soon find themselves in the embarrassing position of granting to the Negro an inalienable right which he already constitutionally possessed. The timing was actually quite close. Only two weeks after the Press Conference, the Fifteenth Amendment was ratified, thereby guaranteeing that the right to vote not be abridged or denied because of race, color, or previous condition of servitude.

The ratification was widely celebrated by the black citizens of South Carolina. Every city, town, and county courthouse had a Fifteenth Amendment celebration, and Negro statesmen were in great demand during the month of April to appear at one occasion after another. If the number and importance of each man's speaking assignments were marks of his prestige, Elliott clearly ranked very high, for he took part in the observances at Edgefield, Abbeville, and Charleston, and was one of the principal orators in the capital city of Columbia on April 29.

By that time the initiative generated at the Press Conference had led to the organization of a new political entity, known at first as the Citizen's party, but ultimately called the Union Reform party. "History but repeats itself," editorialized the *Charleston Courier*. "Parties spring up, perform their mission and then give way to new combinations and the formation of new ideas and issues." Allegedly the "new idea" of the Citizen's party was to court and win the immense Negro vote and to use it to rid South Carolina of corruption and misrule. In reality its objective was to eliminate Negroes from office and thus re-establish a white man's government; 1870 was to be the "Year of Happy Deliverance."

Elliott was merciless in his derision of the new "reformers": "Today, instead of being spurned away as brutes, we are welcomed by those who have always declared that we were not fit to occupy a position entrusted to us," he said in his Columbia speech. "The men who in the fall of 1868 declared that we would never be citizens . . . are now for us. We now find them more loud-mouthed than any to accord us the rights that have already been solemnly declared ours. Today we find that our only danger is that, in their anxiety, they will swallow us entire. . . . The danger is that our people might be too easily led to believe the arguments of our new friends and be won over to their side. But let me say that today, clothed in the rights of citizenship, elevated to the proper position of manhood, it behooves us to be careful of these men whether they come in the name of the Democrat, Conservative, or Citizen's party." [2]

Equally mocking in tone was the *Charleston Daily Republican,* the largest and, in the year 1870, almost the only daily Republican paper in the state. As prejudiced in its Republican sentiments as the *Charleston Mercury* was in the opposite direction, the fledgling *Daily Republican* tried to emulate the bitter sarcasm of the venerable *Mercury.* Its favorite target was the "Broad Street Clique." Broad Street was Charleston's elite financial-legal center, and the clique was made up of men who, although they did not necessarily have offices on Broad Street,* were eligible because they were members of the professions, holders of large wealth, or "had a grandfather, no matter how big an ass he was," which somehow entitled them to a strong voice in the affairs of state.[3] "What is the dilettante of Broad Street really worth to the world?" asked the *Daily Republican.*[4] "What has he done, what is he doing for his fellow men?" For one thing, he was masterminding the forthcoming June convention of the Citizen's party or, as the *Daily Republican* liked to put it, the "June Bug Convention of the Palpitating Party."

To give credibility and potency to the new reform party, two types of delegates were being sought for its convention: aristocrats who had been members of the former ruling class and Negroes, the first being considerably easier to come by than the second. Numerous blacks were allegedly hired at $2.00 a day to attend the

---

* There were also some men who had offices on Broad Street who were not members of the clique, to wit, Robert B. Elliott, William J. Whipper, and Macon B. Allen, of the firm Whipper, Elliott, and Allen, 61 Broad Street.

convention. "Those who have other work, more respectable and less dull, will refuse," wrote the *Daily Republican,* "but two dollars is not to be rejected by an idle man because the work is disagreeable." [5]

Other Negroes maintained that they had been appointed as delegates to the Citizen's (or Union) Reform Convention without their consent, in some cases without their knowledge. One black, after informing his Republican friends in Lancaster County that he had no intention of attending the convention to which he had been named a delegate, wrote, "I regard the meeting and my nomination as nothing more than a repetition of the devilish duplicity that has been practiced upon our people for the last four years by the pro-slavery party." [6] Some Negroes said they went to the preliminary Union Reform meetings in their counties just out of curiosity, but few evinced much real interest in the new party or could be persuaded to attend the convention without some financial inducement.

When the 150 delegates finally assembled in Columbia on June 15, 1870, there were some thirty Negroes present, none of whom had been delegates to the 1868 Constitutional Convention or were members of the state's General Assembly. This was hardly surprising since the new party was being formed explicitly to oppose what one Democratic newspaper referred to as "that abomination of abominations known in Columbia as the Legislature of South Carolina." [7]

To the Conservative press the occasion was a grand one. "For the first time in the history of South Carolina," exulted the *Charleston Daily Courier,* "her people, her entire people, her wealth, her intelligence, her bone and sinew, all, irrespective of race, color or previous condition, meet in convention for the common weal." [8]

Although most of the Union Reformers were Democrats, it was considered important that they chose at least a nominal Republican to head the ticket. Some delegates felt that they should not even try to nominate candidates for the offices of governor and lieutenant governor, believing that opposition to Governor Scott might consolidate strength behind him. This sentiment did not prevail, however, and the convention chose for governor a Kentuckian, Judge Robert B. Carpenter, who was characterized as "a Southern gentleman *but* a Republican." [9] The *Courier* described Carpenter with qualified enthusiasm as a circuit judge who had "discharged his duties impartially and given general satisfaction." Under the circumstances they did not think a better nomination could be made.[10]

In contrast, there was great enthusiasm about the candidate for lieutenant governor, General M. C. Butler, a gallant and valorous Confederate general, who was an ardent Democrat and had never shown the slightest inclination to act upon the pious words on racial equality he had manufactured for the occasion as chairman of the platform committee.

Before Butler's nomination was voted upon, however, the convention delegates played out a patently prearranged little drama designed to demonstrate the biracial, nonpartisan viewpoint of the new Union Reform party. As soon as General Butler's name was placed in nomination, General J. B. Kershaw, a prominent Democrat, sprang to his feet, "I am requested by General Butler, who has left the room, to state that he labors under political disabilities and is thereby disqualified." As a Confederate general Butler was indeed disbarred from holding state office without a pardon from the president (which would doubtless have been granted, as many similar ones had been). Knowing this, Kershaw added, "I do not wish it to be understood by this statement, however, that General Butler's name is withdrawn." [11]

Up stepped actor number two, Dr. J. E. Byrd, vice-president of the convention. He nominated F. L. Cardozo, the black secretary of state who was a solid Republican and obviously not present at the Union Reform Convention. Next came a black delegate, A. Harper, from Charleston, a willing cat's-paw, to say that, while he was quite satisfied with the choice of General Butler, if he was indeed disqualified, his supporters' votes might be thrown away; therefore he would like to nominate another colored man, Mr. William E. Marshall, also of the Charleston delegation.

Marshall did his part: "I do not think I possess the necessary qualifications. . . . I decline an honor which I would be proud to own, I cheerfully transfer it to General M. C. Butler whom it will be my pleasure to support." [12]

Two more Negroes were then nominated. Two more declined fulsomely in favor of Butler. At this point General Kershaw, the star of the piece and probably coauthor (with Butler) of the script, rose to say "in all candor and sincerity" that he would prefer an honest and capable colored man on the ticket, "but, Mr. President, we are embarrassed by the fact that the only colored man who now remains in nomination [Cardozo] already holds a high office in the state and would, as I am almost directly informed, decline the office." (In this Kershaw was entirely correct. Cardozo, though a more cautious and conciliatory man than Elliott, would have been no more willing to run on the Union Reform ticket than they would have been to have him do so.)

"So far as I know," Kershaw continued unctuously, "he would have been altogether acceptable to this Convention as he certainly would be to myself. If I believed that he would accept the nomination I would counsel this Convention to render it to him unanimously. . . . As I said before, however, I have reasonable cause to suppose that Mr. Cardozo would not accept the nomination. On the other hand my esteemed and respected friend [Butler], than whom there is none I would more delight to honor, labors under a disability. Still [and here Kershaw moved in for the denouement] our colored friends present have taken this matter into their own hands, and put words into our mouths, and since they continue to press the nomination of General Butler, I am satisfied to let it go forth as the will of the Convention." [13] Great applause.*

By thus exploiting a few weak, ignorant, or easily bought Negroes, the new party, the "bone and sinew" of the state, began its campaign for reform by an act of blatant hypocrisy.

The Conservative press, which had had little reason to be happy or hopeful since the Reconstruction acts of March 1867, responded to the convention with enthusiastic fervor: "The movement initiated at the Reform convention last week by honest men without regard to political prejudice will, if vigorously pushed forward, eventually crown our efforts with success," said the *Marion Star*.[14] "An honest and patriotic effort to uproot ignorance, vice and dishonesty and establish in its place virtue, competency and worth," gloated the *Kingstree Star*.[15] "A pure and noble gentleman," rejoiced the *Charleston Daily Courier* about General Butler. "No reader of this paper, in fact no citizen of this state can fail to approve his nomination." [16] There were, of course, 85,475 black voters in the state who could certainly have failed to approve the nomination of a man who had fought to preserve the institution of slavery.

* As everyone concerned must have known they would be, Butler's disabilities were shortly thereafter removed by presidential pardon.

The rise of the Union Reform party was not without its advantages as far as the Republican party was concerned. Heretofore they had had only the shadow of the Bourbons and planters as their targets; now they had flesh and blood antagonists who looked on themselves as the South's new "natural leaders." But, at the same time, the Republicans were involved in some rather sharp infighting. Perhaps emboldened or, more likely, inspired by the passage of the Fifteenth Amendment, certain black statesmen began to demand a greater share of the public offices.

At a Republican mass meeting held in Charleston on June 24, 1870, two weeks after the close of the Union Reform Convention, some inflammatory speeches were made, the most insistent by the renowned Negro, Martin Delany. Delany was a physician who had attended Harvard Medical School for a year, as well as an inventor, explorer, philosopher, and cofounder and editor with Frederick Douglass of the newspaper *North Star.* He had been an early abolitionist and an advocate, long before the Civil War, of black separatism; in fact, he is often referred to today as the father of that movement.

"I take the ground," said Delany, "that no people have become great people who have not had their own leaders, and black men must have black leaders. We have the strength and we want a fair share of the offices. We don't want more than one half; we don't want a colored governor, for our good sense tells us differently . . . but we want a lieutenant governor, and two colored men in the House of Representatives and one in the Senate and our quota of state and county offices." [17]

At that time Delany was careful to specify that he had no idea of forming a black man's party, but the devious Robert C. De Large, appearing at the same meeting, hinted that this might be his objective, and implied that blacks might be better off placing their trust in blacks than in whites: "I hold that my race has always been Republican from necessity only," he suggested ominously.[18]

The *Daily Republican,* which proclaimed itself the official organ of the party, lashed back at the "extreme and impractical views of race" expressed by Delany and De Large. Fearing that a black party was indeed in the making, they protested, "It is a return to the old curse of South Carolina. Have Republicans fought so long for the disenthrallment of the colored people from the whites and the destruction of all political lines founded on race, only to see the colored people return evil for evil, and seek to pit their race, as a race, against the whites?" [19]

For almost a week the sparks flew. Then, with the Republican convention only a month away, matters began to simmer down. De Large vowed that he was making his fight for Congress strictly on Republican principles and within the Republican party. He was not in favor of a black man's party and never intended to say a word that could be construed that way.

The *Daily Republican* answered that they had been convinced that such a movement was in the wind and that, if successful, it would have proved "direfully disastrous" to both the Republican party and to all the people. In an editorial headed "The Conclusion of the Whole Matter," they wrote that fortunately the response to their strong protest had met with universal approval among Republicans. The controversy had not injured the party because it had stopped in time, but it had gone just far enough to point up the serious evils of making distinctions of race or color in the party.[20]

Elliott, who was not at the Republican meeting with Martin Delany in Charleston, did not appear to have taken any part in the subsequent dispute, but doubtless he was involved in some way because he later said that his opponents had "misrepresented and misunderstood" him when they called him a leader of the "proscripted black party." There is certainly no evidence that he was a leader, and it does not even seem likely that he fully endorsed the idea of a black man's party. At the very least, his actions and utterances lead one to believe that he was of two minds about it. Beyond question he had worked hard and fought consistently for greater recognition of Negroes in public office. On the other hand, he had clearly demonstrated his conviction that the destiny of his race lay in its close ties with the Republican party. He well understood that the new "natural leaders," as personified by the Union Reform party, sought to gain the Negro vote and then to use it ultimately to oust blacks from power. He realized too that certain Republican carpetbaggers and scalawags might also try to exploit the blacks for selfish purposes, but these efforts would be parochial, limited in scope. If ever they encroached on the Negroes' basic rights, he felt assured that they would be speedily balked by strong Radical Republicans in Congress and even by President Grant. Elliott had great faith in the statesmen who had worked to achieve the Fourteenth and Fifteenth amendments. In sum, he reasoned that the Negroes were in a safer, stronger position when closely allied to the party which had successfully built those two towering monuments to racial equality than when cast adrift in a black party where they might easily founder.

At the same time, with his fierce racial pride, Elliott must have been very much stirred by Martin Delany's conviction that black men needed black leaders. His ambivalence was reflected at the Republican State Convention where he was elected permanent chairman. From the moment he took up the gavel on July 25, 1870, a strong sense of party unity and loyalty prevailed. Delegates affirmed their Republicanism first, foremost, and always. Nevertheless the blacks were intent on forcing the racial issue. They demanded and received greater power and far more public offices.

With almost no contest, A. J. Ransier won the nomination for lieutenant governor, the first Negro in any Southern state to achieve this position. The four congressional districts met after the convention to choose their candidates for Congress, and when they had done their work, three out of the four nominees were black.* Within the party structure, the Negroes also dominated in all areas. The state central committee consisted of Ransier, as chairman, along with Cardozo and W. B. Nash, and only one white, E. W. M. Mackey. Three of the four congressional district chairmen were blacks, and the convention, of course, was under the chairmanship of a black (Elliott), with two others, Robert Smalls and J. H. Rainey, as vice-chairmen.

No one, black or white, challenged R. K. Scott's hold on the governorship; he was renominated without contest. The chairman of the platform committee was B. F. Whittemore, a white carpetbagger from Malden, Massachusetts, whose appointment caused much gloating among the Conservative press since he had recently resigned his seat in the federal House of Representatives just be-

* At the convention itself two congressmen-at-large were chosen prospectively, in the belief that as a result of the 1870 census and the Negro counting as a whole man, the state would be accorded a larger congressional delegation. Of these two men (who were never actually seated) one, Lucius Wimbush, was a black. The other J. P. M. Epping, was notable chiefly as the originator of the soft drink sarsparilla.

fore he was due to be expelled by the Congress for selling a cadet-ship to West Point. (His extraordinary explanation for this action was that he wanted the money to give to his needy constituents.)

Whittemore's connection with the platform gave the press an opportunity to mock it. "We have read and re-read with some care and much amusement the platform of the corruptionists, styling themselves the Republican State Convention," wrote the *Courier*. The platform was in reality a straightforward document, possible to disagree with, certainly, but hardly to be read with amusement. The Republicans expressed sincere satisfaction with the fidelity evinced by President Grant and committed their support to him; they cordially endorsed the administration of Governor Scott and insisted on continuous close economy in all departments of government. They hailed with gratitude the adoption of the Fifteenth Amendment and pledged the Republican party to a "firm, fearless and unfaltering support of the Civil Rights Bill." They urged the United States to purchase land for the landless in the Southern states under the Homestead Law. They declared finally that they were entering the 1870 campaign confident of victory with the noble words "equality before the law, free speech, a free press, a free ballot, and free schools emblazoned on our hearts." [21]

Scott and Ransier each gave supper parties on the night of their nominations. There is no way of knowing if these affairs were integrated, but it seems probable that they were not. Scott had had trouble on that score early in his administration, when, following the time-honored custom of his predecessors, he gave a ball for state officials at the Governor's Mansion at which no Negroes were present.* Commenting on this, the *New York*

---

* Even though no blacks were invited, there were enough carpetbaggers and scalawags on the guest list to cause most of the "old residents" to decline with thanks. Columbians then delighted to tell a story about how Scott allegedly spoke to one of his guests, Timothy Hurley, a white legislator, adventurer, and sometime owner of the *South Carolina Leader,* of his disappointment in the attendance at the ball: "We have here an outstanding party," the governor was supposed to have said to Hurley. "Beautiful decorations, delicious food, good whiskey, old wines and the orchestra is the best obtainable. No expense has been spared. Aren't you surprised so few Columbia gentlemen accepted my invitation?" To which Hurley was alleged to have replied "bluntly," "No sir, if I were a gentleman I shouldn't be here myself" (Nell S. Graydon, *Tales of Columbia* [Columbia: R. L. Bryan, 1964]).

Times correspondent wrote, "Although the Governor had ventured to extend his recognition to a mulatto or quadroon girl when travelling upon the cars, he had not the courage to invite his colored friends to his entertainment." [22] His failure to do so gave rise to a storm of protest, less among the Negroes themselves than among certain whites who sought to improve their political positions by constituting themselves champions of Negro equality. Prominent among these was Franklin J. Moses, Jr., who was at the time speaker of the House and was looking toward the Governor's Mansion himself.

Scott solved the problem later in his regime by instituting a series of Thursday evening "levees" which were open to both races but which were almost invariably attended only by blacks. However, if his post-nomination celebration had fallen into this category, it seems unlikely that Ransier would have given a party of his own.

In any event, at one or the other of the affairs Elliott was serenaded, presumably in gratitude for his able handling of the Republican Convention. In response he said that if he received the nomination for Congress at the Third Congressional District Convention, he wanted it clearly understood that it would be as a sound Republican and not as a black man.

He did win the nomination with relative ease, defeating his opponent, S. L. Hoge, by a vote of 19 to 9. Hoge's nominator then did his gracious duty and made it unanimous. Elliott's acceptance speech was purely political and full of platitudes: He was incapable of expressing the deep emotion he felt; the Third Congressional District might have chosen a worthier man but certainly not a sounder Republican; he bore no ill will to any Republicans in the district (i.e., Hoge and his supporters); he would labor not just for himself, but for all Republican candidates. "You might get along without me," he concluded, "but you could ill afford to do without R. K. Scott. My heartiest efforts will be given to secure his reelection." This latter statement could hardly have been less sincere, since it will be remembered that Elliott and Scott were not on good terms as a result of Elliott's angry resignation from the office of assistant adjutant general. Nonetheless, good party man that he was, Elliott did devote a great deal of time between his nomination and election day campaigning for Robert K. Scott.

The governor, employing the traditional political gambit of an incumbent and heavy favorite, refused to risk his lead by meeting his opponent, Judge Carpenter, on any speaking platform. A list of twenty-two prominent Republican speakers—Elliott among them—was offered instead, but the opposition insisted on only candidate-for-candidate encounters and refused to invite any of the other men to speak on the same program with Judge Carpenter.

The alert Elliott, however, noted that on one occasion the Reformers called upon Scott either to come himself and answer the charges made against him or "designate a Demosthenes to speak for him." Accordingly, Elliott showed up at a huge outdoor meeting held at Sidney Park, Columbia, in mid-August and, standing in the crowd, began to heckle the chairman to be heard as Scott's Demosthenes.

The chairman tried first to put Elliott in his place by responding that he did not propose to "shoot our big guns against Scott's little ones," and Carpenter himself said contemptuously that he did not feel bound to meet every Tom, Dick, or Harry who came along, or—quickly switching metaphors—a new horse at every road.[23]

Elliott, undaunted, persevered, waving a copy of a newspaper containing the Demosthenes suggestion. General J. B. Kershaw then took a hand and tried honey instead of vinegar. He had heard Colonel Elliott speak once before and was bound to say it had been a very good, straightforward speech. But, under the circumstances, since the Demosthenes suggestion had not been officially authorized, he did not think that Colonel Elliott could claim a hearing, and hoped he would understand the difficulties under which they were laboring in trying to present a new party to the public.

Colonel Elliott professed magnanimity, and some of the Union Reformers were so favorably impressed with his suitable demeanor that they decided to set up an impromptu meeting for that evening on the lawn outside of the Columbia Hotel so that Elliott might have an opportunity to be heard.

Elliott was too canny to fall into the trap. The meeting was proposed for late at night when most of the country people who had heard him in the morning at Sidney Park would have gone home. Furthermore, it was not to be an official meeting of the Union Reform party, but a hastily conceived affair by which the

Reformers were hoping to gain quick credit for their open-minded willingness to listen to opposition speakers when, in fact, they were not prepared to do so on any formal prearranged basis.

Elliott framed his written refusal in his usual elegant, courteous language.[24] At that point the Reformers had not yet chosen a candidate to run against him in the Third Congressional District and perhaps it was Elliott's style on this occasion which suggested to them the idea of running him as their candidate as well. A week after the mass meeting, the *New York Times* reported that such a possibility was being talked of.[25] The advantages to the new party were plain: They would be gaining a polished, competent, ambitious and, they probably thought, tractable Negro, Eton-educated to boot (at least so the story went). What was more, Elliott was probably going to win no matter who they ran against him. By making him their candidate they would turn defeat into victory and win plaudits for their progressive biracial ticket in the bargain.

The only drawback to the plan was that there was no advantage whatsoever as far as Elliott himself was concerned. Even less than Cardozo would he have been willing to be a dupe for the Reformers and he must quickly have so informed them. They then chose one of their own as the congressional candidate from the Third District. Major John E. Bacon was the son of one of the low country's most aristocratic families. Just before the war he had been attaché at the Court of St. Petersburg to the ambassador, F. W. Pickens, who subsequently became the secession governor of South Carolina. Bacon's wife, who was Pickens's daughter, was the principal organizer of the Daughters of the American Revolution in the state.

Meanwhile the Reformers had received a very considerable setback when highly respected former Governor James L. Orr announced his intention of voting for Scott and Ransier. By every inclination and persuasion, Orr, who had been the first governor elected by the whites after the war and before the start of Radical Reconstruction, belonged in the forefront of the new party's ranks. Yet his reasons for endorsing the Republican party, as eloquently propounded in a lengthy public statement, were both pragmatic and eminently sensible.[26] The Union Reform party was trying to reform the Republican party by destroying it, he said. There was not the remotest chance of their success because the Negro majority in the state would not be lured away from its ardent devotion to the Republican party, and quite understandably and properly so.

Suppose our conditions were reversed, Orr suggested. Suppose that our white ancestors had been slaves for two hundred years, and that then a political party had fought a war and given us freedom. Suppose that same party had periled its own supremacy by guaranteeing to us our civil rights, and above all the ballot. Suppose in the face of all this, we were asked by those who had opposed all these great boons to join with them in overthrowing the party of our deliverance and redemption? "Would any white man for a moment tolerate such a proposition?" [27]

Governor Orr then stated his conviction that the white race in South Carolina would never again be able to influence the management of governmental affairs until it secured the confidence of the colored race. Declining to dwell on what he referred to as constant and often exaggerated references to corruption and misrule, Orr chose to concentrate on some of the positive accomplishments of the Republican administration. He then called upon the "good and true men" of the state to accept the Reconstruction acts of Congress and the new conditions growing out of them: "If they will affiliate with the Republican organization, we will profit largely by what they have done correctly and much can be accomplished to correct abuse and malfeasance that may have grown up in the anomalous state of affairs surrounding us." [28]

Yet even without the votes of the "good and true men," the blacks and the Republican party triumphed completely—if only temporarily—in the election of 1870. Their victory was in every way decisive. Scott and Ransier defeated Carpenter and Butler by almost 35,000 votes. In the heavily Negro First Congressional District, J. H. Rainey, who finally replaced B. F. Whittemore as the candidate, walked away with a 17,191 majority over his white Union Reform opponent. By contrast, in the Second District, where two Radicals opposed each other, De Large won—or claimed to have won—by a majority of only 986 votes. His opponent, C. C. Bowen, contested; after De Large was seated in the House of Representatives, a congressional committee ruled that he had not received a majority of the votes cast and was therefore not entitled to retain his seat. Bowen was not seated either, however, because of alleged election irregularities.

Elliott's majority of 6,567 was substantial, particularly since his opponent, Bacon, had proved a very effective candidate who was given a slight edge to win by the *New York Times* in their prediction a few days before the election. The contest in the Fourth District was between two white men: Alexander S. Wallace, the Republican, defeated I. G. McKissick, his Union Reform opponent, who also contested the election for "irregularities," but in this case the congressional committee decided the evidence of the contestant was inadequate and Wallace retained his seat.[29]

Before, during, and after the election both parties charged violence and intimidation; and certainly there was evidence in the activities of the militia and the Ku Klux Klan to support each of their contentions. Furthermore, on the Republican side, the Union League (or the Loyal League, as this secret organization was sometimes called), which had been largely responsible for galvanizing the Negroes to register and vote in 1868 and which had been more or less quiescent in the intervening years, again sprang into action. Francis L. Cardozo, president of the Grand Council of Union Leagues of South Carolina, addressed the League's annual meeting in July 1870. Mincing no words, he reminded the membership that it would be "simply suicide" to adhere to any but the Republican party, which had distinguished itself as being the "generous protector of the freedmen amidst their greatest dangers." [30] In numerous counties various local Leagues joined together to form military companies within the militia and thus to back up their determination to win a united Negro vote for the Republicans with a show of force.

Most of the sorties of both the militia and the Klan took place in the up-country, where the Union Reformers felt they had a better chance, since the whites had a majority in more counties there than they did in the seacoast areas. Accordingly, Scott sent most of his arms to these counties, where it was alleged that 7,222 stands of arms and 88,000 rounds of ammunition were issued during the months of June, July, and August. Yet even the Union Reform candidate for governor, Carpenter, admitted that, although the militia was "sometimes very offensive and did a great deal of mischief," he knew of no instance where a colored company had attacked any person.[31]

Still, the presence of any bands of armed men, whether white or black, was always potentially dangerous. To prevent bloodshed in Spartanburg County, where racial feelings were running extremely high, one black militia commander deemed it unwise even to issue the 192 rifles and the 5,000 rounds of ammunition which had been allotted to him until the election was over. And indeed, on the day *after* the election, when their motive could only have been revenge, the Klan did lash out in Spartanburg, attacking and beating an estimated five hundred persons known to have voted the Republican ticket. They also killed several persons, including the only Negro magistrate in the county.

Uprisings of the same or even greater magnitude occurred almost simultaneously in Laurens, Union, and York counties. Thus began a period of rampant Klan activity which was to last well into the next year and have profound repercussions, not only in South Carolina but in the entire country, and to lead to an unprecedented federal intervention.

Although widespread outbursts were kept under control until after October 19—election day—more subtle means of intimidation were employed by both the Republican and the Union Reform parties. Evidence taken by the congressional committee investigating the Ku Klux Klan situation in the South indicated repeatedly that many a poor white who said he was satisfied with Scott's administration and expected to vote for him was "persuaded" by the Klan to vote for the Union Reform candidates. By the same method, a wavering Negro, lulled by the conciliation tactics of the Union Reformers, was "reminded" quite clearly by the militia of his duty to the Union Leagues and the Republican party. In the town of Cowpens, for example, while the Negro election manager was busy with his duties, an armed party of six or seven undisguised men approached the polling place and, while loudly proclaiming the white man's government, snapped the straps of their rifles and pointed the weapons threateningly at each black or white Republican who came to vote. Just as obstreperous were the armed militia companies around Charleston who, on election day, fell into line ominously behind any Negro suspected of having Union Reform sympathies. In Newbury, a black believed to have voted Union Reform was set upon by a group of unarmed militiamen. While whites drew pistols to defend him, the blacks shouted, "Go for your arms, go for your arms" and dashed for the armory.[32]

In addition to claiming violence and intimidation, the Union Reform party even more loudly cried fraud. And not without reason, for the machinery of the election laws did, without question, favor the party in power, since it was the governor who appointed the three election commissioners for each county. These commissioners, in turn, appointed the managers for each of the several precincts and furnished them with sealed ballot boxes. Naturally Scott chose commissioners favorable to himself and naturally the commissioners chose managers equally partisan. The Reformers were fond of saying that only in precincts where no Republican manager could be found who could read or write was the commissioner forced to appoint a Conservative. Many of the commissioners were themselves candidates for the General Assembly, and it was alleged that they carefully put the polling places in locations most convenient to Negroes, while often forcing whites to travel forty miles to vote. Union Reform candidates and sympathizers appearing before the congressional committee charged that in some instances the polling places were actually in the homes of Republicans. Furthermore, they charged that women and children voted by proxy for sick husbands and brothers who then regained their health in time to vote themselves, and that the ballots were tampered with by the election commissioners before being turned over to the state canvassers for verification.

Even if each of these reports had been entirely true, however, the outcome of the election would not have been different, as both the defeated Carpenter and Butler admitted. So too did the Democratic *Charleston Daily News,* which wrote, "The ingeniously contrived frauds of the Radical party . . . do not, it must be confessed, account satisfactorily for the election of Governor Scott by a majority of thirty or thirty-five thousand votes." [33]

What the election results did indicate was that most citizens in 1870 had voted predictably and that almost no blacks strayed from the Republican party. In the first attempt by the Conservatives to redeem the state from Negro-carpetbagger rule, the Union Reform party had failed utterly. Perhaps the Conservatives deserved to fail. Governor Orr, much more than they, seemed to have understood what they needed to do to restore balance in the South. But they had not done it. They had not succeeded in winning the confidence of the blacks because they had not sincerely tried to do so; they had merely patronized them. Much as they knew that they needed the support of the majority race to regain control of the state government, they still could not find it in their hearts to dignify the Negro's role as a citizen by extending to him the hand of genuine friendship. Over and over again, as Robert Elliott was to point out in a later speech, the blacks had appealed to the "intelligence, the virtue and the patriotism of the white citizens of South Carolina to aid them in inaugurating a free good government." But over and over again they had been rejected by the same "intelligent, refined gentlemen, who told them 'We will have nothing to do with you. . . . This nigger government . . . will fall of its own weight.' " [34]

Eventually, of course, the Negro-dominated government in South Carolina would be brought down, but not, as has far too often been asserted, by its own weight. Rather, its collapse would be due to the deep racial antagonism which ran in the veins of white men, both in the South and in the North, and which ultimately prevailed.

7

In the Congress of
the United States

ROBERT ELLIOT was not the first man of color to
take a seat in the Congress of the United States, but he was
the first full-blooded black to do so, and the distinction was an important one in the nineteenth century.

One year before Elliott took his oath and became a member of
the Forty-second Congress, Hiram Rhodes Revels, an octaroon,
had been sworn into the Senate, but only after considerable controversy. Revels was the first colored man to claim election to the
Congress; furthermore, he had been elected from the state of Mississippi (which like South Carolina had a black majority) to fill the
seat formerly occupied by Jefferson Davis. His credentials, however, were questioned by certain implacable opponents on the
grounds that, according to the Dred Scott decision, Revels, as a
Negro, could not have been counted a citizen of the United States
before the passage of the Fourteenth Amendment, and thus was not
eligible to take his seat in the Senate, which required nine years'
prior citizenship.

Revels's supporters argued that Chief Justice Roger B. Taney, in
his majority opinion in the Dred Scott case, had specifically limited
the noncitizenship dictum to those blacks with pure African blood
in their veins; therefore Revels, who had more white than black
blood, was exempted and had in fact been a bona fide citizen all
his life. This argument prevailed in the Senate, and the pale Revels
qualified when the jet-black Elliott perhaps would not have.

Enough of a precedent was established by Revels's admission to the Senate, however, to insure that when the first Negro, Joseph H. Rainey, came to take his seat in the House of Representatives, he was accepted without question—in fact even with a certain fanfare. Rainey (who was also very light-skinned) was elected from South Carolina at the same time as Elliott, but he went to Washington a few months ahead because he was filling the seat left vacant by the resignation of B. F. Whittemore. He was sworn in on December 12, 1870.

A few weeks later Rainey was joined in the House by Jefferson Franklin Long of Georgia, whose entrance had been delayed by a confusion over Georgia's readmission to the Union. Long, although a light mulatto, was somewhat darker than Rainey and thus regarded as more characteristic of his race. To him belonged the honor of being the first Negro to make a speech on the floor of the House. Otherwise he served without great distinction for the few months remaining in the Forty-first Congress.

Elliott was sworn in with the rest of the Forty-second Congress on March 4, 1871. The other new Negro members were Benjamin S. Turner of Alabama, a thickset bearded mulatto described as a schoolteacher in the *New National Era* (the newspaper edited by Frederick Douglass, Jr., and his brother Lewis), but depicted in other sources as a livery stable owner of scanty education who could write his name and nothing more; Josiah T. Walls of Florida, a lithe, intelligent young man (he and Elliott were both twenty-nine) who represented the entire state of Florida, which at that time had only one congressman-at-large; and Robert De Large, who entered the new Congress with the others but kept his seat only briefly.

Elliott arrived in Washington at the end of February 1871. At that time the city was still a long way from achieving the look of spacious beauty which designer Pierre L'Enfant had planned for the nation's capital. Most of the District streets, which were paved with cobblestones, were a mass of ruts and potholes; sidewalks sloped inward, gutters were overgrown with weeds. However, the capitol building itself looked much as it does today. The new House and Senate wings had been completed just a few years before the Civil War, and in 1865 the capitol's old wooden dome had been replaced by the present cast-iron structure. The White House, with its familiar Ionic portico and ballustrade, also looked much like the present-day structure, unmarred of course by the east and west executive offices, added later. The other major landmark, the Washington Monument, was still only half completed; begun in 1848, work on the 555-foot marble obelisk had been abandoned in 1855 and was not to be continued until 1877. Pennsylvania Avenue, which had been partially repaved since the war, was then, as it is now, the city's main thoroughfare. Lined with wooden buildings which housed saloons, pawnshops, gambling houses, and most of the District's second- and third-rate hotels (there were practically no first-rate hostelries), it was a boisterous street enlivened by the jangling of trolley car bells and the cries of street vendors selling oysters and vegetables. While less progressive than most Eastern cities in 1870, Washington had, by the time of Elliott's arrival, begun to cast off its sleepy Southern image and had become an active seat of government with a population of one hundred twenty thousand people, of whom approximately forty-five thousand were black.

When Elliott went to visit the capitol a few weeks before his actual swearing-in, he was accorded the traditional courtesy extended a congressman-elect; he was permitted to sit on the floor of the House, in fact to sit in the seat of his white predecessor and recent opponent, S. L. Hoge. Reporting on his visit, the *Charleston Daily Courier* remarked that as a "genuine African" he attracted general attention, but that even the Republican members did not seem inclined to give him a very warm welcome—certainly not so cordial a one as was extended to Rainey and Long.[1]

Apparently Elliott's coal-blackness came as something of a shock which accounted for his luke-warm reception in the Congress. There was, after all, a certain ambiguity about the light skins and acquiline features of the other Negro congressmen which made their presence bearable to the many Southerners and Negrophobes in the House. But Elliott's pure African blood, his wide nose and thick lips, doubtless assaulted their sensibilities and brought home the unpalatable truth that a member of the "inferior race" was now occupying a position equal to their own.

Even Frederick Douglass's *New National Era* used a faintly disparaging tone in describing Elliott, although it did acknowledge that among South Carolina politicians he was generally considered the ablest man in the state delegation.

Elliott lived in a boardinghouse at 1828 K Street during his first term in Congress. Boardinghouse living was common among legislators, even those who brought their wives and families to the capital. Apparently Grace Elliott was with her husband part if not all of his time in Washington. It is known that she was there in February of 1872, when her presence in the gallery reserved for the wives of members of the House of Representatives caused the wife of a Radical congressman from Ohio to leave in indignation. Thereafter Mrs. Elliott found it more comfortable to sit in the regular Ladies' Gallery.[2] There is no way of knowing whether or not Grace Elliott accompanied her husband when he first came to Washington. Probably she did not. Although the Elliotts had no children, they were by then established in their own home on Taylor Street in Columbia and in all likelihood Grace stayed behind to care for the house during Elliott's early absence.

For Elliott, more than for most freshmen congressmen, the time in Washington must have been particularly strange and lonely. Coming from a state where the majority of his legislative colleagues were black and where many of the whites, by necessity, curried his favor, he was accustomed to a full and lively daily contact with his fellow men. In Washington, where he knew no one and had not been very graciously received in the House of Representatives, such relationships, except with the other Negro congressmen, were largely lacking. He not only suffered from the ennui experienced by all men who were formerly big frogs in little ponds, but he faced some racial problems in Washington which, surprisingly, were more severe than in South Carolina. For example, although Negroes were the backbone of Republican politics in their Southern home states, they were excluded from the Republican Club of the District of Columbia.

Restaurants in both places posed social difficulties, but at least in South Carolina the blacks could enjoy the refreshment room in the state capitol, which, although much maligned by contemporary observers and later historians for its luxuries, at least made no racial distinctions. It was famous for its good food and drink and boisterous companionship at all hours of the day or night.

In Washington an ordinance similar to the one Elliott had helped push through in South Carolina made segregation illegal in places which required licenses to operate. As a result many restaurants attempted to circumvent the loss of license by posting a list of exorbitant prices for food, while noting in smaller letters "a liberal

reduction for our regular customers." Not being "regular customers," Elliott and Rainey and later Cain had trouble finding suitable
places to eat. On one occasion Elliott's presence in a public restaurant so disturbed a young man seated at the next table that he
created a considerable scene and noisily stormed out of the dining
room. Elliott remained seated, but managed to find out the young
man's name. Subsequent investigation revealed him to be an em-
ployee of the Treasury Department, from which post, "upon a representation of the case, he was promptly dismissed." [3]

Even traveling to the nation's capital Elliott had faced the
humiliation of being refused service in the station restaurant in
Wilmington, North Carolina, where, with only twenty minutes between trains, he tried to get a quick meal. This incident was reported by Richard Cain in one of his speeches to the House of
Representatives: "My colleague . . . was compelled to leave the
restaurant or have a fight for it," he said. "He showed fight, however, and got his dinner but he has never been back there since."

The next time the South Carolina congressmen traveled to Washington, Cain said, they decided not to "draw revolvers and present
the bold front of warriors," so they ordered their dinners brought
to them in their railway cars. "Still there was objection on the part
of the railroad people," Cain reported, "because they said we were
putting on airs." [4]

Joseph Rainey felt so strongly about integrated public accommo-
dations that he once refused to leave the dining room of a hotel
in nearby Virginia until he, a congressman, was forcibly ejected.

There were some political compensations for the blacks in Washington, however. Just before Elliott arrived in the city the District
had enacted a bill creating a new "territorial government" which
consisted of a presidentially appointed governor with an eleven-man
upper house or governor's council and a twenty-two-man lower
house to be elected by popular vote. Elliott, who was doubtless
homesick and missed the stimulation of a good partisan fight,
promptly got involved with the election of delegates to the lower
house. In fact, he was one of the principal speakers at the opening
Republican rally held on the corner of Seventh Street and Pennsylvania Avenue on March 25, only three weeks after his arrival.
The Republicans won handily in the mid-April District of Columbia
election, although there were only two Negroes among the twenty-
two delegates.

However, in selecting the eleven-man upper chamber, President Grant appointed three first-rate Negroes: Frederick Douglass; John Gray, a well-known Washington caterer; and Adolphus Hall, a highly regarded member of the Negro community. In addition, John Mercer Langston,* a distinguished mulatto who had been chosen to head the Howard University Law School, was made legal counsel to the Washington board of health.

These men ranked high among the black elite of the District of Columbia. There is no way of knowing, however, if Elliott or any of the other newly elected black congressmen were taken up by this aristocracy when they first arrived in Washington. Judging by the somewhat restrained tone used about them in Douglass's *New National Era,* it seems likely that each man was expected first to prove himself in the Congress of the United States.

The floor of the House of Representatives was a more lively place in the nineteenth century because most members had no place else to go to do their legislative work. There were few if any offices for representatives, and no secretaries or staffs. Congressmen sat at their desks in the House chamber (Elliott's was number 115), reading constituent mail or home newspapers, studying new bills, or preparing motions. Elliott spent his first ten days in this atmosphere, hardly conductive to coherent thought, composing his maiden speech, which he delivered on March 14, just ten days after he was sworn in. As he was later to recall,

> I shall never forget that day, when rising in my place to address the House, I found myself the center of attraction. Everything was still. Those who believed in the natural inferiority of the colored race appeared to feel that the hour had arrived in which they should exult in triumph over the failure of the first man of "the despised race" whose voice was about to be lifted in that chamber. The countenances of those who sympathized with our cause seemed to indicate their anxiety for my success, and their heartfelt desire that I might prove equal to the emergency. I cannot, fellow citizens, picture to you the emotions that then filled my mind.[5]

His subject was a matter of grave importance to his constituency: It concerned an amnesty bill to remove the political disabilities of all persons lately engaged in rebellion against the government of the United States. Elliott rose to enter his "solemn

* The great uncle of Langston Hughes.

protest." The bill, he said, was "nothing but an attempt to pay a premium for disloyalty and treason at the expense of loyalty." His fierce objection to amnesty was at least partially a manifestation of his unforgiving nature, but more particularly it represented his strongly held belief that the members of the former ruling class who were still disenfranchised were the men largely responsible for the outrages then being committed throughout the South. If they were not the men who actually pulled the triggers, he said, they encouraged, aided, and abetted the men who did—the Ku Klux Klan—by their "evil examples, their denunciations of Congress, their abuse of the President . . . and by their money and the money sent from northern states—money furnished by Tammany Hall for the purpose of keeping up these outrages in order to insure a Democratic triumph in the South in 1872." [6]

Instead of passing a proposal for amnesty, Elliott suggested that Congress should turn its efforts, "and that speedily," to halting the lawlessness and protecting the life and property of the loyal citizens of the South. The majority of the House believed, however, that the continuation of disabilities imposed for complicity in a rebellion ten years earlier could serve no further useful purpose: The vote on the amnesty bill was 132 to 57; three Negroes, Elliott, Rainey, and Walls, voting nay, with De Large—conscious no doubt of his tenuous hold on his congressional seat—voting yea. Still the bill, which required a two-thirds majority, did not pass.

Two days after Elliott's speech, the liberal, Republican *New York Tribune* took him to task editorially (thereby affording him exceptionally good news coverage for a freshman representative): "Mr. Elliott . . . asserted on Tuesday that the Ku Klux disturbers of the South are the 'very class whom it is proposed to relieve of their political disabilities,'" they wrote. "Mr. E.'s naked assertion does not suffice to prove that the midnight riders and raiders in masks . . . are the ex-colonels, ex-legislators and ex-magistrates of the old slave holding regime. . . . If Mr. E. asserted that pears and watermelons are generally stolen by clergymen and deacons fifty to eighty years old, his mistake would not be more obvious." [7]

Elliott responded immediately (gaining even greater publicity when his answer was printed on the front page of the *Tribune*) that he had never said the ex-colonels were the midnight riders; only that they had encouraged those who were doing the killing and terrorizing.[8]

The *Tribune,* which was certainly not sympathetic to the Klan, had taken a surprisingly forbearing attitude toward it in this particular editorial, characterizing its members as wild, reckless youngsters whose lawless acts might be justified because they saw "those they loved and respected proscribed and disfranchised for their part in a rebellion which they esteemed righteous and patriotic."

Elliott, of course, would have none of this tolerance. "Possibly, Mr. Editor, your graciousness to recalcitrant Confederates would be somewhat modified if you lived, as I do, within the theatre of their operations. Men often bear the misfortunes of their neighbors with great equanimity, and are ready most graciously to forgive wrongs to which they cannot be personally subjected. Thus the philosopher Seneca, seated in his magnificent villa, surrounded by symbols of opulence, wrote upon tablets of gold his famous 'Essay on the Beauties and Advantages of Poverty.' " [9]

His answer is noteworthy, among other things, for this classical reference. Similar classical or historical allusions appeared in all the speeches Elliott delivered from Washington (and to a lesser degree in those he delivered elsewhere), thus giving rise to rumors that someone else was writing his material, since it was not believed possible that a black man would even have heard of Seneca or Demosthenes or Milton or Burke, let alone be familiar enough with their words to quote them. But, in fact, Elliott's numerous historical and literary references clearly bear witness to his fine classical education.

Elliott was properly aroused by the outrages perpetrated by the Ku Klux in his state: The atrocities which had begun to accelerate during the November 1870 elections continued at an ever-heightening pace until the summer of 1871, when they reached their peak. By that time more than six hundred men had been murdered in South Carolina alone.

In June 1871 Congress appointed a Joint Select Committee to Inquire into the Condition of Affairs in the Late Insurrectionary States. The committee, consisting of seven senators and fourteen representatives, thirteen Republicans and eight Democrats, collected nine thick volumes of testimony, three of which dealt with South Carolina. Horror stories of every degree abounded in the massive record. An incident at the town of Union Court House serves as well as any of countless others to document the brutalities of the times:

Just before Christmas in 1870, a white whiskey peddler named Matt Stevens was killed by a group of Negro militiamen. Stevens, an ex-Confederate soldier, had come to South Carolina from North Carolina and was selling whiskey illegally—that is, without a license—a not uncommon practice of the day. In this particular case, however, he sold just enough whiskey to the Negroes, who were already in high holiday spirits, to get them drunk and then refused to sell them any more. The blacks, "crazy and mad because they could not get all the liquor they wanted when only partly satisfied," set upon Stevens and killed him.

Thirteen Negroes were arrested and jailed, either as murderers or as accessories. On January 4, 1871, at ten o'clock at night the Ku Klux Klan arrived at the Union jailhouse where the blacks were incarcerated. Armed with guns and wearing their white disguises, the Klansmen moved up to the jailhouse and formed into line. Their discipline was perfect, according to the testimony of David T. Corbin, United States attorney for the District of South Carolina, before the Joint Congressional Committee.[10] The officer in command ordered, "Number one, number two, number three, ten paces forward." No names were called. The three men stepped forward and demanded the keys to the jail. The sheriff resisted, was put under guard and threatened; he gave up the keys. Six of the prisoners were taken from the jail, put into line, and the troop marched silently out of town.

In the woods two miles out of town the company halted. Numbers one, two, three, four, five, and six stepped to the front. The prisoners were instructed to walk ten paces forward. The order was given: "Ready; aim; fire." One prisoner fell, then another. Two others followed. As the four Negroes lay dead on the ground, there was a moment's hesitation among the Klansmen. One of the prisoners started to run. He was fired on and died on the spot. Another managed to escape, though wounded, only to be recaptured a few days later and eventually killed, but not before he had given his eyewitness account of the shootings.

When Governor Scott heard of the murders he took immediate steps to protect the other seven men arrested for the same crime who were still in the Union jail by suggesting to the judge of the circuit court that he order their removal to Columbia for safety. Circuit Judge William M. Thomas did issue an order to that effect to the sheriff, who promptly told everyone in Union that the men were about to be taken from the jail. That night (January 12) the armed and mounted Klan arrived again, this time in greater numbers—some estimates went as high as a thousand men—took out the remaining eight Negroes (seven plus the one who had escaped and been recaptured), and shot them all in cold blood.

The KKK left a note on the door of the Union jail, supposedly to explain their action in killing the second set of prisoners: "In silence and secrecy thought has been working, and the benignant efficacies of concealment speak for themselves," they wrote with characteristic mumbo jumbo, "once again we have been forced by force to use Force. Justice was lame and she had to lean upon us. . . . We yield to the inevitable and inexorable, and account this the best. 'Let not thy right hand know what thy left hand doeth is our motto.' " [11]

If the exact meaning of that message was somewhat obscure, the action itself was all too clear. Although some Southerners justified the thirteen ruthless murders on the grounds that the drunken black militiamen had, after all, started the trouble by killing the white whiskey peddler, most whites were appalled by the Union jail raids. There were loud repercussions in the state legislature and reverberations were felt in the nation's capital as well. In fact, by March 1871 there was growing agitation on the part of certain Radical Republicans to push President Grant for legislation which would curb the dangerous lawlessness at the South.

Both Senate and House Republicans held caucuses on March 10. The Senate session was entirely dominated by the dethroning of Senator Charles Sumner of Massachusetts from his long-held chairmanship of the Committee on Foreign Relations. This action was undertaken by the Republican caucus committee ostensibly because Sumner's deteriorating relationship with the president and his secretary of state, Hamilton Fish, was alleged to be jeopardizing his effectiveness in foreign affairs. Sumner, of course, was furious; had he not been so bitterly hurt, he might well have taken the lead in introducing some sort of strong anti-Ku Klux Klan legislation. But, although the Senate had a Committee on Southern Outrages which was collecting facts, it was in the House that legislation was actually introduced.

The House Republican caucus led by Benjamin Butler of Massachusetts was called specifically to get a commitment from the members that they would push for a Ku Klux bill before adjournment. Although the Forty-second Congress had just convened, many members—holdovers from the Forty-first—had been in session since early December (in those days a period long enough to cause complaint) and were eager to get home by the end of March.

At this, his first Republican caucus, Elliott chose not to maintain a suitable freshman listen-and-learn silence. Feeling that the acute situation in his home state warranted federal action, he spoke up at once to urge members to postpone an adjournment until a bill was passed to punish the Ku Klux and protect the citizens of the South.

Such a bill had just been introduced in the House by Samuel Shellabarger of Ohio. The measure, based on the power conferred in the Fourteenth Amendment, gave the president the right to intercede with federal forces in cases of insurrection or obstruction of laws, *even if* the state legislature or executive did not summon such a force.

On March 23, 1871, Grant, who had been holding back on the Southern-outrage question pending action by the legislative branch, finally decided to move matters forward by sending a message to Congress. He deemed it so important that he delivered it in person. The president pointed out that a condition now existed in some states of the Union which rendered life and property insecure and which (from the federal point of view) endangered the carrying of mail and the collection of the revenues. He did not doubt, said Grant, that the power to correct these evils was beyond the control of state authorities. But it was not clear whether the power of the president, "acting within the limits of existing laws," was sufficient for the present emergencies. Therefore he urgently recommended "such legislation as, in the judgment of Congress, shall effectually secure life, liberty and property in all parts of the United States."

Five days after the president's message, Shellabarger's bill was reported out of committee and Shellabarger graciously announced, for the benefit of his Democratic opponents, that he would not call the question until a week for debate had been allowed. He himself opened the discussion with an able defense of his bill. He was followed by Michael C. Kerr of Indiana, a Democrat and a strong states-righter, who challenged the constitutionality of the measure and denied the necessity for its enactment.

The stage was thus set for Robert Brown Elliott to make the

most mature and thoughtful speech of his career to date. At twenty-nine he must have been one of the youngest, if not the youngest, men in the House; his legal training was admittedly sketchy, yet his grasp of the constitutional issue was sure. Boldly and skillfully he set out to answer Representative Kerr, who was considered the most experienced constitutionalist on the Democrats' side of the aisle.

The capstone of Kerr's position was that the Ku Klux bill was unconstitutional because, by permitting the intervention of federal troops without a specific request from state authorities, it ran counter to Article Four, Section Four, of the Constitution which reads, "The United States shall guarantee to every State in the Union a republican form of government, and shall protect each of them against invasion, and on application of the Legislature or of the Executive (when the Legislature cannot be convened) against domestic violence." Kerr contended that the article clearly meant that it was the duty of the federal government to go to the aid of a state *only when* that state applied for such aid.[12]

Elliott vigorously denied this interpretation. The clause, he said, was "not inhibitory but mandatory." It was designed not to "restrict the rights but to enlarge the duties" of the federal government. The phrase "on application of the Legislature or Executive" did not mean that such an "application" should always be an essential condition, but rather that the United States could not refuse to give protection when the application was made. "Otherwise a faithless and undutiful Executive, giving his personal aid to or covertly bestowing his official sanction upon the insurgent authors of 'domestic violence' might, by withholding his 'application' render the Government of the United States a torpid and paralyzed spectator of the oppression of its citizens."

His opponents' point of view, Elliott said, reminded him of the "rigid etiquette of the Frenchman who, on being upbraided for not saving the life of a fellow passenger whom he saw drown before his eyes, attempted to justify himself by pleading that he had 'not been introduced to him.' "

Kerr in his "able but ill-timed speech" had referred frequently to the eminent constitutionalist Justice Joseph Story. "I think," said Elliott, "that to quote Justice Story in defense of the position assumed by the gentleman from Indiana and his political coactors on this floor is to 'steal the livery of Heaven to serve the devil in.' "

Thereupon Elliott himself invoked Justice Story to bolster his own arguments, quoting at length from the great jurist's writings, which, like the Constitution itself, were open to varying interpretations.[13]

Elliott delivered his speech on a Saturday afternoon to an empty gallery and a rapidly thinning audience on the floor. Although the Republicans listened with close attention, the Democrats treated him with open contempt, laughing, talking aloud, and eventually noisily leaving the chamber almost en masse. Those in the press gallery noted that still he appeared undaunted: "His manner was easy, his voice clear and penetrating, and his sentences, though delivered somewhat hurriedly owing to a desire to bring the argument within the hour's limit, had a finish and elegance not often heard in Congress oratory." [14]

Kerr, the gentleman from Indiana whose argument Elliott was so carefully refuting, had made the mistake of belittling the gravity of the troubles in the South. It was a gross perversion of truth, Kerr insisted, to assume that any desire to incite rebellion existed anywhere. The utmost extent of insubordination, he said, was confined to a very small number of persons in a few localities who were merely common criminals without political aims or "higher motives of action."

Elliott took full advantage of his opponents' refusal to face incontestable facts. To prove that more than just a few Southerners manifestly had political aims and were trying to "defeat the ballot with the bullet," he chose excerpts from a voluminous record of harassment and intimidation of blacks and Radicals. For example, the Democratic Club of Charleston had called upon its members to enter into solemn agreement to "employ no mechanic who does not belong to the same Democratic organization, neither to patronize any mill, tannery or other place dependent on public patronage, owned or superintended by another than an out-and-out Democrat." Even doctors and lawyers were enjoined not to attend professionally any Radical or his family. From another Democratic Club, Elliott read a resolution passed by the membership that no freedmen be hired who could not show certificates proving that they were members of some Democratic association.

He cited Democratic newspaper editorials which called for a "straight and severe line between the races" and for the immediate return of the white man's government. He read documents from

KKK headquarters: *"Resolved,* That in all cases of incendiarism ten of the leading colored people and two white sympathizers shall be executed in that vicinity." Or another, from the KKK headquarters, Ninth Division, South Carolina, a demand that members of the legislature, the school commission, and the county commissioners of Union should "resign their present inhuman, disgraceful, outrageous rule" forthwith, or else "fifteen days from this date . . . retributive justice will as surely be used as night follows day." (And indeed many of the officers in Union and other upper counties of the state not only did resign, but fled to Columbia for safety.)

Following these and other "manifold proofs" demonstrating how the bloody purpose of the Democrats and secret societies of the South had been executed, Elliott climaxed his speech with an anecdote:

> It is recorded that on the entry of Louis XVIII into Paris, after the fall of the great Napoleon, an old marshal of the empire who stood in the vast throng, unknown, was addressed by an ardent Bourbon who expatiated on the gorgeous splendors that marked the scene, and exclaimed "Is not this grand? Is it not magnificent? What is there wanting to the occasion?" "Nothing," said the war worn veteran as his mind wandered over Lodi and Wagram and Austerlitz, . . . "nothing is wanting to the occasion but the presence of the brave men who died to prevent it."
>
> Such, sir, will be the bitter reflection of all loyal men in this nation, if the Democratic party shall triumph in the States of the South through armed violence.[15]

Elliott's compelling rhetoric helped to move the Ku Klux bill (officially known as the Enforcement Act) through Congress with unprecedented speed. It passed the House on April 6 and the Senate (with some amendments) seven days later; final passage came on April 20, 1871, and on that same day President Grant signed the bill into law.

Meanwhile the situation in South Carolina had deteriorated to such an extent that Governor Scott asked for federal assistance; as the state's chief executive, having asked for help, he did not need to wait for the passage of the Ku Klux bill to get it. A limited number of troops (one infantry and one cavalry company to each of four Northern counties) were promptly dispatched.

Once the bill was passed, the operant clause as far as South

Carolina was concerned was the provision making it mandatory that conspiratorial and violent offenses against freedmen be tried in a United States District Court. One of the greatest difficulties heretofore had been that if, by any remote chance, a Klansman was arrested after an outrage, there was no possibility that a jury in a state court would dare render a verdict against him. Still, it was not until late November 1871, six months after the passage of the Ku Klux bill, that the first United States Court convened in Columbia to hear evidence.

Prior to that, Ulysses S. Grant had taken direct action of his own in South Carolina. On October 12, using the power which the Ku Klux bill specifically gave him, Grant suspended the writ of habeas corpus in nine South Carolina counties. It was a drastic step, more in keeping with arbitrary justice in the so-called banana republics than in the United States of America.

The writ of habeas corpus assures that the legality of an imprisonment can be tested in a court of law. Without this vital safeguard, wholesale and unjustifiable arrests are possible. Yet, considering the large membership in the Klan and the huge number of white sympathizers, the military authorities were relatively temperate in their arrests. The strongly conservative, pro-white historian John Reynolds states that there were only 195 persons arrested in York County, 200 in Union County, "some hundreds" in Spartanburg, "several" in Chester, 35 in Newberry, and none in Fairfield, Lancaster, Chesterfield, or Laurens.[16]

A few weeks after the arrests, the trials of the Klansmen began in the United States Circuit Court at Columbia. Indictments were brought against approximately five hundred persons—fewer, incidentally, than the total number of persons who had been killed by violence in the state in the past two years. Court proceedings lasted for two months. Fifty-five persons were found guilty and imprisoned. An endless recital of horrifying details of Ku Klux brutality had sufficient impact to diminish—at least temporarily—the lawlessness which had gripped the state.

It is quite possible that such a tapering off would have taken place and comparative sanity would have been restored even without suspension of the writ of habeas corpus, but perhaps not so swiftly and not before a greater number of lives (mostly black) had been lost. It is also possible that Grant's action was to some extent politically motivated. Certainly he was not unaware that his dramatic intervention on behalf of the blacks would help insure their continued faithfulness to the Republican party.

There is some reason to believe that Robert Elliott may have been personally involved in the president's decision to suspend habeas corpus. Some months earlier he had been a member of a delegation of South Carolina statesmen who had met with the president to discuss the difficulties in their state. He was a leading advocate of strong federal intervention and, as the most articulate of the Negro congressmen, it would have been altogether logical for him to counsel the president—or at least one of his aides—on a matter of such grave importance, both morally and politically.

In any event, the fact that Elliott was in Washington on the day that Grant's habeas corpus suspension was signed is notable because it was at a time when Congress was not in session. On the next day, which happened to be Friday, October 13, he left for home. He must have been in some fear of his life, for before leaving he wrote the following letter to Grace Elliott:

Dear Wife—
I write this to inform you that I shall leave for home at 7 o'clock tonight, by the Richmond and Danville R.R., and expect to reach home by the Charlotte and Columbia Rail Road on Sunday morning before day. If anything should happen to me, I have a draft on the Bank for $1800.00 (Eighteen hundred dollars.) If it should be stolen, write immediately to Hon. N. G. Ordway, Sergeant-at-Arms of the House of Representatives and have him stop the payment of it, and send you a new draft. Mr. Ordway has also a life-insurance policy on my life for $10,000—which he will collect and after taking out what I owe him, the balance he will turn over to you. I do this, my dear, because life is uncertain.

I hereby constitute you my sole heir. All my property is yours.

If anything happens send for Whipper at once, and have him arrange your business for you.

Your affectionate husband,
Robt. B. Elliott [17]

8

High Crimes
and Misdemeanors

WHEN Robert Elliott answered present to the roll call at the reconvening of the Forty-second Congress on December 4, 1871, he was, like many politicians of that troubled time, caught in a swirl of conflicts. Corruption, fraud, and malfeasance in office, which had been simmering below the surface for several years, both nationally and in his own state, now began to bubble up into public consciousness, threatening the future not only of Governor Robert L. Scott, but of President Ulysses S. Grant himself. In South Carolina a movement to impeach Scott was underway, with Elliott's friend and law partner, William Whipper, in the vanguard. In Washington a growing sentiment against Grant—spearheaded by Charles Sumner—led to plans by some Republicans to replace him as the 1872 presidential nominee.

In both cases Elliott's divided loyalties forced him to take stands that must have cost him painful hours of indecision. Elliott revered Senator Charles Sumner as the "friend, advocate and fearless associate of the colored man," and Sumner was thought to have looked on young Elliott as a protégé. Although there is little evidence to indicate that their relationship was that intimate, it is certain that there was a particular bond between the two men which probably developed for the most ironic of reasons.

Fifteen years earlier, in 1856, just after Charles Sumner, then forty-three years old, had delivered one of his most passionate antislavery polemics, he was physically attacked on the floor of the

Senate by a Southern aristocrat. Representative Preston Brooks of South Carolina set upon him with a cane and rained a series of murderous blows upon his head and body in a brutal assault from which Sumner took three years to recover. (In South Carolina a collection was promptly taken up to buy Brooks another cane.) There must, then, have been some grim satisfaction for the senator when the same South Carolina district which had sent Preston Brooks to the House sent Robert Elliott, a full-blooded black, to represent it in 1870. To the aging, embittered statesman, the youthful Elliott symbolized the tangible fulfillment of his early struggles for racial equality. In addition, Elliott's convictions, his daring and persistent efforts on behalf of the Negro, his intellect, his style of oratory, modeled in some ways on Sumner's own style, must all have endeared him to the senator.

Elliott, for his part, recognized that in Charles Sumner his race had an advocate who not only believed with every fiber of his being that the American black man was the peer of the American white man, but who strove ceaselessly to assure that blacks were accorded the same safeguards to liberty and freedom which protected whites. Sumner's endeavor in this regard was embodied in the civil rights bill which he introduced (or rather reintroduced, it having been previously defeated) in the winter of 1872.

At the same time, however, he was doing all in his power to discredit Grant, even though the president's objectives of insuring social equality were often consonant with his own. The animosity between Grant and Sumner stemmed largely from a fundamental difference in character, personality, and style. Charles Sumner was a man of lofty eloquence, egocentric, ever-desirous of power, complex, overbearing, highly intellectual, conscious always of the righteousness of his cause. Ulysses Grant, on the other hand, was a plain man, stolid, unemotional, taciturn, excessively loyal to his friends, naïve politically, sincere in the decency of his beliefs, effective in battle, but unimposing in the White House.

During the early months of the Grant administration (1869), Sumner had had considerable influence with the president. Grant's initial cabinet appointments showed his abysmal political ineptitude. He chose men of no special capability merely because he liked and trusted them. He soon found, however, that he needed the experienced guidance of some of the more prestigious Republican senators; thus, for a brief time at least, he relied on Sumner's wisdom and authority. Although Sumner had looked with considerable scorn upon Grant's nomination, he could not fail to recognize that Grant, in his downright way, had accepted the tenets of Radical Republicanism and, in so doing, had gained the confidence of the Southern blacks.

But the *entente cordiale* between these two men—unnatural at best—was short-lived. Sumner opposed a favorite presidential project to annex a part of the Dominican Republic (then called Santo Domingo) because he thought the scheme ill-conceived and shoddy. Furthermore, he believed that, although the United States should give moral support and counsel to the Dominicans, it should primarily encourage them to establish a firm and energetic republican government of their own.

Grant, who had probably never felt comfortable with Sumner anyway, retaliated by supporting a complicated political maneuver which culminated in Sumner's removal from the chairmanship of the Senate Committee on Foreign Relations. From the moment of his ouster, Sumner became the president's implacable foe, seeking to discredit him in subtle but deadly ways. The pecadillos of Grant's administration were fair game for the senator's skillful exploitation.

Grant himself was an easy mark. His staff was full of people appointed because of their personal ties to him, rather than for any qualifications which they did, or in most cases did not, possess. In addition to cronyism, charges of nepotism were rife; the president was accused of putting in office all his brothers-in-law (plus his son-in-law, whom he made minister to Turkey). Said Charles Sumner in one of his numerous speeches denouncing Grant, "Thirteen relations of the President are billeted on the country, not one of whom, but for this relationship would hold office. Beyond this list are other relations showing that this strange abuse did not stop with relatives but widened to include relatives of relatives." [1]

More serious for the country than Grant's ineptitude and bad judgment about hangers-on was his penchant for the company (and unfortunately for the gifts) of rich, powerful men. His intimacy with Jay Gould and Jim Fiske and his alleged, although never proven, connivance with them in their attempt to corner the gold market brought about the "Black Friday" of September

24, 1869, which ruined thousands of gold speculators on Wall Street and would have been even more disastrous if Grant had not stepped in, albeit belatedly, to release $1 million in gold.

Still to be exposed, although fulminating at the time of Sumner's attacks in late 1871 and early 1872, were the operations of the St. Louis Whiskey Ring whose illegal tax abatement on large amounts of whiskey cost the government some $2,786,000 in revenue. The money was ostensibly used by the leaders of the ring to aid in Grant's campaign for his second term (and ultimately for the third term which he briefly attempted to seek). Grant personally was said to be the recipient of many extravagant favors, including a pair of fine horses plus carriage and harness. His private secretary, Orville E. Babcock, was supposed to have received a pair of diamond shirt studs costing $2,400 plus other surprise trinkets such as a $1,000 bill tucked in a box of expensive cigars.

But probably the most famous scandal of the Grant administration was the notorious Crédit Mobilier affair. The mid- and late 1860s were the years of a great railroad boom. Expansion, slowed by the Civil War, picked up at a much quickened pace as the demand grew to link together an ever-growing country. Everyone was talking, thinking, and investing in railroads. Between 1865 and 1873, thirty thousand miles of new track were opened. In 1869 the first journey by rail from one end of the continent to the other became possible when the Union Pacific, laying its road westward, and the Central Pacific, building eastward, finally joined at Ogden, Utah.

Congress had authorized the vast construction of the Union Pacific by land grants and by an initial loan of $27 million in government bonds, plus authorization to issue further first mortgage securities. Simultaneously, a second construction company was formed to build the roadbed. Called the Crédit Mobilier, it was capitalized by private investors, mostly Easterners, and headed by an impeccable Boston Yankee, Oakes Ames. The Crédit Mobilier Company had an interlocking directorate with the Union Pacific Company.

In much-simplified terms, what happened was that the Union Pacific Company began to show a loss and needed further injections of government money to complete the railroad. But at the same time, Crédit Mobilier was yielding a profit because money was being funneled from the Union Pacific into the subsidiary Crédit Mobilier "construction" company. Later investigation revealed that $73 million were diverted from the Union Pacific and put to the credit of the Crédit Mobilier for only $50 million worth of construction work, thereby paying C.M. stockholders dividends of $23 million, and swindling the Union Pacific and the government of the same sum.

Oakes Ames, the instigator of the Crédit Mobilier, had been a member of the House of Representatives since 1862. By October 1867, when the Union Pacific Railroad reached Cheyenne, word of the questionable machinations of its operation also reached the ears of some members of Congress. Questions began to be asked, and it soon appeared that a nosy congressman, C. C. Washburn of Wisconsin, was threatening legislation which would be inimical to the best interests of Crédit Mobilier.

At that point Ames decided to take steps. He had 343 shares of Crédit Mobilier transferred to him as trustee; these, he decided, in his own often-quoted words, to distribute among congressmen "where they will do most good to us." Beginning in December 1867, he sold shares to influential legislators at par, with interest retroactive from the previous July. Ten shares cost the members of Congress only $1,000, although the stock was then worth twice that much. Some members who did not have the cash available to make the initial payment were carried by Ames. One year later their $1,000 investment (or gift) was worth $3,418.50.[2]

Shares of Crédit Mobilier were held at one time by 160 congressmen and senators, including some of the most important statesmen of the day; the most famous of these were James A. Garfield, a future president of the United States, and Schuyler Colfax, who had been speaker of the House when he acquired two hundred shares and who was Grant's vice-president when the scandal broke.

Oakes Ames blandly denied any suggestion of bribery in his actions: "I never dreamed of it," he replied to Luke P. Poland, chairman of the House committee subsequently investigating the affair. "They were all friends of the road and my friends. If you want to bribe a man, you want to bribe one who is opposed to you."[3]

Although the Poland committee recommended that Ames be expelled outright from the House of Representatives, the members took a more lenient view. On February 27, 1873, they agreed to "absolutely condemn" but not to expel Ames. (Elliott voted nay, whether because he thought Ames deserved a stronger punishment or none at all is not indicated by the record).[4] Apparently in letting him off so lightly, the congressmen considered that Ames had suffered enough humiliation for his understandable although perhaps overzealous desire, as he himself put it, to "connect my name publicly with the greatest public work of the present century." He had also managed to pocket close to a million dollars as a result of this connection; yet he was condoned, not only by many of his colleagues (including perhaps Elliott), but by contemporary and future historians as "a product of his time . . . who had no idea he was doing an immoral or indelicate act." [5]

No such forbearance was ever shown toward the carpetbaggers and Negro legislators of the South for their railroad manipulations or other financial transgressions. In fact, until the advent of the mid-twentieth-century revisionists, both contemporary and later historians looked on the misdeeds which occurred in the Southern states during Reconstruction as unprecedented, unheard-of acts of barbarism: "A parallel which can only be imagined in the lost records of Sodom and Gomorrah," wrote one John Leland, Ph.D., headmaster of a school for young ladies and a sometime Klan member.[6] "The barefaced fraud and moral perjury . . . can scarcely be realized by civilized people," stated the sanctimonious South Carolina Investigating Committee in their *Report on Public Frauds*.[7] Yet these same "civilized people" were not only aware of the $23 million Crédit Mobilier swindle, but as taxpayers they had been cheated by it just as severely as they were by the local corruptions.

The national furor over railroad expansion was particularly feverish in South Carolina, where the state's entire railway system, from roadbeds to rolling stock, was in a deplorable condition as a result of the war. Immediate decisive action was imperative, and many South Carolinians, as much "products of the time" as Oakes Ames, took a leaf out of his book. In their zeal to build railroads which would link every part of the state to the thriving port of Charleston and would then tie the entire state to the Gulf region and to the great Northwest, some politicians and financiers found ways to benefit themselves at the expense of South Carolina.

A case in point was the Blue Ridge Railroad.[8] In 1852 the road had only thirty-three miles of track, running through the northwest part of South Carolina from Anderson to Walhalla. But the Blue Ridge had great plans; its ultimate objective, before it was interrupted by the war, had been to run the line through North Carolina and Georgia into Knoxville, Tennessee, where it could link up with other lines going west.

To pick up and continue building the Blue Bridge tracks after the war it was necessary first to tunnel through Stump Hole Mountain northeast of Walhalla, an expensive project but one which was, in all good faith, considered worthwhile by Governor Scott and by the House Committee on Railroads of the South Carolina legislature, of which Robert Elliott was then chairman. In September 1868, therefore, the state guaranteed a loan of $4 million to the Blue Ridge Railroad reserving the statutory lien on the road—an action equivalent, one might say, to the federal government's loan to the Union Pacific.

Although the parallel between the United States' and South Carolina's railroad enterprises cannot be carried too far, there were obvious similarities in the main outlines. The initial public loans in both cases were insufficient; private capital was required. To this end the South Carolina legislature was persuaded to relinquish the state's lien on the railroads (the Blue Ridge had by then consolidated with the intrastate Greenville and Columbia) in exchange for mortgages to certain individuals. This action was perfectly sound; in fact, it was even approved by the ultraconservative Taxpayers' Convention, then meeting in Charleston, on the grounds that a mortgage was better security for the state than a statutory lien.

The individual mortgage holders then formed a corporation not unlike Crédit Mobilier. In positions comparable to that of patrician Oakes Ames were such Southern bluebloods as James L. Orr, former governor; General M. C. Butler, recently defeated Democratic candidate for lieutenant governor; M. C. Gary; W. D. Porter; James Connor; and numerous others, all falling into the "natural leader" category.

To head the new corporation, however, the stockholders went outside their "class" and brought in a professional railroad man, a wily entrepreneur named John J. Patterson who had been president of the Greenville and Columbia Railroad and was full of money-making schemes. Along with Patterson came a number of Republican carpetbaggers (but no Negroes) who were members of the original Greenville and Columbia crowd now expanded into the Railroad Ring—notably Niles Parker, the state treasurer; D. H. Chamberlain, a future governor of the state who was to run on a reform platform; Joseph Crews; Tim Hurley; C. P. Leslie; and a man who was always referred to as "cherubic," the powerful H. H. Kimpton, South Carolina's financial agent operating out of Wall Street. These Republican names were always associated with the infamous Railroad Ring; Orr, Butler, Gary, and their ilk were never mentioned, although they too profited.

The new corporation promptly bought 13,100 shares of Blue Ridge stock from the state at the greatly devalued price of $1.00 per share, thereby gaining titular control of the road. So far nothing illegal had transpired. But it soon did when Patterson arranged to have a bill introduced into the state legislature which asked the state to issue $1.8 million worth of scrip (tax-guaranteed treasury certificates) as an outright loan, instead of merely guaranteeing $4 million worth of bonds. The ostensible purpose of this bill (called the Revenue Bond Scrip Act) was to "relieve the State of South Carolina of all liability for its guaranty of bonds of the Blue Ridge Railroad Company." The real reason was to enable the Railroad Ring to get control of scrip which was unendorsed and thus, under certain conditions, could be readily converted into cash.

To push a bill of such obvious financial gain to the ring through the legislature (especially after Governor Scott had voiced strong opposition to it) required that considerable funds be earmarked for out and out bribery—in effect, once again, a situation analogous to Oakes Ames's distribution of Crédit Mobilier stock in the United States Congress "where it would do the most good."

Elliott was in the federal House of Representatives, not the state legislature, at the time, but he definitely was involved, if only marginally, in the Blue Ridge Bond Scrip Act. Evidence which is incontrovertible (even though it appeared in the highly partisan 1877 *Report on Public Frauds*) indicates that he was present at a key meeting held at John Patterson's house on March 4, 1872. On this occasion, after some very ugly words between the participants during which a pistol was drawn by Patterson, a letter was drafted ordering the state treasurer, Niles Parker, to deliver to H. H. Kimpton the sum of $114,250 in scrip at par ($.70 on the dollar). Of this sum, $43,857 was to be used for the "expenses of passing the revenue Scrip Bill through the state House of Representatives," and $50,000 for the expenses which had already been incurred in getting the bill through the state Senate two days earlier.

This document was witnessed by R. B. Elliott and was the only matter on which he was ever questioned by the Joint Investigating Committee on Public Frauds. His answer to the committee hardly did him justice. He was present at Patterson's house on a day in the spring of 1872, he said when questioned in 1877. He did remember having witnessed a paper of some kind, but he had "no knowledge of the substance of the paper." [9]

On the other hand, C. D. Hayne, a black legislator from Aiken who was in the House of Representatives at the time the revenue scrip bill came to its final vote, testified later that he had first voted for the revenue scrip bill and then reversed his position on the advice of his friend General R. B. Elliott, who told him the bill was clearly unconstitutional. Apparently then, as far as Elliott was concerned, it was a case of do as I say not as I do.

Although Elliott's complicity in the Blue Ridge machinations is clear, there is no evidence of how much—if any—cash he actually pocketed. Since he was never specifically cited in the *Report on Public Frauds* for having made money out of the Revenue Bond Scrip Act, it seems likely that if he did profit he covered his tracks very skillfully.

But, in another connection, he was constantly accused of having been paid a fee, quoted at $10,500, for his part in preventing the impeachment of Governor Scott, an allegation which Elliott himself flatly denied.* It is a fact, however, that Elliott did leave Washington to return to Columbia and work to forestall the impeachment of the governor. But later the *Charleston News and Courier,*† in an open letter to Congressman Elliott, asked a number of questions, one of which was "How much were you paid for your services to stave off the impeachment of Governor Scott?" [10] Elliott answered, "While I was free to charge a professional fee, yet I assert emphatically that I neither charged nor received one dollar for services in connection with the impeachment

---

* There is no indication of how the figure $10,500 quoted in the *Report on Public Frauds* was arrived at, and certainly nothing in that document to support it.

† At the end of 1872 the *Daily News* and the *Daily Courier* merged.

of Governor Scott." [11] Exactly what his services were, however, was never spelled out. The impeachment had many contradictory aspects.

Scott was a man of decent instincts and average intelligence who was, however, very easily led and too weak to guard against his own follies. It is said that on one occasion he was lured into going to New York, taking with him the Great Seal of the state of South Carolina. In the big city his predilection for alcohol and women was played upon until, when the moment appeared propitious, he was persuaded to use the state seal to issue a whole series of new bonds and then affix his signature to them, which made them negotiable.

State agent Kimpton then sold the bonds to members of the Bond Ring * at $.75 on the dollar to bring the price down until they could corner the market. At this point the bonds became a valuable issue which brought the interest on them up. The figures vary, but a conservative estimate is that Scott signed in the neighborhood of $17 million worth of bonds during his two terms as governor.

This depredation of the state treasury was the alleged reason (and indeed it was reason enough) for the attempted impeachment of Scott and State Treasurer Niles Parker. Ironically, however, it was really not Scott's misuse of power, but his proper use of it which, at this particular juncture, brought the wrath of the legislature down upon him. He had vetoed a bill for $75,000 for furnishings for the statehouse. He also had begun to establish better relations with responsible Democrats by consulting with them about ways to lessen the Ku Klux tensions. Furthermore, he had come to relatively friendly terms with various members of the Conservative Tax Payers' Convention which had been organized by the Charleston Chamber of Commerce and was held in that city in the spring of 1871. The governor had even gone so far as to appoint one or two Democrats to office and to promise a general retrenchment and financial reform.

In sum, there were three groups, each with a different motive, pushing for the impeachment of Governor Scott. One group was justifiably concerned about past evidence of his financial irresponsibility. Another was reacting selfishly to such tentative steps

---

* The Bond Ring, like the Railroad Ring, contained some of South Carolina's most honored Democrats.

as Scott was trying to take to curtail graft and to forge a link to the Democrats. A third group, acting out of hostility and venality, was led by C. C. Bowen, sheriff of Charleston County and a member of the legislature, who actually introduced the impeachment proceedings.

Bowen, who fitted perfectly the popularly accepted image of a Reconstruction carpetbagger, had been born in Rhode Island and moved before the war to Georgia. He took up life as a gambler, enlisted in the Confederate Army, was court-martialed for instigating the murder of his commanding officer, jailed in Charleston, and released by the end of the war. Early in 1871 he was convicted of bigamy, then acquitted, then reconvicted, and finally sentenced, but soon pardoned by President Grant—in fact, pardoned just in time to bring the impeachment resolution against Governor Scott, whom he had always heartily disliked.

Working behind the scenes in his usual wily capacity was John J. Patterson ("Honest John"), who by 1871 had become one of the most powerful men in the state. Along with his railroad interests, Patterson also had political ambitions which required large sums of money. Governor Scott's impeachment struck him as a good potential source of revenue. Patterson had a henchman, a dandy named H. H. Worthington, and together they played on Scott's fear that the impeachment might become a reality. Patterson and Worthington convinced Scott that his situation was dire and persuaded him that they could save him, given sufficient sums of money with which to bribe the legislature. It was this ugly machination which probably brought Elliott to defend Scott, with whom, it will be recalled, he was not on very good terms.

The easiest state money Scott could get his hands on was the armed forces account, which had been loosely earmarked by the 1868 legislature as "for the preservation of peace." It is asserted in the *Report on Public Frauds* that Scott dipped into these funds to write three bogus warrants totaling $48,645, made payable to three fictitious characters named John Leggett, John Mooney, and David H. Wilson. Conspiring with the head teller and the president of the South Carolina Bank and Trust Company, Patterson and Worthington managed to collect the cash on the warrants made out to the nonexistent men. They distributed these funds to certain members of the legislature for a vote against impeachment, but obviously kept plenty for themselves, since the average bribe was around $200 and the aggregate sum spent not more than $20,000.[12]

The impeachment resolution came before the legislature just before the General Assembly was to recess for the Christmas holidays. Scott and Treasurer Niles Parker (whom Elliott officially represented in the proceedings) insisted that the issue be settled before the recess on the grounds that it was "neither decent nor proper, but injurious to the state" for the General Assembly to adjourn on December 22, 1871, and to begin the New Year with a charge of "high crimes and misdemeanors" hanging over the governor and treasurer.[13] Actually, the pro-Scott forces sensed that Patterson and Worthington had achieved a majority of anti-impeachment votes through their bribes, but they were by no means certain of holding them over the Christmas recess. It therefore seemed imperative that the vote be taken quickly. However, W. J. Whipper was a strong force in favor of impeachment, acting apparently in good faith in his belief that Scott was playing havoc with the state credit. Whipper had the floor on December 22 and did not intend to yield it until adjournment the next day.

One can imagine Elliott arguing with his friend that for the good of the state and the Republican party Scott should not be impeached. But when he failed, Elliott must have decided he would have to gain the floor from Whipper by use of his skill as a parliamentarian, for which he was renowned.

To this end a meeting was held at Scott's house on the night of December 21. Present were Franklin J. Moses, speaker of the House and soon to be governor, and Samuel J. Lee, a black who was to become speaker. For a price, Lee was instructed to make certain "points and motions" which would be ruled on (for an even larger price) by Speaker Moses "in strict accordance with parliamentary law," but in such a way as to force Whipper from the floor and permit the vote before adjournment. The results were 63 to 27 against impeachment of both Scott and Parker.

When Scott testified before the Joint Investigating Committee in 1877 on this subject, he stated that he had never heard of Mooney, Leggett, or Wilson, to whom the warrants were made out, and could only conclude that a few signed warrants, which were kept locked in the desk of his private secretary in the event of the governor's absence from the state, must have been stolen and made out to these three men. However, as to Treasurer's Voucher No. 1584½ for $5,000 made out to R. B. Elliott from the armed forces fund, Scott contended that this was in payment for expenses which Elliott claimed he had incurred when he was assistant adjutant general, and that after a year's delay, by which time Elliott was in Congress, Scott had decided his claim was just and had ordered the $5,000 to be paid.[14]

Treasurer Parker also testified before the Joint Committee that he had hired Elliott as one of his lawyers during the impeachment proceedings because he was a "member of Congress and had considerable influence." Although he did not feel that Elliott had done much to prevent his impeachment, nonetheless Parker said he paid him a salary of $1,000 for his services, which made a total of $6,000 for Elliott on the record.[15] A good salary, no doubt, for a few days' work, though hardly a swindle. Moses, by his own admission, received $15,000 for his "rulings."

Elliott had been granted a brief leave of absence from the Congress to attend to the crisis in his own state. He returned to Washington in mid-January after the problem was resolved, thus setting a pattern of divided time and, more importantly, divided concern between the nation's and his state's capital.

During the winter and early spring months of 1872, Representative Elliott was relatively silent on the floor of the House, limiting himself to a few private bills * and an occasional incidental remark. However, during these months—he was then living at a boarding house at 1208 Sixteenth Street—he became friendly with most of the leading blacks in the District and won their esteem. He was chosen by them to give the principal oration at their celebration on April 16, 1872, marking the tenth anniversary of their emancipation in the District of Columbia.†

The occasion was a splendid one; the day was fine, though windy. At ten o'clock the procession began forming at Washington's City Hall, led by a chief marshal (in corn-colored sash) and his two top aides (in purple and white sashes), followed by several

---

* One of these was to remove the political disabilities of James D. Tradewell, a white Democrat who was for a few months in 1874 a law partner of Elliott's in Columbia.

† History has made little of the fact that on April 16, 1862, eight and a half months before President Lincoln issued the Emancipation Proclamation, he signed a bill, originally introduced in the Senate by Henry Wilson of Massachusetts, which specifically provided for the abolition of slavery in the District of Columbia and for the payment to the masters of $300 for each of the thirty-one hundred slaves thus manumitted.

dozen district aides and staff officers (in blue and purple sashes). Next came the Philadelphia Excelsior Cornet band of twenty-one pieces, in "showy uniforms," after which marched a batallion of one hundred Howard University cadets in blue uniforms with white belts, succeeded by several companies of Zouaves "in full zouave uniform, white leggings, blue pants and jacket stripped with red, red shirts, yellow sash, white and blue turban, yellow fez, accompanied by field music." [16]

Various companies of territorial and home guards, several more bands and the Lincoln Hook and Ladder Company immediately preceded the carriage containing the dignitaries, who included the orator of the day, the Honorable Robert B. Elliott. Finally scores of representatives from all eight of Washington's district "working-men's clubs" paraded together, each contingent carrying banners or riding in wagons decorated with pictures of Abraham Lincoln, the twelve apostles, the "Goddess of Liberty," and, in one case, a streamer bearing the somewhat puzzling motto, "Bone and sinew. United we will live, but *investigation* will make us fall." [17]

A hundred-gun salute signaled the start of the procession's lengthy march down Second Street to Pennsylvania Avenue passing by the Executive Mansion,* where they were saluted (but not addressed) by President Grant and members of his cabinet. The ceremonial ranks then marched to Georgetown and back to Judiciary Square (now Post Office Square), where a platform had been erected for the occasion. A huge throng was present. With difficulty, the chairman of arrangements, R. W. Tomkins, Esquire, managed to quiet the crowd long enough to introduce Robert Elliott, whose appearance set off such prolonged applause that it was some minutes before he could begin his oration.

Since he was addressing a vast multitude of men and women who were obviously in a celebratory mood, Elliott might have elected to give a fairly routine speech glorifying the act of ten years earlier which officially made the District of Columbia's black population the first freedmen of their race. But instead Elliott chose a sterner tone; perhaps, as a result of the recent imbroglio in his home state, he was more keenly aware of the frailties which underlay the current political situation.

He did begin, however, with the obvious tribute to the Thirty-

* The presidential residence was not called the White House until 1902, when Congress formally so designated it.

seventh Congress, which had pushed through the legislation that led to the "great declaration of human freedom." He paid homage to the martyred president who had signed the bill manumitting Washington's blacks; he thanked God for Charles Sumner and Henry Wilson of Massachusetts ("When did a noble cause have two such noble advocates? When did advocates have a nobler cause?"); and, good Republican that he ever was, he managed to remind his listeners that throughout the struggle for emancipation the Democratic party had opposed the measure "inch by inch, and it has preserved its ignoble record for *consistency,* upon this and kindred measures, untarnished to the present day."

The overall theme of Elliott's oration, however, was a grave warning against complacency: "All history teaches that there is a constant reflux, or flowing back of the current of human events," he said. "There are in the moral, as in the physical world, centripetal and centrifugal forces, the one tending to repel the good and the other to attract it." This tendency, Elliott contended, demonstrated the fallacy of the "trite aphorism that 'revolutions never go backward.'" Revolutions, he warned, do go backward and have done so. In proof of this he first cited the freeing of the Israelites from the yoke of the Egyptians and their resubjugation, two generations later, to the domination of the Assyrians and Babylonians, because "they proved false to the principle to which they owed their first deliverance."

Example followed example, some of which must have seemed erudite and distant to his generally unsophisticated audience. The Torgote Tartars, emancipated from slavery in China in the fourteenth century and then re-enslaved; the Magyars of Hungary, free for two centuries, but then again in shackles because they too forgot the principles to which they owed their independence. In France, after her Revolution of 1792 had culminated in a great and powerful Republic founded upon universal suffrage, "the sun of their freedom went down in blood, and an imperial diadem was substituted for the cap of liberty." Why? Because her people were untrue to their own liberties. And finally there was the American Revolution of 1776, built on the broadest recognition of the rights of man; yet, eleven years after the declaration that "all men are created free and equal," the founding fathers, through "an almost fatal spirit of compromise adopted a Constitution recognizing property in man"—slavery!

Thus the course of history afforded manifest proof that the rights of man, far from being held by a "perpetual or irrevocable charter," were subject to constant hazards. "Yet," said Elliott, "perhaps, by the inscrutable order of Providence, the very dangers that menace our rights are intended to admonish us to be vigilant in guarding them."

To this end tools had been put in Negroes' hands in the form of the Fourteenth and Fifteenth amendments, the "brightest jewels in the crown of the Republic," which constituted the "new charter of American liberty."

> This natal day of our freedom comes to remind us of our responsibilities as well as our rights. It teaches us not only that we are American citizens but reminds us that we owe it to the world . . . to use all our rights in firm resolve to leave those who follow us a heritage enriched by our accumulation and adorned by our triumphs. Citizenship and a participation in the government are guaranteed to us—let us now go faithfully forward. . . . Let us lift ourselves to the height of our responsibilities . . . and fear no danger. . . . So living and so acting we shall be worthy of the high privileges we possess, worthy to perform our part in preserving the temple of liberty, and in perpetuating our Republican institutions.[18]

Charles Sumner was one of the many dignitaries who, unable to attend the ceremonies, sent a message which was read to the gathering. In words closely reflecting those of Elliott, he too warned that, besides celebrating victories already won, the blacks must at all times insist on their rights and then vote to advance them.

Perhaps it was just as well that Sumner did not appear in person before the largely black assemblage, for by that time, unhappily, considerable resentment was building up against the senator among the Negroes because of his increasing opposition to Ulysses S. Grant and his fervid attempts to displace him as the 1872 presidential candidate. A Liberal Republican faction had developed within the party, animated originally, and with Sumner's blessings, by a conviction that some other candidate should be their next Republican standard-bearer. Furthermore, in December 1871, Sumner had proposed a constitutional amendment to limit presidents to one term in office. Clearly designed to embarrass Grant (although it would not have become effective until after the 1872 elections), the amendment was said to be " 'the first big gun to be sent booming over the surface of the land' to announce the drop-Grant movement within the Republican party." [19]

But Grant was not to be so easily dislodged. His hold on the blacks and on the other regulars was secure enough that by the fall of 1871 his chances of renomination seemed inevitable. Therefore, the Liberal Republicans (but not Sumner, who still clung to the hope that Grant could be dumped) turned their attentions toward a third-party effort. To almost all blacks, including Robert Elliott, such a possibility was disastrous; they had cast their lot firmly with the regular Republicans and were convinced that any split in the party would benefit the Democrats and seriously imperil the future of their race. Thus when the Liberal Republicans met in Cincinnati in May 1872 and nominated Horace Greeley (over Charles Francis Adams) for the Presidency, Sumner's dilemma was an agonizing one. Greeley (perhaps best remembered in history for his famous phrase, "Go west, young man,") had been an early supporter of the abolitionist cause. He was the editor of the liberal *New York Tribune* and a strong advocate of Negro suffrage. Clearly such a man was preferable in Sumner's eyes—as almost anyone would have been—to Grant. Still, although Sumner was under great pressure from the Liberal Republican party publicly to support their ticket, he hesitated—and with good reason. He knew that his endorsement of Greeley would alienate his enormous Negro following. Besides, he agreed with the Negro leadership that Greeley would need considerable Democratic support to make any kind of showing against Grant (as it turned out the Democrats did ultimately endorse Greeley at their July convention) and he feared that under Democratic influence the Liberal Republicans would renege on their campaign pledge to protect the rights of the black.* So, instead of coming out for Greeley, Sumner decided to make a last-ditch stand against Grant.

---

* Sumner's longtime friend Wendell Phillips was violently opposed to Greeley, whom he considered a man without principles, a secessionist whose candidacy had been hatched by Southern white rebels. "I advise anyone who means to vote for him to find out first what agreements have been made by Mr. Greeley's friends with Jeff Davis," he wrote to a friend. "If Greeley enters the White House, Jeff Davis will be as truly a part of the Administration as Seward was in Lincoln's days. . . . If he is elected, let the negroes live in squads of fifty whom no coward will dare shoot down, and show no property after sundown" (*New National Era*, May 30, 1872).

On May 31, three days before the regular Republican Convention convened in Philadelphia, Sumner gave an oration on the floor of the Senate, "Republicanism vs. Grant"—a vitriolic blast designed to read the president out of the party.

Greeley and the Liberal Republicans were delighted: "Our greatest senator has made the greatest speech of his life," wrote Greeley's *New York Tribune*.[20] But to the Negroes, their greatest senator's speech—tantamount to a break with the Republican party —was a disaster. By placing his hatred of Grant above his commitment to the protection of their rights, Sumner seemed to have deserted them. They were dismayed and apprehensive.

The regular Republican party men, of course, were furious. At the Philadelphia convention they not only nominated Grant by acclamation but further rebuked Sumner by selecting the other Massachusetts senator, Henry Wilson, as the vice-presidential candidate. Even then Sumner did not retaliate; he waited almost two more months before he finally endorsed Greeley and the Liberal Republicans. On July 29, in an open letter to Negro voters, he announced his decision to support Greeley: "I have not taken this step without anxious reflection," he wrote to Henry Wadsworth Longfellow, "and I know the differences it will cause, but I cannot help it. I felt it my duty which I could not avoid." [21]

Robert Elliott led the South Carolina delegation to the Republican Convention, which met at the Academy of Music in Philadelphia. He, Joseph Rainey, and a rising young Negro politician from Mississippi named John Roy Lynch made headlines as the first blacks ever to address a national party convention.

Elliott's speech to the enthusiastic Republican delegates (who claimed that they, rather than the self-appointed soreheads from Cincinnati, were the properly elected representatives of the party) was brief and wholly political. His very presence among them, along with the other members of his race from the several states, he said, was an illustration of the accomplished fact of American emancipation. "We stand here in your midst, gentlemen . . . not only to give our vote to this body in behalf of our constituents for the nomination of president and vice president, but to pledge to you the earnest cooperation of 900,000 voters whose complexions are unlike yours." [22]

A few months later he made a similar pledge to President Grant himself, in a letter, Ciceronian in style, which was written to lay at rest a suspicion that Grant must have had about the South Carolina congressman's lingering loyalty to Charles Sumner.

Columbia, S.C.
September 19, 1872

His Excellency, U.S. Grant
Washington, D.C.

Sir—Having been informed that a rumor is current in Washington, that I am hostile to your election, or at least, view your nomination with sullen coldness, I desire, in justice to you, to remove any impression that such false rumor may have created.

The statement referred to, doubtless owes its origin to the fact that I was reared at the feet of the most distinguished assailant of your administration; one whom all New England long delighted to honor. I was not dazzled, however, by the lustre of a deservedly great name. I saw the duty and the danger of the hour, and, unhesitatingly, I performed the one and hastened to aid in rallying my race to meet the other. Had I done otherwise, I would have proved false to my record as a Republican. I had the honor of presiding over the Convention that nominated the Republican electors in this State in 1868 and have presided over every State Republican Nominating Convention that has met in South Carolina since that date. As Chairman of the delegation from this State in the Philadelphia Convention, I had the honor of supporting you and your distinguished associate by my voice and vote; . . .

I need not here refer to the fact, that throughout the 42nd Congress, I have sustained actively the salient measures of your administration, and . . . I expect to support such measures again, assured that, in the future as in the past, they will commend themselves to my judgment, as calculated to advance the best interests of our whole country.

Hence, Sir, my position cannot be mistaken. It is that of the great mass of my race in the United States. We stand by you because you have stood by us. In this we but obey that intelligent instinct of the true soldier which teaches him, when without orders, to move in the direction of the heaviest firing. We perceive too, that the heaviest firing is against you, and blazes from the guns of the same party that confronted you in 1864, and whose defeat has always signalized the advance of free government in this country. No, Mr. President, I am for the ticket which your name leads. Republicans of South Carolina, standing self-sustained without any appreciable aid from official patronage, poor and needy in purse, and confronted by the organized capital of the State, are advancing to your support with their thirty-five unpurchasable majority, as a just tribute to the man who, in the gravest conjuncture of his country's affairs, has been tried in many high trusts and has proved faithful in all and superior in every emergency.

With best wishes for Your Excellency's good health, and satisfied of your assured triumph, I have the honor to be,

Very respectfully,
Your Obedient Servant,
Robert B. Elliott [23]

Noteworthy in the letter is his reference to the "official patronage in this state," doubtless a slap at South Carolina's United States Senator Francis Sawyer, a white carpetbagger who, although elected by a black majority, had failed throughout his tenure to appoint any blacks to office and who was moving more and more toward the conservative (white) side of the state Republican party. And by this time Elliott must also have decided that within a few months' time he himself would try to win Sawyer's seat in the United States Senate.

Also significant in his letter to the president is his bland reference to having been "reared at the feet of" Charles Sumner, thus perpetuating what must certainly have been the myth of his Boston birthplace. Perhaps as he penetrated more and more deeply into the mainstream of American politics, Elliott began to believe his own story of his origin.

9

The Almighty Dollar

IN THE elections of 1870 South Carolina Republicans had pulled together with a great show of harmony to combat their adversaries in the so-called Union Reform party, which was actually the Democratic party under a more palatable name.

In 1872 there was no such organized opposition and, lacking a common enemy, the Republicans loosed all their belligerency upon each other. A fiercely fought, rambunctious state convention was presided over by Robert Brown Elliott, who earned himself many enemies between August 21 and 27 for the partiality of his rulings from the chair.

There were many strange alignments during those five hectic days; old friends became bitter antagonists, long-standing enemies suddenly united against a mutual foe. The battle raged over the nomination for governor of two major white candidates, Franklin J. Moses, Jr., and Daniel H. Chamberlain.

The two men, both of whom eventually were to be governor of the state, offer a variety of contrasts, most markedly perhaps in the place each occupies in history. Moses, a native Charlestonian, son of a highly respected judge, is remembered as a renegade, an immoral weakling who trafficked with Negroes, a scoundrel who, having robbed the state blind, became a derelict and a drug addict, dying in abject poverty in Winthrop, Massachusetts.

Chamberlain, on the other hand, enjoys considerable respect of pre-revisionist historians (and of many revisionists) as an honest reformer who battled against crushing odds to save the South Carolina Republican party from ruin by its own corruption, but who ultimately denounced Negro rule, after which he became acceptable to many Democrats. Neither account gives a full picture of the men nor of the events in which each played a key role.

Elliott was a strong Moses backer. One might wonder if his loyalty to this man of doubtful ethics did not reflect his own questionable morality. Perhaps, Elliott, after all, knew at first hand from the time three years earlier when he had been assistant adjutant general how much use Moses had made of his position as adjutant general to pocket unearned dollars. But, realistically, Elliott was also well aware that he would have had to search far and wide to find a politician completely without taint to endorse for the governorship.

Moses was an exceedingly attractive young man. The strong probability was that Elliott liked Moses and that Moses liked him; that what seemed to many contemporary whites to be Moses' truckling to Negroes was, in fact, a genuine sense of kinship which he felt for many blacks and which was exemplified by his friendship with Elliott. The two men certainly had much in common. They were of an age, both were lawyers, both had been newspaper editors, both were well educated and highly intelligent; they were excellent orators, facile politicians, luxury-loving, adventurous, and, at the same time, dedicated to racial equality.

Elliott's relationship to Daniel Chamberlain was quite different and much more complex. On the surface there was ample reason for him to have admired Chamberlain, who was also an extremely intelligent, well-educated lawyer and a skilled politician. But Elliott disliked Chamberlain, and it is possible from much evidence to postulate the reasons why.

Chamberlain, who was attorney general of the state in Scott's second administration, was a short man, prematurely bald, reserved, and rather humorless. While one can easily imagine Elliott and Frank Moses enjoying an evening of drinking and talking in Fine's Barroom, it is difficult to picture Chamberlain in any such cheerful camaraderie with a black. He had a cool elegance of manner which Elliott probably regarded as patronizing. There is little doubt that Chamberlain believed intellectually in the rights of Negroes and in the Republican party as the instrument and protector of those rights. But he somehow never conveyed any emotional fervor to back up his stated convictions, and his detachment must have galled Elliott.

In his native New England, before joining the Union Army, Chamberlain, who had gone to Yale and to Harvard Law School, mingled naturally with the intellectual elite, numbering among his friends men like Wendell Phillips, Henry Wadsworth Longfellow, and Charles Eliot Norton. Thus it was perfectly understandable that he should have sought similar companionship in South Carolina. But that level of society, which of course included the Southern aristocracy, was closed to him because he was a Republican. Or at least it was almost closed. Chamberlain managed to keep the door ajar by ingratiating himself—here also some might have called it truckling—to the natural leaders. For "coquetting with Democrats" and for publishing "love letters for their support," Elliott bitterly mistrusted him.[1]

Still, things must have been very awkward for Chamberlain. He was a Republican carpetbagger but, with some justification, he felt himself an exception to the stereotype of the adventurer gone South in quest of a fortune gained at the expense of ignorant blacks and helpless whites. Although he set himself apart as an honest man and a reformer, there is ample evidence that he was a member of the infamous Bond and Railroad rings. In the case of the Greenville and Columbia Railroad, for instance, Chamberlain, using his position as attorney general, was instrumental in procuring for the ring from the state 21,698 shares of stock in the road —stock which had cost the state $20 per share and which was sold to the ring for $2.75 per share: "There is a mint of money in this, or I am a fool," Chamberlain wrote to state agent Kimpton about the Greenville and Columbia Railroad maneuver.[2]

There was, of course, nothing exceptional in the 1870s (or in the 1970s, for that matter) about public servants who advocated reform on the one hand while systematically defrauding the public on the other. Men like Moses, Naegle, Patterson, Tomlinson, Cardozo, Whipper, Smalls, and even on occasion Robert Brown Elliott, to mention only a few who played prominent roles in the 1872 Republican Convention, all talked a noble game while often playing an ignoble one. But there was something excessively sanctimonious about Chamberlain's zealous call for reform, which, in view of his own not unblemished record, caused men like Elliott to want to expose his hypocrisy.

The hostility between these two politicians was to have a profound effect upon the destiny of South Carolina, beginning with the August 1872 state Republican Convention and continuing for the next four years.

The drama began on Wednesday, August 21, with delegates jamming the floor and lobby of the state Senate chamber while Trial Justice Thompson's brass band, stationed in the gallery, played such numbers as "Shoo Fly," "Dixie" and, when appropriate, "See the Conquering Hero Come." Over the hubbub, Lieutenant Governor Alonzo J. Ransier called the 1872 Radical Republican nominating convention to order.

After a few remarks of his own, Ransier asked for nominations for chairman of the convention. Robert Elliott was nominated by his fellow congressman Joseph H. Rainey. Francis Cardozo was nominated but declined. (In this fight Cardozo, who was later to become Chamberlain's most loyal Negro friend, was strongly pro-Moses—or at least strongly anti-Chamberlain, so much so that a few days before the convention he had publicly accused him of malfeasance in office, specifying bond, railroad, and land commission frauds.) C. L. Wilder, a black from Richland County, was the only other nominee.

Elliott was elected 108 to 28, was conducted to the chair by Rainey and B. F. Whittemore, and introduced to the convention by Ransier, after which he took up the gavel and, according to the *Charleston Daily News,* made a "short speech devoid of significance." [3] After a brief recess Elliott appointed a committee on credentials, which he packed with Moses men, so that on the first day all signs pointed to a relatively easy Moses victory. There was, however, one contrary note of interest. U.S. Senator Francis Sawyer had arrived in Columbia with what was reported to be a mandate from Washington. [4] Because Franklin Moses was an anathema to some of the more conservative (and in many cases the more respectable) elements of the party, a bolt by them was considered possible if he were nominated. To prevent such a split in the party, Grant himself, according to the rumor, had declared that Chamberlain must be the nominee. To effect this, Moses was to be bought off, but not until a bitter battle with all semblance of reality had been waged for a few days so that he could retire as if beaten in a fair fight.

Some credence was given to this rumor when June Mobley,

black leader of the Union County delegation for Chamberlain, saw Sawyer on the floor at the start of the evening session and moved that the senator be allowed to speak. W. C. Jones, black, a stooge for Elliott and Cardozo (he was Cardozo's clerk in the office of secretary of state), spoke tartly against Mobley's motion, saying that Senator Sawyer had done nothing as a Republican to entitle him to a voice in the councils of the party. Furthermore he, Jones, did not appreciate anyone coming from Washington to "chalk in big letters on a blackboard for poor niggers to read the orders by which they should be governed." [5]

Mobley defended Sawyer, but his motion to have him speak was defeated, and before any additional conflicts could develop, the gas lights began to flicker and Elliott called a recess to "resuscitate the meter," after which the convention adjourned for the day.

By the next morning there were so many charges of bribery flying around the Senate chamber that the unsuccessful attempt to buy off Moses, even if it had been dictated by Grant himself, lost most of its steam. After the business of seating the contesting delegations from six counties was settled, predictably in Moses's favor, the convention proceeded to the nomination for governor.

Moses was nominated first. His name was greeted with "tremendous and continued cheering." "Daddy" Cain made an effective seconding speech, reminding the convention that, although Moses was the scion of an old South Carolina family, he had become the poor man's champion and was thus the candidate of the "bone and sinew of the state."

John L. Naegle, comptroller-general of the state, then rose to nominate Chamberlain. He began graciously by saying that he had no intention of attacking anyone; Moses was his firm personal friend and he would therefore "throw the mantle of charity over him to conceal his nakedness." The thrust of his speech was directed toward the acknowledged possibility that if Moses were the nominee there would be a bolt which, Naegle predicted ominously, would mean the dissolution of the Republican party and the disenfranchisement and re-enslavement of the colored man. Whereas the man who could prevent a break, the man who would be acceptable to all Republicans, who would cement the party together and avert all schisms, was D. H. Chamberlain, a Northern soldier who could guard the rights and liberties of the Negro.

Here T. J. Mackey, a Moses man, interrupted to ask if being a

Union soldier was a test of Republicanism. Not necessarily, Naegle replied, but such a man could "touch the chords in the hearts of Union soldiers that other Republicans could not." [6]

At this point Robert Elliott relinquished the chair temporarily in order to join the fight. He denied that Chamberlain had any such power. He himself had been a soldier in the Union Army, said Elliott, and Chamberlain could touch no such chord in his heart. Here again was an example of Elliott's ability to invent any aspect of his background that suited an immediate situation. There is not a shred of evidence to indicate he had ever been a soldier in the Union Army. On the contrary, there is every reason to believe that he was not even in the United States during the Civil War. However, as usual, his words were accepted at face value.

Once he had divested himself of the theoretical impartiality of the chair, Elliott held the floor and proceeded to a vivid attack on Chamberlain's attempts to win the nomination by bribery. Citing chapter and verse, he said that one member of the Edgefield delegation, a black named Simkins, had been approached by a state official and asked to support Chamberlain and name his own price. Who was that state official? "There he is," Elliott cried dramatically, pointing to Comptroller Naegle. "Behold the man!" The words caused a tremendous uproar.

Three times, in three separate instances, Elliott demanded that the delegates behold the man Naegle, who had offered bribes in Chamberlain's behalf. Could the convention support a man whose nomination was to be procured by such means, he then asked righteously?

Needless to say, Naegle did not permit Elliott's virtuousness to go unchallenged. Was Elliott aware, he demanded, that Moses had offered Owens of York $1,000 for his vote?

"That is false as hell," Elliott shot back. "Moses has no money." [7] A realistic answer, certainly, but hardly one dictated by moral indignation, there being no suggestion that if Moses had had the money and thought there was a chance of winning the delegate he would have hesitated to offer the bribe.

Into this maelstrom of accusation a third name, that of Reuben Tomlinson, the incumbent state auditor, was put forth as a nominee for governor by a Negro, S. A. Swails; he was seconded by ex-governor James L. Orr. Judge Orr's endorsement was particularly important since he carried considerable weight with both the old and new regimes.

In many ways Reuben Tomlinson was well qualified, if not the best and most honorable candidate of the three. A Pennsylvania Quaker, he had been dedicated to the cause of Negro education in the state since 1862. He came South to take part in an early experiment to train and educate the first Negroes who had become freedmen (contrabands, as they were then called) when the Sea Island plantations were seized at the start of the war by the Union Army. Tomlinson had been general superintendent of St. Helena (one of the Sea Islands), then moved on to be head of the Freedman's Bureau educational organization in South Carolina. Elected to the state legislature as a representative from Charleston, he was chairman of the Education Committee of the House, after which he was appointed state auditor.

No sooner had Tomlinson been nominated and seconded than accusations about *his* integrity began to be shouted about the hall, spearheaded by T. J. Mackey. Tomlinson, Mackey said, was a stockholder, and, in fact had been the treasurer, of the Greenville and Columbia Railroad Company while he served as state auditor. Furthermore, Mackey charged, Tomlinson had used his position as state auditor to bribe and push through the legislature a bill to gain control of the state's natural phosphate beds and then helped form a private phosphate company of which he was treasurer. Mackey then went after Tomlinson's "eulogist," B. F. Whittemore (the man who had been expelled from Congress for selling West Point cadetships) and proceeded to tear him to shreds, in this case having better evidence to substantiate his wild claims.

From then on the convention rapidly deteriorated into a regular knock down, drag out fight. Elliott, as chairman, appeared quite willing to give the delegates their head and let the political farce go on so long as candidates other than Moses were being reviled. But as soon as Moses once again became a target, Elliott gaveled the assemblage back to order. When he had restored quiet, he abruptly called for the vote on the nominees for governor. His timing was very skillful. If he had waited another day, Chamberlain and Tomlinson might have joined forces and together picked up enough strength to block Moses, especially as some delegates (Smalls, for one) were calling for a two-thirds majority for nomination. As it was, Moses won easily with sixty-nine votes to Chamberlain's eighteen and Tomlinson's sixteen.

As anticipated, once Moses was nominated the dissidents (Bolters) speedily organized and met the next morning for their own convention in the Columbia courthouse. Judge Orr was chosen chairman. The headlines of the *Charleston Daily News* for that day told the story picturesquely. "Rogues Falling Out. The Grand Bolt. Everybody Penitent for the Past and Bent on Reforming Everybody Else's Sins in the Future." [8]

Certainly reform was the keynote of all utterances at both conventions. Orr made the opening speech to the Bolters, denouncing Moses for the fraudulent pay certificates and Elliott for the partiality of his rulings: "Whenever it suited President Elliott, any motion was declared carried; when not, not." South Carolina through her "rascality and fraud" had imposed a heavier burden on the national Republican party than all the other states combined, said Orr. And let there be no mistake about it, he insisted, the purpose of the Bolters was to organize a reform ticket which was exclusively Republican. There would be no toadying to Greeleyites or Democrats. There only purpose was to beat the ticket nominated at the other—the statehouse—convention. [9]

The Negroes remained solidly with the regular Moses party with but a few exceptions, Whipper being one, and his and Elliott's other law partner, Macon B. Allen, another.

Interestingly enough, Daniel Chamberlain, one of the loudest advocates of reform, did not go along with the reforming Bolters, with whom he probably would have felt more at home; he might even have become their candidate for governor. His reason for staying with the regulars was probably twofold; in the first place, he knew that the Bolters, because of their similar motivation, would automatically be associated, despite Orr's protestations to the contrary, with the Greeleyites, and for that reason his alliance with them would displease Grant. Secondly, Chamberlain was a realist; he knew that without the Negro vote, the Bolters could not win. Therefore, it was more judicious for him to remain within the party, mend a few fences, and pick up some political credits which would serve him well when he tried again for elective office two years hence.

The Bolters nominated Reuben Tomlinson for governor; a black, J. N. Hayne, for lieutenant governor; another black, Allen, of Whipper, Elliott, and Allen, for secretary of state; and whites for the other offices.

At the statehouse, the regular convention continued. The departure of the Bolters did not seem to calm the waters at all; in

"HE WANTS A CHANGE TOO."

Cartoon by Thomas Nast, Harper's Weekly, 1876

Engraving of R. B. Elliott (center top) delivering his famous civil rights speech in the U.S. House of Representatives, January 6,

Eng⁴ by Geo E Perine NY

Robt. B. Elliott

HON. ROBERT B. ELLIOTT

THE FIRST COLORED SENATOR AND REPRESENTATIVES,
In the 41st and 42nd Congress of the United States.

Seated, left to right: Sen. H. R. Revels, Mississippi; Rep. Benjamin S. Turner, Alabama; Rep. Josiah T. Walls, Florida; Rep. Joseph H. Rainy, South Carolina; Rep. Robert Brown Elliott, South Carolina. Standing: Rep. Robert C. DeLarge, South Carolina; Rep. Jefferson H. Long, Georgia. *Library of Congress*

"THE BLOODY SHIRT REMOVED."
Governor Tilden: "It is not I, but the Idea of Reform which I represent."

Cartoon by Thomas Nast, Harper's Weekly, 1876

HON. ROBERT B. ELLIOT.

HON. ROBERT BROWN EL-
LIOT, whose portrait appears
in this issue, is the representative
of the South Carolina District that
for many years sent John C. Calhoun to Congress. He was born
in Boston, but is apparently of
unmixed African blood. After a
voyage to England, he passed
through the High Holborn Academy in London, and graduated
from Eton College in 1859. In 1866
he went from Massachusetts to
Charleston, and began his career
there as a printer in a newspaper
edited by his present colleague,
Mr. Ransier. In 1868 he was a
member of the State Constitutional
Convention, and during the same
year he was sent to Congress. In
March, 1869, he was Assistant
Adjutant-General, which position
he held until he was elected to the
Forty-second and Forty-third Congress.

He is 31 years old, and an eloquent orator of experience. In
the early part of last month he
delivered his great speech on the
Civil Rights Bill, in reply to Alexander H. Stephens.

HON. ROBERT BROWN ELLIOT, AN ELOQUENT NEGRO CONGRESSMAN
FROM CALHOUN'S OLD DISTRICT, SOUTH CAROLINA.

Residence of R. B. Elliott, Columbia, S.C.

ge from the Robert McKay scrapbook, "South Carolina Redeemed," a hand-written
count in doggerel verse of the Reconstruction with contemporary newspaper clippings.
uth Caroliniana Library

FRANK LESLIE'S
ILLUSTRATED
NEWSPAPER

No. 1,107—Vol. XLIII.]   NEW YORK, DECEMBER 16, 1876.   [Price, 10 Cents. $4.00 Yearly.

THE NOVEMBER ELECTION.

The Exciting Contest Over the Result in South Carolina.

THE leading topic of discussion throughout the country during the week ending December 2d was the phase of the political situation exhibited in the struggle of the two combinations in South Carolina, each of which claimed to have been legally elected as the Legislature.

The South Carolina State Board of Canvassers completed what they considered their duty, and adjourned, on Wednesday, November 22d. Their action was taken to the Supreme Court, and the counsel of the relators were instructed to draw the order to commit the Board for contempt of Court, on account of having assumed judicial functions in defiance of the decisions and orders of the Court, and issued certificates of election to the Hayes Presidential electors and to the Republican members of the Legislature in those cases where grave questions had arisen, and adjourned *sine die* at the very instant almost that the Supreme Court was issuing a peremptory mandamus directing the Board to issue certificates of election to the Senators and Representatives of the General Assembly ascertained by the Board to have received the highest number of votes, as made in its return to

THE BOARD OF CANVASSERS GIVING THEMSELVES UP AT THE JAIL AT COLUMBIA, NOVEMBER 25TH.

the Court on the day previous, in obedience to an order of the 20th. A fine of $1,500 was imposed on each member.

On Saturday morning, 25th ult., commitments were duly made out and given Sheriff Dent for service, and his deputies constructively arrested the members of the Board of State Canvassers, all of whom were then at their respective offices in the State House. They asked time to arrange private matters and straighten up the books and records of their offices before closing them, and were granted the indulgence until five o'clock in the afternoon, when it was understood with the Sheriff that they were to report at the jail of the county. In a short time the offices of the Secretary of State, Comptroller-General, Treasurer and Attorney-General were closed and their functions suspended.

At the hour agreed upon, Messrs. F. L. Cardozo (colored), State Treasurer; H. C. Hayne (colored), Secretary of State; H. W. Purvis (colored), ex-Adjutant and Inspector-General; T. C. Dunn (white), Comptroller-General; and William Stone (white), Attorney-General, presented themselves at the jail, and were shown to a small room, destitute of furniture, lighted by grated windows and closed by bolted doors. Sheriff Dent permitted them to send to their homes for such articles as were deemed necessary to render them comfortable.

(Continued on page 250.)

SPEAKER MACKEY SWEARING IN THE REPUBLICAN MEMBERS OF THE HOUSE, IN COLUMBIA, NOVEMBER 29TH.
SOUTH CAROLINA.—THE NOVEMBER ELECTION—THE DEAD-LOCK IN THE STATE LEGISLATURE AT COLUMBIA.—From Sketches by Larry Ogden.

National interest was focused on South Carolina during the fateful days of December 1876.

"THE S.C. STATE CAPITOL
OCCUPIED BY U.S. TROOPS."

Leslie's Illustrated Newspaper sent staff artist Harry Ogden to South Carolina to do a series of sketches depicting the conflict which led to the end of Reconstruction. These sketches appeared in the December 23, 1876, issue.

"S.C.—THE DEADLOCK IN THE LEGISLATURE:
DEMOCRATIC MEMBERS LEAVING THE HOUSE IN
PURSUANCE OF A REQUEST BY SPEAKER WALLACE."

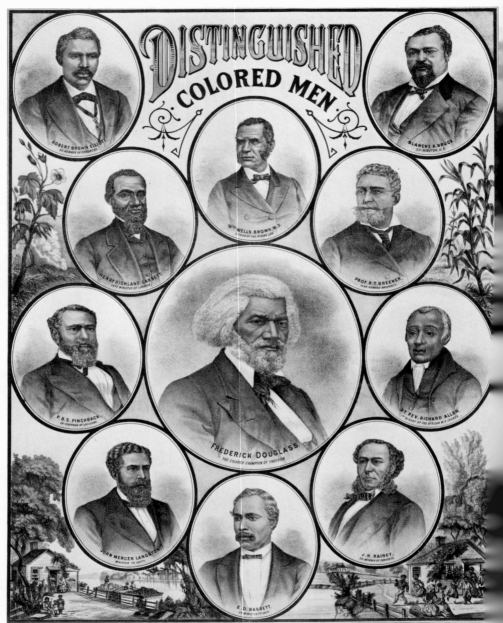

fact, the tempestuousness even reached the point of drawn pistols. Matters proceeded smoothly enough through the nomination for lieutenant governor of a black, R. H. Gleaves; for secretary of state, another black, H. E. Haynes; and for attorney general, Samuel Melton (who received 100 votes to incumbent D. H. Chamberlain's 6). The convention really erupted over the nomination for state treasurer, however.

Cardozo, who had been secretary of state during both Scott administrations, was nominated for the treasurer's post by Joseph Rainey and was strongly supported in seconding speeches by Mackey, Elliott, and Moses himself. A little-known white man named Harry Noah was nominated by B. G. Yocum and seconded by F. H. Frost, both of whom were Chamberlain men. Frost opened his remarks by saying that he supported Noah simply because he did not know him and therefore did not believe him to be a thief. Immediately Elliott called him to order. Frost went on to say that Cardozo, whom he did know, could not be trusted. Again he was called to order by Elliott and again and again, as he attempted to build his case against Cardozo, until June Mobley, described by the *Daily News* as the "plucky little delegate from Union," gained the floor and begged the convention to allow fair play and free speech. He moved that Frost be allowed to bring out whatever points he pleased concerning the character of the candidate, and his motion carried. In a sense this was a rebuke to Elliott, who responded by stepping down and leaving the chair temporarily unattended.

Frost proceeded and was followed by S. A. Swails, who, although he had originally nominated Tomlinson for governor, had not bolted. He now launched into a vicious attack on Cardozo, claiming that frauds "damnable and deep" had been perpetuated by the secretary of state. Swails, however, was more vociferous and savage than specific in his accusations.

While the *Charleston Daily News* gave full play to Swails's attack on Cardozo, the *Columbia Daily Union Herald,* the leading Republican journal in the state, at that time edited by R. Cass Carpenter, a pro-Moses man, referred only to Swails's "extended remarks against the Northern element." [10]

When Cardozo took the floor to answer the charges against him, Elliott resumed the chair and tension rose in the packed Senate chamber. Cardozo attacked Frost; Frost interrupted to demand that he yield the floor for a question; Cardozo refused, and the chair upheld him. Cardozo assailed Mobley for supporting Frost. Mobley rose "greatly excited and made a strenuous effort to get the floor to reply to a personal attack on himself." [11] Elliott ruled him out of order. Cardozo continued to speak. Mobley, Frost, and Swails kept claiming the floor. Confusion and disorder mounted. Elliott hammered down all opponents, while Cardozo attempted to talk over the din.

Mobley, the most insistent, shouted without cease as Elliott tried to drown him out with his heavy gavel. Finally, in desperation, Mobley rushed up to the chair, reached over to the reporters' table, grabbed a heavy inkstand, and began banging it on the table in opposition to the chairman's gavel. Ink flew in every direction; the sergeant-at-arms tried to grab the inkstand away from Mobley and eject him from the hall. Excited members rallied to his defense, and it was at this moment that pistols were drawn, while the crowd "swayed to and fro in innumerable personal conflicts and struggles." [12] In the midst of this pandemonium, Chairman Elliott declared the convention adjourned until ten the next morning. No state treasurer had been nominated.

During the night, an *entente* for the sake of party harmony must have been reached, for Elliott opened the next morning's session with a patently false "personal statement" of the sort politicians are wont to make, in which he assured Mobley that he had not been prompted by partisan feelings in his decisions for the chair, but only by his desire to enforce the rules. Considering the bedlam into which the convention had degenerated the evening before, this quasi apology must have been somewhat difficult for Mobley and his sympathizers to accept. But, when Cardozo followed Elliott with a retraction of some of the things he had said about Mobley in the heat of battle, at least a semblance of peace seemed restored. The delegates unanimously agreed to allow three hours and no more for debate on the subject of the state treasurer. Frost and Swails then resumed their assault on Cardozo, more precisely this time and with fewer polemics. Elliott barely touched his gavel. Cardozo answered the charges effectively and apparently convincingly, for he took the nomination handily with a final vote of 77 for himself to 26 for his opponent, Noah.

The fierce battle for the state treasurer was thus resolved. By contrast, the nomination of Richard Cain for congressman-at-large was achieved in a few hours with only minor conflicts, which was perhaps a reflection on the delegates' view of the relative importance and power of the two offices.

Meanwhile the Bolters, termed by the *Daily Union Herald* "a mutual admiration society of ambitious men," were making an effort parallel to Horace Greeley's at the national level, to hold the Republican votes and to attract the Democrats who, after all, had no place else to go, since there was no state Democratic ticket. But Greeley had actually been nominated for president by both the Democrats and by the dissident Liberal Reform Republicans and thus had no need for pretense. The Bolters did; they therefore went through the motions of endorsing the Republican Grant-Wilson ticket, albeit in the most lukewarm terms possible. At the same time they put on the ticket, as a candidate for the Fourth Congressional District, ex-governor B. F. Perry. Perry, it will be remembered, had been the first provisional postwar governor of the state, and had convened the all-white constitutional convention of 1865 which was made up entirely of ex-Confederate leaders who refused even to listen to any suggestion of Negro suffrage.

"Is it not an insult to every Republican in South Carolina to class B. F. Perry as a true Republican?" asked the *Daily Union Herald,* and then went on to suggest that the Bolters' platform had the "real simon pure Democratic ring to it and will be received with comfort and satisfaction by every unregenerate Democrat from one end of the state to the other." [13]

There were not, however, enough Democrats, unregenerate or otherwise, to turn the tide away from the regular Republican party—that is, not enough who voted, for the returns indicated that at least forty thousand whites had stayed away from the polls altogether.[14] As a result, the entire statehouse ticket, led by Franklin Moses, won overwhelmingly, and nationally Grant and Wilson carried the state by a fifty thousand vote majority.

With virtually no fanfare—in fact, almost incidentally—Robert Elliott had been renominated for Congress by the delegates of the Third Congressional District. He was returned to office with the rest of the Moses ticket. At the time of his re-election, however, he had no intention of serving in Washington in the capacity of congressman, for by 1872 he had other plans which he thought would take him to the pinnacle of his political career.

Members of the House of Representatives, no matter how much they may protest to the contrary, almost invariably have their sights set on the Senate chamber. In 1872 a man's ambition to move upward within the capitol was more easily fulfilled than it is today; until the passage of the Seventeenth Amendment in 1913, senators were chosen not by the electorate itself but by its representatives in the states' general assemblies.

Still, for a black, even during Reconstruction, the Senate chamber was hallowed ground, a lily-white territory which had been invaded only once, and that briefly, when Hiram R. Revels served out Mississippi's thirteen-month unexpired term in 1870. Elliott aspired to be the first man of his race elected to a full six-year term in the Senate of the United States; and, given the black majority which existed in South Carolina's General Assembly, his aspiration did not seem unrealistic. It is impossible to pinpoint exactly when he decided to try to replace incumbent Senator Francis W. Sawyer. Certainly he must have been testing the ground during the August state convention; and the sweeping victory of Moses's (and his own) wing of the party greatly strengthened his hopes. But, even before the election in October, the field of contenders had begun to emerge. Robert Scott, soon to be ex-governor, was an obvious candidate, but Elliott considered him an easy target, tarnished as he was by the stain of corruption during his two terms at the statehouse. Sawyer was another easy mark, since he was unpopular with many Republicans and practically all blacks in the state. But another candidate loomed large. "Honest John" J. Patterson, the railroad entrepreneur from Pennsylvania, had never held public office in South Carolina and was known to the voters primarily as the brains behind the Blue Ridge Railroad stock swindle. Nevertheless, despite the scandal, in fact because of it, J. J. Patterson was a formidable opponent; the Blue Ridge Railroad had yielded him money—a lot of money with which to buy his election.

Early in the fall of 1872, before the legislators had even assembled, Patterson opened his headquarters on Columbia's Main Street, just a stone's throw from the capitol and from the Columbia Hotel where many of the politicians stayed. In his suite of rooms over Fine's Barroom, the best liquors, wines, and cigars were dispensed, while votes were systematically bought by Patterson's general manager, H. C. Worthington, or occasionally by Patterson himself, when he would issue forth from his private room to deal with a particularly recalcitrant prospect.

In the 1877 *Report on Public Frauds,* affidavits from seventy-seven men who appeared before the joint committee attested to Patterson's bribery attempts. The highest sum was the $8,000 allegedly offered to Robert Smalls if he would deliver the Beaufort delegation into Patterson's hands.[15] But this was only rumor; Smalls did not himself testify before the joint committee. It was a fact, however, that the entire (and heavily black) Beaufort delegation did vote for Patterson against Robert Elliott.

On the other hand, Beverly Nash, a staunch black colleague and friend of Elliott's, did appear before the joint committee and stated that he was offered $4,500 by Patterson to switch his allegiance, which he declined to do.[16] Laurence Cain and Paris Simkins, two Negroes from Edgefield, Elliott's home territory, were offered $1,500 and $1,000 respectively, which both refused.[17] The average bribe was more like $300, and in some cases, depending on the sophistication of the legislator, considerably less. One Henry Riley, a freshman representative from Branchville in the county of Orangeburg, said in his testimony that, on arrival in Columbia a few days before the legislature convened, he went directly from the depot to the rooms above Fine's. "A good many members were there," he testified. "General Worthington was there. Liquor and cigars were there. The talk was mostly about Patterson's election—Honest John Patterson some called him. That was my first experience of the Legislature. They drank Patterson's health. They said: 'Now, all that are in favor of Mr. Patterson's election to the Senate, come and drink.' I drank with the others. I had little or no money, and I asked some how I must do. Some members told me to see General Worthington. I saw him privately and asked him to lend me twenty-five dollars. He handed me the money in cash and put it down on a slip of paper. I didn't sign the paper . . . and he said he would make me a present of it." [18]

Scott was said to be paying $100 per vote, and Elliott, who had no money, paid nothing.[19] Characteristically, in the pages of the *Report on Public Frauds* which dealt with the Patterson senate election, Elliott, invariably described elsewhere in the report as a corruptionist, emerged as the innocent—and even worthy—victim of a corruptionist. And, in fact, he was. Not only was Elliott without funds, but many of his influential friends were shilly-shallying about committing their outright support to him; notable among these was governor-elect Franklin J. Moses. Three days before the legislature convened Elliott wrote to the man he had so determinedly helped put into the statehouse:

Columbia, S.C.
November 23, 1872

General F. J. Moses, Jr.
General—

As it has been repeatedly asserted by friends of Col. Patterson on the one hand, that you favor his election to the United States Senate, while on the other hand, the friends of Governor Scott have boldly stated that you are pledged to him, several of my friends have deemed it proper that I should at once advise you of these facts and ask of you an explanation of the matter.

Aside from the foregoing reasons, I think it proper that I should at once be informed of your attitude—as in a contest like this, I consider it important that I should know who are with me in the fight. This is not a time for equivocation. While I have no demands to enforce, I have a right to ask that those who may not feel at liberty to accord to me that vigorous, voluntary, manly and loyal support that I am always accustomed to bestow on *my friends,* will not endanger my success by rendering what they may be pleased to term a "negative auxiliary support."

In view of these things, I would respectfully ask that you settle this question, by a simple explanation, in order that those upon whom I rely for assistance may be correctly informed. I have simply, in addition, to request that those who are really my friends, be not driven off, by that "negative support" which continually preaches to them the certain defeat of a candidate who is without money, through and by the potent influence of the "almighty dollar."

Hoping for an early reply, I have the honor to be,

Very Respectfully,
Your Obedient Servant
Robt. B. Elliott [20]

Outwardly Moses, as governor-elect, chose to maintain a show of impartiality, so there is no way of knowing how much behind-the-scenes manipulating he did and in whose behalf. The final results indicate that he probably stepped in on Patterson's side at the last minute, just before the General Assembly voted on December 10, 1872.

But before that date Elliott must have posed more of a problem than Patterson had imagined he would; or perhaps too many of Elliott's friends, like Nash, Cain, and Simkins, were able to resist blandishments. For whatever reason, Patterson felt obliged to resort to the bribe of bribes, which was one to Elliott himself.

According to Elliott's testimony before the Joint Investigating Committee, borne out by the testimony of Martin Delany, who was a witness, and of John B. Dennis, who acted as go-between, Patterson had been attempting to discover the amount of Elliott's various debts and also tried to buy off the mortgage on his Columbia house. Elliott, on hearing of his rival's probing into his personal life, was "very much incensed," and complained bitterly about the improper interference to his and Patterson's mutual friend John Dennis. The unfortunate Dennis, who had by then been assigned the unenviable task of offering Elliott $15,000 in addition to payment of some debts if he would drop out of the Senate race, was so alarmed by Elliott's anger, before he even knew how much there was to be angry about, that he managed only to say that he had been requested to speak to Elliott on a related matter, before he lost his nerve and refused to continue.[21]

The next day Elliott and Martin Delany were together in the Republican State Executive Committee room when Dennis happened to come in. Elliott at once set upon him and insisted he finish what he had started to say the day before, and Dennis, finally trapped, transmitted Patterson's offer. Just as anticipated, Elliott flew into a rage. Delany had to intercede or, as he said in his testimony, "there would have been a serious difficulty and perhaps bloodshed about it." [22]

Having failed to knock his competitor out of the race, Patterson probably recognized that even the $50,000 he proposed to spend might not be enough to clinch the election; doubtless his fears were further aroused by the clear, strong backing Elliott was receiving in the press. The Republican *Columbia Daily Union Herald,* after sternly calling upon the consciences of the legislators not to barter away their own birthrights and those of their constituents, was unequivocal in its endorsement of Elliott: "We have no hesitancy in saying we believe Congressman Elliott decidedly the best representative of the Republican party. We doubt if there

is another man in the state who has done more for the success of
the party than he. . . . One thing is certain. He will spend no
money to buy votes, nor will he compromise himself in any way.
If the majority in the legislature believe that in addition to devotion to party principles, a public officer should possess merit, intelligence, ability and competency, then we do not know how they
can avoid voting for Mr. Elliott." [23] So, with variations, spoke such
other Republican papers as existed in the state.* Far more significant was the reaction of some of the Democratic press. All
Democratic papers, of course, hated Scott and Patterson; none
had any use for Sawyer, but to many he seemed the lesser evil. Not,
however, to all. The *Charleston Daily Courier* (which along with
the *Charleston Daily News* was one of the most important papers
in the state) could not quite bring itself to come out for Robert
Elliott. What they did, however, was to print, albeit with certain
disclaimers, an editorial from their neighboring Democratic newspaper, the *Columbia South Carolinian,* which did indeed endorse
Elliott. Since this was the first and probably the only time a
Southern Democratic newspaper ever supported a black man for
national office, the *South Carolinian*'s December 10, 1872, editorial as printed in the *Charleston Daily Courier* is quoted here
in full.

> The only candidates who, from present appearances, have any
> chance are Scott and Elliott and Patterson. Between the three
> it seems very clear to us that the conservatives should settle
> upon Elliott. Certainly no honest man in the General Assembly
> can vote for either Scott or Patterson. There is no possible good
> motive which any member could have in doing so and there is
> no escaping the suspicion of bribery which must attach to him
> if he does.
>
> To our mind Elliott is decidedly preferable. If the matter were
> left to us Elliott is not the man who we would want to send to
> the United States Senate, but under the circumstances we can-
> not see how a conservative could do better than to vote for him.
> He is not the candidate of the white people, does not represent
> them and cannot claim to do so. He is, however, the repre-
> sentative of the colored people who form more than half our
> population. Those of his color like him, they have confidence in
> him and he has more influence with them than any other man

---

* An exception was the *Beaufort Republican,* which had been strongly
Bolter and which endorsed Sawyer for senator.

in the state, and is therefore rightly entitled to represent them.

Now the question arises, what is the good to us, the white people of the state in sending such a man as Elliott to the Senate. There is no great positive good to be accomplished so far as we are able to see. But there is much evil to be avoided. It is something to defeat two such wicked men as Scott and Patterson. Moreover Elliott has a constituency of over 400,000 colored people in the state and Scott and Patterson have none. They represent no class, no interest in the state. But the chief prospective good in the election of Elliott is in the influence a seat in the Senate may have upon him. He is the strongest colored man in the state, and if he would exert his influence to bring about a coalition between the real citizens of both races, an approach to good government might be made.

The wisdom of the *South Carolinian,* alas, went unheeded by all the Conservative members of the General Assembly, who, in effect, threw away their votes by casting them for other Conservatives who were not even candidates. Far more unfortunately, the strong recommendation of the *Daily Union Herald* was also ignored by the Republicans; blacks and whites did forfeit their birthrights and voted for J. J. Patterson.

In the Senate, the first ballot was 16 for Patterson to 6 for Elliott, plus 11 for other candidates, which meant there had to be another ballot, since 17 votes were necessary for a choice. The Elliott faction, led by Beverly Nash, tried first to argue that only one ballot could be taken each day; when this was overruled, they moved to adjourn. Apparently they thought that somehow overnight they could appeal one more time to the consciences and better judgment of the black senators, but their motion was lost.

A second ballot was taken. In the interval between the two, H. J. Maxwell, who had nominated Scott and of course voted for him, was blatantly approached on the floor of the Senate by Worthington and offered $2,000 if he would switch. Maxwell kept the Patterson faction in suspense until the actual balloting, at which time, after a pregnant pause, he duly switched and voted for their man. Although his vote assured Patterson's victory in the Senate, Maxwell was punished for the momentary uneasiness he had caused. A few days later he was summoned by Patterson and Worthington and handed a package which contained only $1,000 instead of the promised $2,000; he was never able to collect the rest of his "debt."

In the House of the General Assembly, many spectators were on hand to see the show. Elliott was nominated by W. M. Thompson, a black from Colleton, and seconded by another black, B. A. Bowley, who claimed that the election of Elliott would reflect credit on the state and go a long way toward wiping out the political blot on South Carolina's escutcheon.[24] Samuel Green, one of the numerous black members of the Beaufort delegation, fired the first gun for Patterson by accusing Elliott of trying to dictate to the colored men that they must vote for him or be disgraced. Quite probably the accusation was correct. Another Negro, W. H. Frazier, later testified that Elliott made him and other blacks mad by charging them with selling out their race if they voted for Patterson. Clearly Elliott used strong-arm tactics to make up for his lack of the "almighty dollar." But to no avail. He lost in the House 73 to 27, a defeat more crushing than he and his backers had anticipated. There is no question that Patterson—at this time probably aided by Moses and perhaps even by Chamberlain—mustered a last-minute effort. Prince Rivers, a black trial justice from Hamburg who was for Scott, testified that he was amazed at the number of confirmed Elliott men he saw going in to Patterson's headquarters the night before the General Assembly vote.

Two hours after his election as United States senator, "Honest John" Patterson was arrested on a charge of bribery. A regular comic opera scene followed Patterson's arrest. As the *Charleston Daily News* described it, "Patterson was taken to [Trial Justice R. H.] Kirk's office where a crowd of friends gathered and created a disturbance in the office which came near resulting in a riot. Patterson indulged in most abusive language toward Trial Justice Kirk and, it is said, attempted to get a pistol from Hurley with the avowed intention of shooting Kirk. Minton, a colored adherent of Patterson's, also drew a pistol on [U.S. Marshal] Beatty, and attempted to get possession of the warrant and destroy it. *In the confusion Patterson walked away.*" [25]

He was rearrested at ten o'clock that same evening by two different constables and, "accompanied by a large concourse of friends and spectators," taken to the county jail. No sooner had he been turned over to the Sheriff of Richland County when another special constable appeared with a writ of habeas corpus issued by Judge T. J. Mackey from his improvised "chambers," which just happened for the occasion to be the assembly room over the Carolina National Bank where a large, raucous party was in progress. Patterson was brought there, processed, and duly released from the charge of contempt of court, while the Republican stalwarts, including the new governor, Franklin Moses, and his unsuccessful "reform" opponent, Daniel H. Chamberlain, lifted him on their shoulders and sang "When Johnny Comes Marching Home Again."

It is hardly necessary to add that Elliott was not among the happy throng, and the gall he tasted that evening must have been very bitter. A selfish, unscrupulous cynic, a man who cared for nothing but his often-quoted "ten more years of good stealing left in the state," had been elected to represent South Carolina in the Senate of the United States. And the blacks had put him in office. There was no way that Elliott could blink at that sad truth. What is more, he himself knew that he would have made an incomparably better senator than Patterson. He probably sincerely believed that he would have been an exceptional senator in serving both his state and his race. Certainly with his intelligence, his training, his perceptions, his convictions, and his gifts of persuasion, Elliott would have had a unique opportunity to prove the fitness of a black for leadership and, indeed, to exercise that leadership. Certainly, too, he would have risen to the occasion and, as the *South Carolinian* editorial so hopefully suggested, with his talents and his influence he might well have brought about that "coalition between the real citizens of both races," a coalition that was not then and has never since been truly achieved.

The Senate race was a watershed for Robert Elliott. His failure to win it, brought on by the failure of the Negroes in the legislature to sustain him, sent him into almost a year of obscurity. It would be dramatic to be able to record that during this dim period of his career he got even with those who had robbed him, and that he vented his disappointment in a series of successful moneymaking schemes; that he used his gains to buy the stable of fine horses which some claimed he possessed, or to make Nancy Fat his mistress and deck her out in gaudy finery, each day to ride in her handsome landau through the streets of Columbia.

None of these extravagances occurred. Particularly, they could not have taken place during that year of Elliott's life, which coincided with the national depression of 1873. He bought no property, although in September he did sell a plot he had acquired in

1869, on Sumter Street in Aiken. He received $1,000 for the 160-by-150-foot parcel, and his wife Grace L., in the manner customary on all such deeds, signed away all her dower rights to the land.[26]

Elliott's only innovative act during the year 1873 was a strange one. On January 3 there first appeared an advertisement in the *Columbia Daily Union Herald* announcing "A New Law Firm. Elliott and Tradewell, 6 Law Range, Columbia." Tradewell was James D., who had been a captain in the Governor's Guards, a prewar militia company which was later incorporated into the Palmetto Regiment. He had also served as mayor of Columbia in 1857 and 1858, which office did not disenfranchise him, but his service as an officer in the Confederate Army did. He labored under political disabilities until April 15, 1872, when a bill, HR 2309, to relieve him of these disabilities was introduced in the House, somewhat surprisingly, by Robert Brown Elliott, whose sympathy for ex-Confederates was hardly profuse; in fact, this was the only such bill he ever introduced in behalf of an individual.

That the new law firm was a pay-off for this service rendered by Elliott seems an obvious conclusion, although it is not beyond the realm of possibility that the reverse was true. Tradewell could not have had much influence in postwar political circles at the state capital, and perhaps Elliott acted to give him a leg up. In either case, the partnership brought only minimal rewards as nearly as one can judge, for no record survives of any case handled by either lawyer during the fourteen months of the firm's existence.

When Elliott and Tradewell dissolved in March 1874,* Tradewell became attorney for the city of Columbia. His career, from all accounts, or rather from the lack of them, was an honorable if undistinguished one. Perhaps Elliott's association with this white Democrat amounted to nothing more than a rebuke to the black Republicans who had deserted him.

Meanwhile, of course, Elliott was still a member of the Congress both incumbent and elect. Although he duly returned to Washington for the final, lameduck session of the Forty-second Congress, he spoke only once, and then on a triviality, during the entire session which adjourned on March 3, 1873.

---

* This statement is based on the fact that on March 22, 1874, the advertisement for "A New Law Firm, Elliott and Tradewell" stopped running in the *Columbia Daily Union Herald,* where it had appeared every day since January 2, 1873.

On March 4, Elliott and his wife, along with Cardozo and his wife, and Lieutenant Governor Gleaves and his wife, attended Grant's Second Inaugural Ball.[27] The occasion was marred by the icy weather; the temperature, unprecedented and unseasonable for Washington in March, fell to below zero, and the ball was held in an unheated marquee erected for the occasion on Judiciary Square. The handsome floral decorations froze and wilted, the food was congealed, the coffee turned to an iced frappé; many of the musicians were unable to squeak a sound out of their frigid instruments. Still, the festivities went on. President Grant and Vice-President Wilson arrived with their party at seven-thirty, Mrs. Grant in a white satin gown covered with flounces of black Brussels lace and lavender trimming.[28] West Point cadets were in attendance, and it is often cited as an example of President Grant's racial magnanimity that these young men danced at his inaugural ball with the wives of the black congressmen. Doubtless they sought the favor of a waltz with Grace Elliott, for it was reported by a Southern aristocrat, a former white planter who had little instinct to react favorably toward her, that she was one of the most beautiful and handsomely gowned women at the ball.[29]

The new Congress to which Elliott had been elected did not convene for nine months after the adjournment of the old Forty-second. So, immediately after Grant's inauguration, Elliott, like most other politicians, left the capital to return to his home state. But, unlike most other politicians (and unlike himself, really), he made no waves at all in South Carolina during the spring, summer, and fall of 1873. Then as the year drew to a close, he finally decided that he still had an important role to play in the political arena.

On December 5, almost exactly twelve months after his defeat for the United States Senate, Elliott took his place once more in the United States House of Representatives. Thus 1873, a disappointing year in which he had been largely obscure, ended and 1874, a rewarding year in which he was to be very prominent, began.

10

A Natural Gift for Oratory

"**I** REGRET much to see how little pluck there is among colored representatives," an ailing Charles Sumner wrote to a friend on January 1, 1874. "They are considering how to surrender on the Civil Rights Bill, through fear of the President." [1]

Six days later it fell to Robert Brown Elliott to demonstrate to Sumner how wrong his assessment of the Negro congressmen was, and how strong was their determination never to surrender, but to triumph on the measure which would erase the last legal distinctions between whites and blacks. Elliott had a unique opportunity to help bring to fruition the act for which Sumner had labored so long. Sumner first introduced the bill in May 1870 and reintroduced it in January and March of the following year. In 1872 he attempted to tie it to a bill to provide amnesty for Confederate officers and sympathizers; as a result of his action neither the amnesty bill nor the civil rights measure passed.

The act provided that no public inns or places of public amusement for which a license was required, no stage coaches or railroads, no cemeteries or benevolent institutions, no public schools supported at public expense for public use should make any distinction as to admission on account of race, color, or previous condition of servitude.

In the House of Representatives, one of the principal opponents of the civil rights bill was Alexander H. Stephens of Georgia. A distinguished statesman and superior jurist, Stephens, after waging a hopeless struggle to save the Union, bowed finally to the inevitable, joined the secessionists, and became vice-president of the Confederacy. Even in this capacity he demonstrated his hatred of the war and of Confederate President Jefferson Davis. After the war, along with other thoughtful Southern leaders such as Wade Hampton of South Carolina and General Robert E. Lee, he deplored the Black Codes which were designed to keep the former slaves in a subservient position, and even advocated suffrage for those blacks who owned property and paid taxes.

On January 5, 1874, after some parliamentary maneuvering, Stephens was granted the floor for one hour to speak against the civil rights bill, the understanding being that Robert Brown Elliott would be given an hour to answer him.

The word that a Negro was going to respond to the ex-vice-president of the Confederacy had attracted a large crowd to the House of Representatives. The galleries were jammed with both blacks and whites; Grace Elliott sat in the Ladies' Gallery (rather than the Members' Gallery) to listen to her husband; General William Tecumseh Sherman was also there. On the floor of the House both sides of the aisle were thronged with members; the Democrats, polite to Stephens, made a show of busying themselves with their correspondence when Elliott obtained the floor, but the "eloquence of the speaker soon drew them from their preoccupation and compelled them to listen." [2] Referring later to the moment, Elliott himself said, "No man could have had a more exciting theme, or a more exciting occasion. I must speak under the eyes of crowded galleries, in the presence of a full house, and of many distinguished strangers, attracted by the novel interest of such an occasion. . . . With a profound sense of my responsibility to my race, to my immediate constituents and to my own reputation as a Representative in Congress, I addressed myself to this task." [3]

All the nation's dailies, in reporting on Elliott's performance, recognized his natural gift of oratory and his evident education and culture. They commented on the richness of his voice and the marked cadence of his speech: "The African love of melody was noticeable in the harmony of his delivery," wrote the *New York Times*.[4] *

Both Elliott and Stephens read their speeches from manuscript.

---

* Although there was no Negro dialect in his pronunciation, there was also no indication that he spoke with a British accent.

Stephens, who was sixty-three years old, crippled, and in a wheelchair, began his talk by saying that for the first time in his entire career as a legislator (he had served in the House for sixteen years before the war) he had written out in advance what he proposed to say. He had done so because of the "very great gravity, importance and magnitude of the subject," which involved "the whole fabric of our complex system of government." [5]

His arguments against the civil rights bill, he hastened to point out (and his previous humanitarian stance gave a certain credibility to his words), were not based on the slightest prejudice against man, woman, or child on account of race. It was simply that he did not believe that the civil rights proposed by this bill fell within the jurisdiction of federal legislative powers, but belonged purely to the "several states." The heart of his argument, of course, was states rights versus federal rights.

Adherents on both sides of this most stubborn ideological question have always found answers in a wide range of American constitutional thought. Often, however, quite contradictory views have been drawn from the *same* source. In the debate over the 1874 civil rights bill, that source was the Supreme Court's recent (1873) decision in the famous Slaughter-House Cases—famous because during their adjudication the highest court was for the first time called upon to give construction to key clauses in the Thirteenth and Fourteenth amendments.

"But the Slaughter-House Cases!—the Slaughter-House Cases!" said Elliott in his civil rights speech.[6] One can almost hear the sigh in his weary (and probably calculated) repetition of the words, his despair at hearing his opponents bandy the cases about without truly understanding their significance. James B. Beck of Kentucky, highly partisan and one of the civil rights bill's outspoken antagonists, had initially introduced the Slaughter-House Cases into his argument in the House debate; Stephens also depended heavily upon them in his speech. But Elliott, insisting that the "decision of any court should be examined in the light of the exact question which is brought before it," was the one to state clearly the facts of the Slaughter-House Cases to his fellow representatives.

He explained that the state of Louisiana had conferred upon certain persons and corporations exclusive rights and privileges to maintain livestock landings and slaughterhouses within certain designated areas of the city of New Orleans. The Supreme Court of Louisiana sustained the validity of the act conferring these privileges. Thereupon the plaintiffs contended that the act was void, first because it established a monopoly which was "in derogation of common right and in contravention of common law." Second, they argued, the granting of such exclusive privilege was in violation of the Thirteenth and Fourteenth amendments of the Constitution of the United States.

The United States Supreme Court denied the plea of the plaintiffs and upheld the Louisiana Supreme Court decision in favor of conferring slaughterhouse privileges to certain individuals and requiring butchers to slaughter in a specified place and to pay a reasonable compensation for the accommodation. The Supreme Court held that this was a legitimate and warrantable exercise of the police powers of the state, a power that in constitutional history had always been conceded as belonging to the state.

In bringing their suit, the butchers of New Orleans, who were the plaintiffs, alleged that the Slaughter-House Cases contravened articles of the United States Constitution, that granting privileges to certain individuals and requiring butchers to slaughter in a specified area created an "involuntary servitude" which was forbidden by the Thirteenth Amendment. Although they knew full well that the term "involuntary servitude" was written specifically in the Thirteenth Amendment to apply to African slaves, the plaintiffs tried to use it in this case to suit their own purposes. By the same token, the butchers argued that the Slaughter-House Cases abridged the Fourteenth Amendment's "privileges and immunities" clause and denied to citizens of the United States the equal protection of the laws, while also depriving them the use of their property without due process of law.

Even though the Supreme Court ultimately decided against the plaintiffs, it recognized that they raised issues which were pertinent for the first time in the light of the Thirteenth and Fourteenth amendments. Therefore, the majority opinion, written by Associate Justice Miller in 1873, devoted many pages to a consideration of these grave and far-reaching questions.

In the Court's judicious review of the profound issues involved, Congressmen Beck, Stephens, and Elliott all found passages which each believed corroborated his contentions. To Stephens, certain phrases in the Slaughter-House decision fortified his opinion that Congress could not prohibit the exercise of state powers. For example, he quoted from the decision paragraphs which suggested to him that the right to regulate who could and could not be admitted to public schools (as advocated by the civil rights bill) was "one of those powers which are not transferred for its protection to the federal government." [7] In the same vein, Beck, in his speech, said that, as he read the decision, "rights pertaining to the rights of corporations and inferentially to common schools are not embraced in the powers confided to Congress by the constitutional amendments." [8]

To Elliott such interpretations were entirely and deliberately specious. He maintained that the majority opinion unequivocably stated, and he quoted several lengthy paragraphs to prove it, that the Thirteenth and Fourteenth amendments had as their "all-pervading design and end" the protection and security of the recently enslaved race. What his opponents were doing, Elliott claimed, was to wrench the amendments from their clearly defined purpose and use them as instruments to frustrate the race for whose very good they had been designed. "I am astonished that the gentleman from Kentucky or the gentleman from Georgia should have been so grossly misled as to rise here and assert that the decision of the Supreme Court in these cases was a denial to Congress of the power to legislate against discrimination on account of race, color or previous condition of servitude." [9]

The doctrine of the Slaughter-House Cases, he insisted, was, "What you give to one class, you must give to all; what you deny to one class, you shall deny to all, unless in the exercise of the common and universal police power of the State, you find it needful to confer exclusive privileges on certain citizens, to be held and exercised still for the common good of all. . . . Is it pretended," he then asked the honorable gentleman from Kentucky and the honorable gentleman from Georgia, "is it pretended anywhere that the evils of which we complain, our exclusion from the public inn, from the saloon and the table of the steamboat, from the sleeping-coach on the railway, from the right of sepulchre in the public burial ground, are an exercise of the police power of the state? Is such oppression and injustice nothing but the exercise by the State of the right to make regulations for the health, comfort and security of all her citizens. . . . Does the gentleman from Kentucky say that my good is promoted when I am excluded from the public inn? Is the health or safety of the community promoted?"

Then Elliott attempted to put in perspective the key distinction between the rights of an individual as a citizen of his state and as a citizen of his nation. Beck and Stephens had both quoted from the Slaughter-House decision to show that the Court recognized this difference. "That is true," Elliott said. "There are privileges and immunities which belong to me as a citizen of the United States and there are other privileges and immunities which belong to me as a citizen of my State. . . . But what of that? Are the rights which I now claim [and he here again listed those rights, as if believing that by constant repetition their very reasonableness would finally penetrate the consciences of his listeners] rights that I hold as a citizen of the United States or of my State. Or, to state the question more exactly, is not the denial of such privileges to me a denial of equal protection of the laws? For it is under this clause of the Fourteenth Amendment that we place the present bill: no State shall "deny to any person within its jurisdication the equal protection of the laws." No matter, therefore, whether his rights are held under the United States or under his particular state, he is equally protected by this amendment. He is always and everywhere entitled to equal protection of the laws."

Although the burden of Elliott's speech was devoted to the constitutional issue, he heaped scorn upon his opponents on other matters. Beck had been so intemperate as to suggest that there were doubtless adherents of the civil rights bill on the floor of the House who would "arrest, imprison and fine a young woman in any State of the South, if she were to refuse to marry a negro man on account of color, race, or previous condition of servitude in the event of his making her a proposal of marriage and her refusing on that ground. That would be depriving him of a right he had under the amendment," he suggested sarcastically, "and your conventions of colored men will come here asking you to enforce that right." [10]

"Mr. Speaker," said Elliott, "I have neither the time nor the inclination to notice the many illogical and forced conclusions, the numerous transfers of terms or the vulgar insinuations which further encumber the argument of the gentleman from Kentucky. Reason and argument are worse than wasted upon those who meet every demand for political and civil liberty by such ribaldry as this." [11]

And he was at his most acerbic and effective in his icy blast at

John T. Harris of Virginia, who had the day before voiced a prevalent nineteenth-century sentiment which may have been in the minds of many of the Southern representatives, but which none had been so crude as to put into words on the floor of the House. The civil rights bill, said Harris, was based on the doctrine of absolute equality of the races, "and I say there is not a gentleman on this floor who can honestly say he really believes that the colored man is created his equal."

Elliott's black colleague, Alonzo J. Ransier, who had been lieutenant governor of South Carolina and was serving his first term in Congress, spoke up, "I can."

"Of course you can," snapped Harris, "but I am speaking to the white men of the House; and, Mr. Speaker, I do not wish to be interrupted by him again."

Ransier, a mild-mannered man, was not to be intimidated. A few moments later, Harris, warming to his invidious theme, said, "Admit it is prejudice, yet the fact exists, and you, as members of Congress and legislators are bound to respect that prejudice. It was born in the children of the South; born in our ancestors and born in your ancestors in Massachusetts—that the colored man was inferior to the white."

"I deny that," said Ransier.

This time Harris was even more imperious. "I do not allow you to interrupt me. Sit down; I am talking to white men; I am talking to gentlemen." [12]

Fortunately Elliott had had a day to get his celebrated temper under control before he answered Harris. By the time he got around to dealing with him in his speech, Elliott had the assemblage very much on his side and could afford once again to settle for sarcasm: "To the diatribe of the gentleman from Virginia who spoke on yesterday, and who so far transcended the limits of decency and propriety as to announce upon this floor that his remarks were addressed to white men alone, I shall have no word of reply," he said. "Let him feel that a negro was not only too magnanimous to smite him in his weakness, but was even charitable enough to grant him the mercy of his silence." Laughter and loud applause on the floor and in the galleries greeted this. But, after all, Elliott's magnanimity was not quite unbounded, for he added his assurance to the gentleman from Virginia that the Negro "aims at a higher degree of intellect than that exhibited by him in this debate."

As he moved to his peroration, Elliott harked back to the short-sighted policy of the framers of the Constitution who counted the Negro as three-fifths of a man and thus deepened the cancer of slavery.

> To arrest its growth and save the nation we have passed through the harrowing operation of internecine war resorted to at the last extremity . . . to extirpate the disease which threatened the life of the nation with the overturn of civil and political liberty on this continent. . . .
>
> The results of the war, as seen in reconstruction, have settled forever the political status of my race. The passage of this bill will determine the civil status, not only of the negro but of any other class of citizens who may feel themselves discriminated against. It will form the capstone of that temple of liberty begun on this continent under discouraging circumstances, carried on in spite of the sneers of monarchists and the cavils of pretended friends of freedom, until at last it stands in all its beautiful symmetry and proportions, a building the grandest which the world has ever seen, realizing the most sanguine expectations and the highest hopes of those who in the name of equal, impartial and universal liberty, laid the foundation stone.[13]

The speech was an overwhelming success. The roar of applause was prolonged and deafening; so many Republicans (and even a few of the liberal Democrats) swarmed forward to shake Elliott's hand that they actually "formed in line in the aisle and moved up to his seat in a column." Everyone was talking about the nobility of his appeal to reason, the eloquence of his style, the dignity of his bearing, and the brilliance of his grasp of the constitutional issues. His partisans—and at that moment there were many—as well as some neutral listeners asserted that he had easily bested Alexander H. Stephens by the sheer force of his arguments: "What do you think of South Carolina now?" an exultant member asked Benjamin F. Butler, the representative from Massachusetts who had originally introduced the civil rights bill in the House. Quick to claim the man of the hour for his own, Butler, going along with the myth of Elliott's birthplace (which he may or may not have believed), replied, "What do you think of Massachusetts?" [14]

Even more telling were Butler's words on the following day when he was granted the floor to speak for a second time in favor of the bill: "I should have considered more at length the constitutional argument, were it not for the exhaustive presentation by the gentleman from South Carolina," he said. "He with true instinct of freedom, with a grasp of mind that shows him to be the peer of any man on this floor, be he who he may, has given full strength and full power to that decision of the Supreme Court." [15]

All Republican and most Democratic papers in the North gave prominent and extensive coverage to the speech. The *New National Era and Citizen* devoted its entire front page to reprinting Elliott's speech in full and thanked Elliott editorially for "thoroughly replying by calm, convincing arguments to the conceited assumptions of superiority made by plantation overseers who occupy seats in the House of Representatives.[16] The *National Republican,* a newspaper which often irritated the Negro press by its bland assumption that the blacks ought to be satisfied with what had already been done to ameliorate their condition, went far in praise of Elliott's speech: "No more dignified, skillful, exhaustive tearing down of the false theories raised by caste alone has ever been witnessed in legislative halls." [17]

In South Carolina, the *Columbia Daily Union Herald* also gave over its entire front page to a reprint of the speech,[18] but, not unexpectedly, the *Charleston News and Courier* rose above it altogether. They devoted a full column to a description of Stephens's speech, although commenting that "its delivery did not command or receive the attention of the House." However, the following day, on the editorial page, they noted that Stephens's effort had the "ring of old metal about it," presumably a praiseworthy quality. Reporting Elliott's civil rights oration, they contented themselves with twelve laconic words: "Elliott of South Carolina, colored, delivered a speech in advocacy of it." [19]

In Washington hosannas continued to be showered on Elliott. On the Saturday night following his Tuesday speech, a huge crowd composed largely of blacks, but with numerous whites interspersed, assembled at 220 Second Street, N.E., the boarding house where Elliott and his wife were stopping, to serenade their new idol— both musically and verbally. After several rousing tunes by the band, the first speaker addressed Elliott. He was Daniel Augustus Straker, a recent graduate of Howard University Law School who was soon to go to South Carolina as a customs house inspector and shortly after that to open a law firm in Orangeburg with Elliott as his senior partner. Straker's tender of thanks to Elliott in the name of more than four million human beings belonging to the African race was sincere and touching, if a bit fulsome; Elliott's response was suitably modest. After expressing his appreciation to the assemblage for a tribute which he took not so much as a compliment to himself, but as a token of their devotion to the cause of civil liberties, he repeated—mostly in different words—much of the gist of his civil rights speech, omitting, of course, the complex references to the Slaughter-House Cases. In no sense did he talk down to his audience, which had gathered more to cheer the man than to listen to his sober rhetoric. The result was, once again, eloquent and stirring.

In Columbia, South Carolina, an even more elaborate tribute was in the making. Soon after the civil rights speech, various Republican ward clubs throughout the city met to pass resolutions "complimentary to Robert Brown Elliott" and to further agree that all the wards would join together on February 19 to hold a public reception in honor of their distinguished representative.

On February 6, 1874, although Congress was in session, Elliott returned to Columbia for a six-week visit. He came home a hero, and like most men who have scored a singular success he doubtless enjoyed the adulation which was lavished upon him, especially by many of the people who had deserted him a year earlier in his try for the senatorship.

At the same time he had no inclination merely to sit back and bask in his popularity, for he was statesman enough to know that he could use his current prestige to bring about much-needed reforms and politician enough to want to exploit it for his own purposes. Exactly what his ultimate personal goal was at that time is not documented; however, there is some reason to believe that he was testing the ground for a try at the governorship. Certainly such an objective, coupled with his sincere concern for the welfare of his state and of his race, would have accounted for a stunning speech he gave in Columbia ten days after his return. The occasion was a meeting of the Republicans of Ward Two at the Columbia courthouse, held partly to transact business relative to a forthcoming municipal election, but primarily to hear an address by R. B. Elliott.

The rumor that this "talented gentleman" would be present attracted the interest of a great many of the opposition (whites), who came to hear him and gave him their closest attention.[20] Still, blacks predominated at the meeting and Elliott, instead of telling them what they wanted to hear about his triumph in the area of civil rights, told them what they had to hear about the deplorable conditions at home: The government of South Carolina was a disgrace, the local Republican party a mockery. They, the Negroes, being in the majority, had to bear the responsibility for the shame that had been brought upon the state and they must now take the initiative and institute sweeping and immediate reforms.

Elliott launched his attack on February 16; it was not by chance that he chose that date to fire the first salvo in his campaign for reform (and perhaps for higher elective office), since it was the same day that a Taxpayers' Convention of two hundred delegates— the most influential body of whites to convene since Reconstruction—assembled in Columbia to protest the wretched situation in the state government and their grievous status as taxpayers. "The taxpayers are in despair," reported the *News and Courier*. "They have no civil freedom but are the subjects of plain and naked despotism, the preponderance of political power being in the hands of non-taxpayers who . . . bear no burden and enjoy the spoilation." [21]

The Taxpayers' Convention, Elliott told his black audience on February 16, was "no sorehead movement," but was "seeking to do the work which it was the duty of the Republican party to have accomplished." From there he took off, shocking his audience out of any complacency they might have felt by his recital of one brutal truth after another: A great change was taking place in politics in the country, he said, and it was useless for them to shut their eyes to the facts. "If you go North and mention the name of South Carolina you will find the estimate they put on it there. To mention South Carolina is to merit the sneers of the Commonwealths of the North." Furthermore, when corruption was spoken of in South Carolina it was always blamed on the Negro government. The national Republican party was ready to disassociate itself upon the slightest provocation from the corruption now existing in the state; unless the blacks did something, "and that speedily, they would be compelled to cut off the rotten branch." The state government had violated its most sacred pledges to the people; he, Elliott, washed his hands of all participation in their bad faith and strongly advised his listeners to do the same. It was the duty of the Negroes to vindicate themselves by demonstrating that they wanted an honest government; the only way they could prove their determination for reform was to give notice to all who had maladministered the affairs of state to quit; they must turn the thieves out of office and put honest men in their places.[22]

The *Charleston News and Courier* was as taken aback as his audience must have been by Elliott's "remarkable harangue." Having carefully eschewed all but the barest mention of his civil rights speech, they now allotted an entire column on the editorial page, headed "Plain Talk from a Black Congressman," to his February 16 performance.[23] The *New York Times* also reported in some detail on the speech and, in addition, ran an editorial on the South Carolina taxpayers' quest for reform. They pointed out that in this work the whites could, if they wished it, have the "hearty and effective assistance of many colored men," as evidenced by the "remarkable speech lately made in Columbia by the Hon. R. B. Elliott, the colored member of Congress. With the courage and good sense which have marked his entire career, Mr. Elliott condemned the State Administration and declared that the salvation of the Republican party depended upon instantly putting an end to the existing abuses. Nothing which has been said of the State Government has been more severe than the utterances of Mr. Elliott." [24]

The "utterances" took place on a Monday. On the Thursday following (February 19), in the presence of many who had been responsible for the "abuses" and in the very statehouse where they had been perpetrated, the reception was held honoring Robert Brown Elliott for the civil rights speech he had made on January 6. Possibly, if some of the committee had known in advance what he was going to say in his February 16 speech, they might not have been so eager to pay tribute to him on February 19. Certainly some of those in state office, Governor Moses for one, stayed away. The master of ceremonies, however, was Francis L. Cardozo, secretary of the Treasury, and at that time obviously on good terms with Elliott. If Daniel Chamberlain was present, it was not recorded, but his law partner Sam Melton was not only there but made one of the speeches. The *Daily Union Herald* reported, "Long before the appointed hour, every seat in the hall [House of Representatives] was occupied by members of both Houses and professors at the University and other distinguished citizens accompanied by ladies. The throng was augmented by the arrival of a procession carrying torches and headed by a brass band. At a little after 8 o'clock the Hon. F. L. Cardozo stepped to the speaker's stand and in a few appropriate remarks introduced General Elliott who upon coming to the front was received with hearty applause. He then, in a loud voice and in the most eloquent strain kept an intelligent audience in rapt attention for nearly an hour." [25]

Giving his third major address of the new year, Elliott was at his most gracious as he responded to the tribute of his fellow citizens and constituents. As he reviewed the highlights of his service so far in the Congress, he recalled his initial apprehension about how much was expected of him, "robed with the toga of a Representative as a national deputy of a people but recently infused as a new element in the body politic." But while he knew that he could "scarcely hope to fill the measure of public expectation," he was resolved to contribute his "humble share in illustrating the capacity of the negro for self-government." And, fortunately, in both his earlier Ku Klux Klan speech and in the civil rights speech for which the assemblage was honoring him, it was the conviction that his cause was just which had sustained him in his efforts. These modest disclaimers then permitted him to mention how well he had acquitted himself on those two occasions, how warm and flattering had been the commendation he had received throughout the country, how wide the acclaim, "even where sympathy was withheld, respect was freely accorded."

Wisely, he sensed that the other three black congressmen from South Carolina might feel slightly jaundiced by all the fuss that was being made over him. He therefore made a point of praising J. H. Rainey for his zealous and discreet part in the civil rights debate; A. J. Ransier for his courage in responding to Representative Harris, and R. H. Cain for a recent and distinguished effort which had commanded the attention of the entire Congress. "With such Representatives to sustain our cause, victory cannot be long delayed."

Having thus made all the proper moves, Elliott coolly proceeded to fire another barrage in his crusade for reform, this time hitting many members of his audience at point-blank range:

> It is not the Democracy that will overthrow us, [he declared,] it is our own party with its faithless leaders and the infatuated henchmen. Let us not look abroad for our enemies; they are here, members of our own party, officers elected by our own votes. . . . Ten years ago without a vestige of political power, we are today the absolute political masters of South Carolina.

Such a change is without parallel, not only in its rapidity, but in the momentous responsibilities it imposes upon us. Are we so ignorant as to imagine that God and the world will not hold us to account for our use of all these rights? Never was there a people on whom the eyes of the whole world were fixed with more interest than on the people of South Carolina. This proud state—mother of statesmen—has been committed to our keeping. Our former masters have predicted our failure, . . . they have declared that here, in the highest test, the negro would fail; that he would be victim of the cunning and unscrupulous white man, and the base slave of his own greed and dishonesty. I wish I had 10,000 voices with which to proclaim the great fact that they, the colored people of South Carolina, are now on trial before the whole country.

With the political acuity which characterized all his speeches, Elliott was careful to make clear to his fellow citizens that he approached his subject as a strict Republican and challenged any person who doubted his party loyalty to step forward. He reminded his listeners of their party's 1872 platform, which called for reform and fiscal responsibility and which embodied their expression of faith in the national Republican party: "Upon that platform I shall stand," he said, and added piously, "If others have wandered away, I have not." Then, toward the end of his speech, he returned to this theme in words which clearly suggested his availability for higher state office: "There are men in our party who may be called to the helm of State, and who will faithfully carry out the pledges made in our party platform. Pledges are good, but we must put men behind these pledges who will keep them to the letter and in the spirit. Honesty, economy, good government—in city, county, and in State—let this be our watchword and our firm resolve." [26]

Once again the *New York Times* gave prominent coverage to Elliott's address, noting it on its editorial page and quoting, in a full column, the reform portion of the speech verbatim. The *Charleston News and Courier* returned to its usual policy of sneering at the meeting of the "great unwashed" and referred to the performance of the "hero of the occasion" as "another one of those speeches which are supposed to foreshadow a great political revolution." They did, however, concede that Elliott gave his "colored brethren some excellent advice," and that his remarks were "forcible and conservative," especially given the "well known bitterness and extreme opposition to the white race" which he was known to "entertain." [27] The *Daily Union Herald,* on the other hand, felt it could not do justice to Elliott's "elegant effort" by publishing only extracts, so they printed the oration in full.[28]

Actually, during the months of January, February, and March 1874, the Republican press, particularly the *Daily Union Herald,* seemed so entranced with Elliott that they gave space to items which, under normal conditions, might have been considered quite unimportant minutiae. For instance, on February 27, they reported that he would probably soon lay the "artificial stone sidewalk in front of his place, thereby adding to the beauty and value of his already handsome residence."

The Elliotts had by that time moved from Taylor Street in Columbia to number 50 Lady Street (named for Martha Washington when the city was first laid out in 1786), two blocks north of Senate Street and east of Main. They had bought the property (or rather Grace had ostensibly bought it, since the deed was in her name) in March of 1872 for $7,000, a stupendous sum at that time. The lot was slightly over an acre, the house a sizable three-story building with mansard roof and a wide latticed porch running across the front and along the east side. A tall picket fence surrounded the property.

If Elliott himself took a hand in laying the "artificial stone pavement," he paid for it six days later with an attack of rheumatism (also duly reported in the *Daily Union Herald*) which prevented his scheduled return to Washington and kept him confined to his home until March 23, when he finally left Columbia to resume his congressional duties.

By coincidence (although it could conceivably have been by design), Elliott reached Washington on the same day that a delegation of sixteen of the most elite members of the recent Taxpayers' Convention arrived in the city. They came bearing a memorial to President Grant and to the Congress, praying for relief in the form of federal intervention from the burdens of excessive taxation (they claimed a twentyfold increase since the war) due to the open thievery and gross mismanagement of the affairs of state by those who paid no taxes at all.

When they arrived on Wednesday, March 25, the taxpayers' delegation put up at the Arlington Hotel, which the *Daily News and Courier,* obviously relishing their entire trip, termed one of the most "stylish" hotels in the national capital. On Thursday the group spent their morning arranging preliminaries ("Washington is a city of red tape and nothing can be accomplished in a hurry" [29]); in the afternoon Secretary of State Hamilton Fish arose from his sickbed to receive them. Their visit with the Republican secretary was somewhat more prolonged and cordial than the delegation of Democrats had expected, due no doubt to the circumstance that three of their number were members of that venerable and everlasting pillar of society, the Order of Cincinnati, of which Fish was then the president general.

Such credentials, however, did not appear to greatly impress President Grant when he received the deputation on the following morning, although he greeted them politely and even called one or two of them by name. W. D. Porter, who had been lieutenant governor of South Carolina during James L. Orr's provisional governship, acted as spokesman and addressed the president. To describe fully the pitiable condition of the state, Porter said, it was necessary to return to the situation which prevailed at the end of the war. Then in words hardly likely to appeal to the man who had led the Union Army, Porter pointed out how severe the blow of emancipation had been to the whites who had, with the freeing of their slaves, lost $125 million dollars of *property value.* Still, many of Porter's other statistics—the 268,000 acres of land forfeited for taxes, for example, and the increase of the bonded debt of the state from $6 million to an admitted $16 million—did reinforce the taxpayers' contention that their people were in despair. They would be faced with utter ruin unless the federal government could find some way of relieving them of the tyranny that was oppressing them and cruelly victimizing their wives and children.

President Grant, living up to his reputation for bluntness, responded that he did not see that there was anything either the executive or the legislative branch of the federal government could do to alleviate the situation described: "The State of South Carolina has a complete sovereign existence of its own and must make its own laws," said the president. "If the citizens are suffering from those laws, it is a matter very much to be deplored," he continued. "Where the fault lies may be a question worth looking into. Whether a part of the cause is not due to yourselves, whether it is not due to the extreme views you have held, whether your action has not consolidated the non-taxpaying portion of the community [the Negroes] against you, I leave to your own consideration." [30]

The taxpayers' delegation accepted the presidential snub without surprise and promptly moved to bring their memorial before the Congress. On Tuesday, March 31, it was presented to both branches of the legislature and thence referred without debate to the two judiciary committees. On April 6, the taxpayers appeared before a specially appointed subcommittee of the House Judiciary Committee to defend the memorial; also present were the *counter-memorialists*, whose spokesman was Robert B. Elliott.

In this particular instance there was an ironic reversal of roles, with Elliott taking a position which seemed to defend states' rights, while his opponents of the "old regime" tried to make a case for federal rights, or rather federal intervention on behalf of the tax-payers. They did not, however, have such a case, and shortly there-after both the House and Senate Judiciary committees ruled that the request contained in the taxpayers' memorial was beyond the jurisdiction of the Congress. Although this outcome was pre-dictable, it must have been a source of considerable satisfaction to Elliott, who had taken a leading part in the hearing and whose logical arguments against the taxpayers' memorial had prevailed. However, on this occasion he received almost no publicity,* which, used as he had become in the last months to public acclaim for his every utterance, might have irked him had he not by that time known that a most prestigious assignment lay ahead for him.

On March 11, 1874, Charles Sumner died at his home in Wash-ington. A few hours before the end, Frederick Douglass came to stand for a moment by Sumner's bedside. "My bill, the civil rights bill, don't let it fail," were almost the last words that the noble senator uttered.[31]

In the profusion of public and private tributes, eulogies, and memorial services which followed his death, none would have been more meaningful to Charles Sumner than the ceremony which was arranged by the Colored Citizens of Boston to honor their great champion. At a preliminary meeting held just three days after his

---

* The committee did mention that the "intelligence and capacity ex-hibited by the representatives from South Carolina, and particularly by the countermemorialists, gave them confidence in the ultimate success of the African race in this country" (*Columbia Daily Union*, May 1, 1874).

death, a resolution was passed that "Tuesday the 14th day of April (the anniversary of the assassination of President Lincoln) be set apart for the proper consideration of the life-labors of the Hon. Charles Sumner," and that on that day the colored people of Boston and vicinity would assemble at Faneuil Hall at two o'clock to hear an oration. The committee on arrangements voted unanimously to invite the Honorable Robert Brown Elliott to deliver the address; he "humbly" accepted while knowing that he could not "do full justice to the life and character of the illustrious dead." If anyone could have, however, he did. His effort was a magnificent one, as was the occasion itself.

For the Sumner memorial service Faneuil Hall was thronged with Boston's Negro population, joined by such distinguished whites as Henry Wilson, the vice-president of the United States; William Lloyd Garrison, who had been the spearhead of the New England abolitionists; Reverend Samuel Longfellow, brother of the poet; Mayor Cobb and the board of aldermen of the city of Boston; the secretary of state; members of the governor's council and ex-governor William Claflin (who had met Elliott at the railroad on his arrival and at whose residence he was staying); as well as a host of other luminaries.

The fact that Sumner himself had made his first major address in opposition to slavery on the very same platform at Faneuil Hall on November 25, 1845, provided Elliott with a fortuitous point of departure for his reveiw of "that great warfare . . . in the cause of freedom" to which Sumner's life was so completely devoted. With a richness and variety of language, he touched on all the high points of Sumner's ceaseless struggle for human rights: his first senatorial speech in August 1852, upon the repeal of the Fugitive Slave law ("Sir, the Slave Act violates the Constitution and shocks the Public Conscience"); the unwavering vigor with which he opposed Stephen Douglas and others in their attempt to repeal the Missouri Compromise and thereby remove that "Sacred Landmark of Freedom." His "magnificent Phillipic" in Congress against the organization of the territory of Kansas as a slave state, said Elliott, was more than a speech, it was an event. For it was on this occasion that "slavery in the person of a Representative from South Carolina, struck him to the floor and covered him with murderous blows. . . . In that instant the civilized world stood by the side of Sumner."

Moreover, Elliott reminded his audience, during the nearly four years of Sumner's recuperation "his heart was never absent from the Great Cause." He was in the vanguard of every movement which sought to overthrow slavery. As early as October 1, 1861, he gave a speech entitled "Emancipation, our best Weapon," and in December 1861 another—"Welcome to Fugitive Slaves." However, as the hostilities inexorably began, many who had previously joined Sumner in his attacks on slavery "shrank from the gulf of war and disunion" and offered compromises. But, said Elliott, "let no Negro forget that . . . alone of all the great leaders, Charles Sumner kept his faith to Freedom stern and true."

So too when the "wanton destruction was ended" did the Senator "reach the conclusion, finally accepted by the country and enacted in our national laws and Constitution, that the colored race must be made citizens of the United States and voters in their respective states."

At this point in his recital of Sumner's life and service, Elliott reached the single distressing deviation (as far as he and most of the Negro race were concerned) in the senator's splendid career—his failure to support Grant and the Republican ticket in 1872. Adroitly, the orator managed to face Sumner's defection squarely and at the same time to turn it into an encomium: "Differing, as I could not but differ, from his judgment in the last national campaign, I point to it today as one of the highest proofs of his utter devotion to the call of duty. . . . Draw no veil of silence over this passage; but write it high on his monument—that in old age, when his weary frame longed for repose, he could again brace himself for the conflict in which nearly all the friends of a lifetime stood arrayed against him." [32]

Throughout the eulogy the many quotations from Sumner's speeches blended so smoothly with Elliott's own style of oratory that it seemed almost as if all the prose had been written by the same person. There was, however, one significant omission in Elliott's performance. Had he actually been born in Boston, it is difficult to imagine a more appropriate time or place for him to have referred with pride to that fact than from the platform of Faneuil Hall, a building whose very name symbolized the great traditions of Boston and New England. Yet Elliott made no mention whatsoever of a return to his birthplace; he did not boast, as he had occasionally done in other speeches (delivered at a geographi-

cally safe remove from Massachusetts), of the state he was proud
to claim as the place of his nativity. Neither did the distinguished
black Bostonian, William C. Nell, who introduced Elliott at Faneuil
Hall, capitalize on the extra fillip of presenting a native son, which
he logically would have done had he believed it to be true. Nor
did the *Boston Evening Transcript* make any such connection in
the prominent coverage it gave the speech and in the praise (tinged
with faint condescension) it accorded the speaker: "The orator
fully met the duty and privilege of the position. In the unity of his
topic, the correctness and beauty of his style . . . he really needed
no considerations drawn from circumstances, former condition and
relations to make the performance worthy of a high commendation." [33]

Although there was no indication of his having been present to
hear the speech, Frederick Douglass sent Elliott a letter from
Washington the next day thanking him for his eloquent and beautiful tribute to their honored departed friend. "As a colored man as
well as an American citizen and a man among men," he wrote, "I
am proud that one of my race, contumed and scorned for ages, has
been able to make a speech at Faneuil Hall, Boston, in all respects
so worthy of the place and the occasion as you have now delivered.
The thought brings satisfaction to my heart and to my grey hair." [34]

A few months later, the *News and Courier,* in an open letter to
Elliott, demanded to know "who wrote the speech on the Civil
Rights bill [and] . . . the eulogy of Sumner which you delivered
as your own composition?" [35] Elliott answered, stating unequivocably that he and he alone had composed and written the speeches
and that they were in every sense his own production. Furthermore,
he pointed out that his "professional and other public efforts, made
under such circumstances as to preclude the idea which your questions insinuate"—in other words, his unprepared ad lib speeches—
should entitle him to freedom from any further innuendoes on that
subject. It was certainly true that his extemporaneous utterances
displayed the same splendid rhetoric as did his more formal orations.

Strangely, the *Columbia Daily Union Herald,* perhaps because
it was a Republican paper and had still not forgiven Sumner his
1872 transgression, made no mention of Elliott's eulogy, either in
its news or editorial columns. The memorial address did, however,
receive prominent and repeated notice in that newspaper, if in a

somewhat bizarre fashion. On the front page was an advertisement linking two entirely incongruous items: "The Hon. Robert Brown Elliott [in large-point type] greatly pleased the citizens of Boston by his eulogy on Charles Sumner. The 'Indian Girl' has delighted the citizens of Columbia by the sale of those celebrated five cent cigars." Whether with Elliott's approval or not, this awkward and somewhat far-fetched nineteenth-century version of a present-day commercial ran for several weeks after April 14, 1874. It would be a long time before Elliott's name would again appear in such an innocuous context.

11

Seeds of Discord

A F E W weeks after he delivered the Sumner Memorial, Elliott had to return to South Carolina to attend to a piece of business which was as sordid as his Boston appearance had been prestigious. Franklin Moses, abundantly earning his sobriquet the "Robber Governor," was in severe difficulties; his wild extravagances had finally caught up with him.

Shortly after his inauguration, Moses had given up his suite of rooms at the Columbia Hotel (leaving behind an unpaid bill of $500) to move, not as people naturally assumed he would, to the executive mansion on Arsenal Hill, but instead into the magnificent Preston Mansion, the showplace of Columbia, which he had just purchased for the sum of $42,000 (easily the equivalent today of $500,000). The stuccoed, white-columned edifice, with its museum-size rooms and its marble inlaid floors, was said to have been designed by the great American architect, Robert Mills.* The formal gardens, occupying a full city block and laid out by a gardener brought from Scotland, were complete with boxwood hedges, pools in which swans floated, and a fountain created by the sculptor Hiram Powers. The mansion had been bought by the first General Wade Hampton, a Revolutionary War hero, in his declining years and remained in the possession of his daughter Caroline Preston until she was forced by financial pressures to sell it to Franklin Moses, or rather to his wife Emma.

* The Washington monument is probably his most famous creation.

To go with his aristocratic house, Moses of course needed a string of horses and carriages (allegedly valued at $30,000), suitable furnishings (he owed a Baltimore furniture dealer $30,000); he needed proper clothing ($1,500 owed to his tailor), and to set a lavish table ($2,000 of unpaid butcher's bills).

Despite these and other debts (listed on May 24, 1874, as totaling $227,150 [1]), Moses decided that he wished to acquire what he termed "political control" of the state's leading Republican newspaper, the *Columbia Daily Union Herald*. It was this relatively small bit of overexpansion which led to his undoing. In September 1873, Moses had agreed with Thaddeus C. Andrews, then owner of the newspaper, to pay $12,000 for one-half interest in the *Daily Union Herald* in which he, Moses, was to share neither expenses nor profits. Characteristically, Moses had no hesitancy in using public funds for this purpose, and he promptly ordered the state treasurer to make a draft to Andrews for $6,000 (the first installment), to be drawn from the state's contingency fund.

It was one thing, however, for Andrews to possess a signed draft (or certificate of indebtedness) and another to convert it into actual cash. To this end, Andrews persuaded the governor to appoint as treasurer of Orangeburg County one of Andrews's henchmen, John L. Humbert, a young Negro whose "intelligence and peculiar fitness for this position" Andrews personally vouched for. In March 1874 Humbert, demonstrating these characteristics, duly paid Andrews cash on the $6,000 draft. But when the county treasurer then presented the warrant to the state treasurer (Cardozo) for redemption, payment was denied on the grounds that no funds were available. Shortly thereafter Humbert was arrested for "defalcation"; the case went before a grand jury in Orangeburg County, which brought in a "true bill" for breach of trust and grand larceny against both County Treasurer Humbert and Governor Franklin J. Moses, Jr., charging the latter with having "counselled and advised" the former to use $6,000 of state funds to pay the governor's private debts. A bench warrant for Moses's arrest was issued by Republican judge Robert F. Graham on May 18. Bail was set appropriately at $6,000.

At this point Robert Elliott was called upon to serve as attorney for the governor. His co-counselor, also defending Moses, was none other than Daniel H. Chamberlain, a strange alignment under the circumstances and certainly one fraught with political implications. Here was Elliott, who had been accused two years earlier, during the Republican state convention, of favoring Moses at the expense of Chamberlain, now working with Chamberlain to save Moses from disgrace. If Elliott's efforts in Moses's behalf were consistent with his previous sentiments, Chamberlain's certainly were not.

Meanwhile, the excitement in Columbia was intense. Governor Moses refused to allow himself to be arrested; to protect himself against such an eventuality he ordered out four companies of the Negro militia, including one company of Zouaves, glittering in red uniforms, to stand guard at the statehouse and around the Preston Mansion. With the troops in place and streets crowded with interested spectators, Moses made the most of the occasion by driving in an open carriage right through the middle of town from his home to his office and back again.

While the governor was enjoying his derring-do in Columbia, Elliott telegraphed him—or was reported by the *News and Courier* to have so done—from Orangeburg, where he had been surveying the situation, and advised him to surrender to arrest and pay the bail.[2] The same edition of the paper, in a later dispatch, stated that the governor had capitulated and was surrendering, not to the sheriff of Orangeburg County, who had come to Columbia with a warrant for his arrest, but to the coroner of Richland County, whose law-enforcement qualifications Moses seemed to prefer.

The next day, however, the *News and Courier* had to retract the entire story. "Moses was not arrested last night as reported," began their lead story.[3] "Coroner Coleman was sent for yesterday to receive the submission and was taken to the executive mansion in Moses' carriage." While the coroner was hesitating to act, since he had some doubt as to his authority to arrest Moses, a dispatch was received from the lawyers in Orangeburg advising Moses *not* to allow himself to be taken and *not* to give bail.* Whether this meant that attorneys Chamberlain and Elliott had never sent the first telegram or had never sent the second contradictory telegram or had sent both, having reversed their opinion in the interval, is not clear. It is known that Elliott and Chamberlain, joined by S. W. Melton,

---

* Coroner Coleman must have been so frustrated at being robbed of his moment of glory in arresting the governor that the following day he did the next best thing. The coroner persuaded Moses to issue a warrant for the arrest of the sheriff of Orangeburg County on the grounds of having attempted an illegal arrest of the governor!

and several other unnamed prominent Republicans, had caucused between the two messages to discuss the situation.

Moses held one trump card: He threatened, if indicted, to appoint none but Conservatives as election commissioners in the forthcoming October elections. It therefore seemed prudent to those Republicans attending the meeting not to abandon the governor to justice and to the fate he obviously deserved. Instead the conferees made a counteroffer; if they managed to get Moses off the charges, would he promise to stand aside and not seek renomination as governor? Moses apparently agreed.

At this point it is perhaps worth pausing to consider what could have been in the minds of the two principal characters at the caucus, Daniel H. Chamberlain and Robert B. Elliott. It is safe to say that neither man was acting in Moses's behalf for purely altruistic reasons; both doubtless knew he was guilty beyond question. Both doubtless saw Moses's dilemma as a means of getting rid of him as governor, and both saw an opportunity to step into his shoes. Both were qualified to do so. Of the two men, Chamberlain's bid for office was the more forceful (even though his own reputation for probity was not spotless), partly because he had already made one try for the nomination, but mostly because he was white. Thus he could, and probably did, point out to Elliott that at that parlous moment in the state's affairs, a Negro could not—and should not—assume the responsibility of the governorship, since a failure on his part to reverse the downward trend in state affairs would reflect adversely on his entire race. Chamberlain may also have indicated that to run a Negro for governor might cost the Republican party the statehouse altogether. Elliott may have been at least partially persuaded by these arguments, particularly remembering that even Martin Delany, the most active black nationalist, had said emphatically, "We don't want a colored Governor, for our own good sense tells us differently." [4]

However, at that particular juncture, in the spring of 1874, Elliott had far greater political muscle than Chamberlain: He was an incumbent congressman, while Chamberlain held no elective office at all; Elliott had just gained a national reputation through his civil rights speech and his Sumner Memorial address and had already staked a claim on the reform movement in the state by sounding a clarion call for an immediate end to corruption and mismanagement. Therefore Chamberlain was not in a position to dismiss the black politician nor to ride roughshod over Elliott's aspirations for higher office. What is more, he needed Elliott and Elliott's influence with the blacks to win the nomination (and election) for himself. What Chamberlain was perfectly capable of doing, and what he very likely did, was to make a deal with Elliott; ensuing episodes suggest the possible substance of such a proposition.

It is fair to speculate that Chamberlain's ultimate goal was the Senate of the United States. He was an intensely ambitious man, a stateman who would certainly have considered the nation's highest legislative body a more suitable arena for his talents than the highest executive post of a lone Southern state. Furthermore, as has been suggested, his social life in South Carolina (and, more importantly, the problems it created for his delicate, sensitive wife, to whom he was devoted) was awkward, forced as he was to spend his time in the company of riffraffish Republicans rather than the Bourbon Democrats with whom he had a more natural affinity. In Washington, however, his Republicanism would not be a social burden, since many of the most elite Northerners were of the same political persuasion.

But Washington was out of the question in 1874, because neither of South Carolina's Senate seats was due to be contested until 1876. Meanwhile, Chamberlain really wanted to be governor, not merely, it should be pointed out, to gratify his own desire for power, but because he knew that the state was in desperate need of sweeping reforms, reforms which he earnestly believed he had the ability and the courage to carry out, provided that he had a legislature also committed to the same ends. Here again he needed Robert Elliott, who controlled the black majority in the state more firmly than any other Negro politician. Thus the first part of Chamberlain's proposition probably was that Elliott resign his seat in the federal Congress, return to South Carolina and get himself elected to the state House of Representatives. At this point Chamberlain would help him to become speaker of that body—a position of considerable influence and power. Together, then, the two men would work miracles in cleaning up the state's administrative and legislative stables.

Fortunately, Elliott seemed to prefer Columbia to Washington for precisely the same reasons that Chamberlain leaned in the opposite direction. Clearly he felt his best arena was the capital of

South Carolina, where he could more directly affect the destiny of his race. And certainly the social life was also a factor in his preference. Having lost his try for the United States Senate two years earlier, Elliott appeared to have lost his taste for the office as well.

Still, it is highly doubtful if merely being speaker of the state House of Representatives would have been enough of an incentive for Elliott to have renounced Washington altogether. Although no more than a very plausible conjecture, it is logical to assume that Chamberlain would have had to offer more, and that almost certainly he did so. Chamberlain knew that if he won the gubernatorial election of 1874 and if he were successful in ridding the state of its ills, he could run for re-election in 1876 with every expectation of being returned to the governorship, but perhaps with no expectation of actually serving in that office. With this in mind, he would be able to use his by then considerable prestige to hand-pick his lieutenant governor, and one might postulate that his choice would fall to R. B. Elliott. Then, according to this scenario, when the General Assembly met in 1876 to elect a senator, Chamberlain would present himself as a candidate and, if chosen by the legislature—and he could envisage himself as practically invincible by 1876—Lieutenant Governor Elliott would succeed him as governor.

First, however, they had to cope with Frank Moses. When the court convened in Orangeburg on Friday, May 29, 1874, the opening gambit of attorneys Elliott and Chamberlain was to move for a change of venue on the grounds that the governor could not get a fair hearing in Orangeburg, which, freely translated, meant he could not as easily manipulate the jury box as he could in Columbia. The astute presiding judge, Graham, responded that he would certainly grant the motion provided that a proper showing was made—that Moses came into court himself to be arraigned and plead to the indictment. Accordingly, the sheriff was instructed by solicitor E. L. Butz, the prosecutor, to call F. J. Moses, Jr. The *News and Courier,* taking special pleasure in this particular moment, reported, " 'F. J. Moses Jewnier-r-r' called the sheriff with a loving lingering on the final r of the junior. An ominous silence followed. 'Call him again,' said the solicitor and again the plaintive cry for Moses rang out in the still air, but again there was no response save the rustling of the surrounding pines. 'Call him three times,' said the solicitor, but no Moses answered to that affectionate call and the sheriff gave it up, sat down . . . and wiped the perspiration and dust from his oily black countenance." [5]

At this point Chamberlain and Elliott, now joined by E. W. Moise, a lawyer from Sumter and a Democrat, offered their chief argument: Based on the theory of English law that a king can do no wrong, they contended that a process could not be issued for the arrest of the chief executive of the state. In other words, following the same immunity accorded to members of Congress, a governor would first have to be *impeached* before he could be indicted. Since the General Assembly was not then sitting, this would have meant that Moses would have had to call the legislature into special session for the purpose of impeaching him, an absurdity which the prosecution was quick to point out. Nonetheless, Elliott, in his usual rational, scholarly way, argued that the constitutional provision which called for impeachment before indictment was intended to benefit the office not the man, and that if it were not duly respected, the entire state could be engulfed in anarchy.

Ultimately Judge Graham upheld this view. His ruling must have been painful for him, since he, like everyone else, including the defense attorneys, knew that the governor was guilty, not only of this particular larceny, but of numerous other offenses as well for which he deserved punishment. But the judge's opinion, which was filled with legal precedents, apparently cited in good faith, in effect quashed the case against the governor.

Once freed of the charges, Moses, as anticipated, paid no attention whatsoever to his promise to withdraw as a candidate for re-election. In an interview he gave to the *New York Times* on June 21, 1874, he blithely stated that he would run again for governor and that he still retained full control of the machinery of the state's Republican party. This time, however, the "Robber Governor" had miscalculated. Without Elliott and, equally importantly, without state treasurer Francis L. Cardozo in his camp, Moses's days in public life were numbered. As for Chamberlain, even with Elliott and Cardozo working for him, all was not quite clear sailing.

As president of the Republican state executive committee, Elliott issued the call for a state convention to be convened on Tuesday, September 8, in Columbia. At the same time, he wrote a charge to the Republican voters of the state calling, needless to say, for reform. In this document, co-signed by the entire executive committee, Elliott pointed out, as he had done in his February speeches, that the deplorable condition of South Carolina was "made chargeable to the colored race who constituted a majority of her citizens." Upon their shoulders rested the responsibility of redeeming their state from "obloquy and disgrace," or, if her credit were not re-established, from "utter and complete annihilation." [6]

This warning was well received at the North, although the *New York Times,* while finding his words commendable, thought they were "not so definite or bold as they should be." The *Daily Union Herald* was unreserved in its praise of the "stirring and eloquent appeal," [7] perhaps influenced by the fact that by that time Chamberlain, along with Cardozo, Melton, and a few other "leading Republicans"—not including Elliott—had acquired control of the paper (Andrews, from whom Moses was to have bought his share, had sold out).

However, after an auspicious start for Elliott, Chamberlain, and reform, matters began to go awry when the delegates to the convention met at the statehouse. At the two previous nominating conventions, Elliott had breezed in as temporary chairman. In 1872 he defeated his nearest rival, the black postmaster of Charleston, C. M. Wilder, by a vote of 108 to 28. But in 1874, Wilder defeated him by a vote of 88 to 68; with this unexpected turn of events the Elliott-Chamberlain forces lost control of the convention.

To make matters worse, Wilder, who was suspicious of the Chamberlain-Elliott axis, did not appoint Elliott to represent his county (Aiken) on the all-important credentials committee, but instead chose another member of the delegation, C. D. Hayne. At that point Elliott showed he was not to be trifled with. If he no longer held the upper hand in the convention, he at least had the delegation from Aiken safely within his grasp. One after another of the remaining Aiken delegates declined to serve on the credentials committee and asked that Elliott's name be substituted. Each refusal elicited a spate of "motions, counter motions, and motions upon motions hurled at the chair." [8]

Wilder made one last effort to dodge the inevitable by saying that he would make an appointment from the Aiken delegation and give the name of his appointee directly to the committee on credentials. Elliott put up a howl; all the other names, he said, had been put before the convention. Poor Wilder, knowing when he was licked, at last yielded, stating that "while he was as tenacious to hold to the right as anyone, he was as ready as anyone to acknowledge an error." [9] He then announced the name of R. B. Elliott as a member of the committee on credentials.

The committee at once retired to begin its deliberations about the five counties that had contesting delegations, with Charleston and Beaufort the largest. For three days the convention was held up while the committee was deadlocked over the seating of delegates favorable to Chamberlain or those committed to no candidate.* Moses, although very much in evidence at the convention, was by then almost certainly ruled out, so it appeared to be a battle in which Chamberlain stood against the field. And in this field, incidentally, Elliott was on at least one occasion mentioned as a possible contestant.

As the convention continued to be delayed by the failure of the committee on credentials to report, word began to circulate that Chamberlain was using money supplied by the state's most durable political briber, John J. (now Senator) Patterson, to buy off the resisting committee members. On balance it seems unlikely that Chamberlain would have resorted to such a method of persuasion. Although his enemies accused him of complicity in the fraudulent Bond and Railroad rings (even some of his friends admitted that he had been a silent and willing participant), out-and-out bribery was hardly his style. At any rate, the results, when the committee on credentials finally reported on the fourth day of the convention, did belie such an accusation: Of the five contesting delegations, they recommended the seating of three which were anti-Chamberlain. Once again Elliott did not manage to have things go entirely his way.

In the end, what was by then being referred to as the Chamberlain-Elliott-Patterson Ring prevailed. It was said that their success was due to the fact that they had got the delegates drunk on freely dispensed whiskey before the vote was taken. While this simple and time-honored tactic may have had some good effects on Chamberlain's victory, what doubtless helped him more was his opponents' inability to come up with a strong candidate to pit

---

* Bowen in Charleston and Whipper in Beaufort favored Chamberlain, while Mackey in Charleston and Smalls in Beaufort remained uncommitted.

against him. The two other men nominated were a venerable doctor named John Winnsmith, introduced to the convention as a "good Republican, an old man, and above all an honest man"; and John T. Greene, a middle-aged judge, indisputably honest, but only marginally a Republican. Both men were white. Against this competition Chamberlain received 72 votes, to 40 for Greene and 10 for Winnsmith.

The *News and Courier* was outraged, which was nothing new for the *News and Courier* when reporting on Republican affairs in the state. In the light of the change that was soon to take place in their attitude toward Daniel Chamberlain, their reaction to his nomination was noteworthy: "The supporters of D. H. Chamberlain, those who procured him the nomination on Saturday night, are the men who devised and carried into execution every fraud of magnitude which has been committed in South Carolina during the past six years," they wrote in their editorial of September 15, 1874. Among the "criminals" who backed Chamberlain, Elliott had the dubious honor of being first on the list. "1. R. B. Elliott, ex-member of the Legislature where he was never known to have voted for a good measure or against a bad one; the agent who saved Gov. Scott from impeachment, and is charged with having received a large sum of public money for the job; the champion of Moses two years ago and his counsel in the Orangeburg larceny case; the man who delivered a Civil Rights speech and a Sumner eulogy which D. H. Chamberlain is declared to have written for him."

This last charge was, of course, the most preposterous. As mentioned earlier, Elliott himself effectively silenced such insinuations by pointing to his numerous successful impromptu speeches, which even the *News and Courier* could not have attributed to a ghost writer. But the Southern white press could not accept the fact that a Negro could be gifted enough to have written the brilliant civil rights and Sumner Memorial addresses.

Second to Elliott on the *News and Courier*'s "guilt by association" list was "Honest John" Patterson, followed by Whipper, Leslie, B. F. Whittemore, T. J. Mackey, F. L. Cardozo, and so forth. Each man was described in lurid terms, true in some cases, exaggerated or false in others. The editorial closed by saying, "Chamberlain was first convicted by the public records of complicity in great crimes; he was next convicted by his own admissions of winking at fraud; he is now convicted of being the willing instrument of knaves and adventurers of the most mischievous class. We know him by the company he keeps."

As was expected and as had by then become almost routine, a Bolter party speedily organized (this year called the Independent Republicans) and nominated Judge Greene for governor and Martin Delany for lieutenant governor. What was not so routine was the size of the vote the Independents managed to garner on election day—the largest of any dissident faction since Reconstruction. The total vote cast was 159,221, of which Chamberlain received 80,403 and Greene, 68,818—a majority of only 11,585 for the regular Republicans, as opposed to the majorities of approximately 34,000 which Scott and Moses received in the three previous elections. Still, if not quite resounding, it was a victory.

Meanwhile, Elliott had resigned his seat in Congress to run for the state legislature, to the accompaniment of some sarcastic comments about how he could afford to give up his $6,000 position in Washington for a $600 office in Columbia. As always, the white press assumed the worst and conveniently forgot that Elliott did, after all, have a law practice to help sustain him. Although there were some lean times for Elliott financially in late 1874 and early 1875, he was soon to open yet another new law firm, this time with two bright young Howard University Law School graduates, T. McCants Stewart and Daniel Augustus Straker. The firm of Elliott, Stewart, and Straker flourished in Orangeburg until the end of Reconstruction.

On election day Elliott won easily as state representative from Aiken. Then, on November 24, when the General Assembly convened he was duly, though narrowly, elected speaker of the House of Representatives, that body containing fifty whites and seventy-five blacks. "A very bad beginning," the *News and Courier* called his election. "Elliott has the reputation of being as big a rascal as can be found anywhere within the ranks of Radicalism and is besides, supremely insolent, arrogant and arbitrary. Mr. Chamberlain and Attorney General Melton supported Elliott and the consequence is that the worst man that could have been found has been chosen to preside over the deliberations of the lower branch of the General Assembly. A leopard seldom changes his spots, and we are constrained to believe that the victory of Elliott is the defeat of reform. The age of miracles, however, may not be past, and if Elliott be only reasonably fair and honest, the whole people will give him praise." [10]

So, at last, the Chamberlain-Elliott master plan (if one accepts the premise), after coming close to derailment on several occasions, was finally back on the track. It was not to remain there for very long, however.

One of the most enlightening glimpses into the workings of numerous key South Carolina politicians during this period is provided by the handwritten diary of Josephus Woodruff, a white man who was clerk of the state Senate throughout the Reconstruction. A former Democratic newspaperman, Woodruff and his partner, A. O. Jones, a mulatto who was clerk of the House of Representatives, were the state printers. The contract of their company, The Republican Printing Company, with the state was probably the most padded of the many overstuffed contracts of the time. To win their huge appropriations for state printing—$348,000 for the year 1872, for example, which was $172,000 more than state printing costs for the previous twenty-five years combined—it was necessary to spend large sums on bribes and commissions to "the friends," as Woodruff referred to them. But even once those friends had done their work in the legislature and pushed through the printing appropriations, Woodruff still had to pry the money—usually in the form of certificates of indebtedness—out of State Treasurer Cardozo. By 1874 this was becoming increasingly difficult, either because Cardozo, as his many admirers believe, was honestly holding tight to the state's purse strings or because, as Woodruff repeatedly insisted, the state treasurer wanted a bigger slice of the proceeds for himself: "Cardozo will never issue those certificates of indebtedness unless he can see a way of getting half," said Woodruff's May 11, 1874, diary entry. Or again, "Cardozo, [Beverley] Nash and [Robert] Smalls are all hard cases. They ought to be satisfied with what they have made out of the printing company. . . . It has been hard to keep peace among the friends this session." [11]

Woodruff regarded both Cardozo and Chamberlain with grave misgivings. On September 12, 1874, he wrote that "Chamberlain was put in nomination by Cardozo who said the party was sick and needed a physician like Chamberlain. It was a gross libel on doctors." [12] Cardozo, he believed, had no honor. "So it is with Cham-

berlain. Chamberlain is a consummate hypocrite and scoundrel." [13]
Yet, when Chamberlain was elected governor, Woodruff wrote
nervously, "Chamberlain gave me to understand that he proposes
to grind the R.P. Co. [Republican Printing Company] on the
wheels of reform tomorrow. . . .[14] Must try to see Cardozo and
get him to conciliate Chamberlain and let me know how much or
what he wants. Will do all I can to make it right with Chamberlain." [15]

Woodruff's attitude toward Elliott was always respectful—sometimes wistfully so, sometimes fondly, sometimes apprehensively:
"Wish Elliott would support me for State Treasurer. Would at
once commence study of finance in earnest." [16] "Arrived in Columbia in company with Chamberlain, Elliott, Whipper and others.
Gracious what a company. Believe Elliott to be a good-hearted fellow. He was the first to give toward helping a poor white woman
on train who had been injured by some railway accident." [17] And
after Elliott's election as speaker: "Fear Elliott will always be hard
now on those who have business with the Treasury." [18]

Although Elliott was not one of "the friends," in that he neither
asked for nor received regular payments from Woodruff, he was
not above appealing to him for assistance in times of dire need:
"Received letter from Elliott asking assistance from us. Will have
to see Jones [Clerk of the House] about him. Elliott expects to be
elected member from Aiken County and will be candidate for
speaker." [19] Then, a few days later, "Jones and self agreed to send
$500 order to Elliott to help him out with his campaign expenses.
Cardozo will want to know how Elliott got that order." [20] A few
months later, Elliott was less fortunate. On December 30, 1874,
Woodruff recorded in his diary, "Elliott made another appeal to
save him from starvation. Told him I had nothing which could
save him. Have given out all my paper." Elliott must have been
really desperate, for the next day Woodruff noted, "This is the
end of the year. Do not expect any such good luck as to make a
settlement and fix up things with Cardozo. Elliott tried me again
for New Years but failed."

December had been a strange and conflicted month for Elliott.
If he was—figuratively speaking—close to starvation, he was also
suffering from the further disability of having his nose out of joint.
Everyone was talking reform, reform, reform! Elliott had, after
all, made one of the earliest and hardest-hitting pleas for reform

in his February speeches. He had meant what he said and, more-over, he had proved his sincerity by giving up his seat in Congress and coming home to put his words into practice. He had used his considerable power to help put a reform governor in the state-house. He had gotten himself elected speaker of the House to help that governor implement his rehabilitation of the state. As speaker he had begun by making good and fair committee appointments. Even the *News and Courier* grudgingly admitted that, and the con-servative press in Columbia conceded that he had been "liberal to his opponents," that he was thoroughly familiar with parliamentary law, and that he was the "acknowledged leader of his race over whom he exercised a controlling influence." [21]

Then along came Chamberlain on December 2, 1874, to give a really splendid inaugural address in which he carefully pin-pointed each abuse and spelled out how he proposed to correct it. Instantly the Democratic press, led by its most powerful organ, the *News and Courier,* did such a complete turnabout in Chamberlain's favor that one would have thought the new governor was the first per-son ever to have advocated sweeping reform. Naturally this an-noyed Elliott, who was all for giving credit where credit was due, especially when some of it was due him. But, more than that, the sudden Democratic about face made him question—not for the first time—Daniel Chamberlain's loyalties. Was he truly faithful to the Republican party and to the Negroes? Or was he, as Elliott in-creasingly suspected, a Conservative at heart, eager to pander to the Democrats and jump their way as soon as they gave evidence of being willing to accept him? The question was soon put to a test.

One of the first duties of the new legislature was to fill a vacant judgeship in the First Circuit, which, because it covered the city of Charleston, was an extremely important post. There were three major candidates for the office, as described by the *News and Courier:* Elihu C. Baker, white, an ex-Massachusetts man, "a sot," who was candidate of the Whittemore "extreme liberal anti-ad-ministration" faction of the party; William J. Whipper, black, "utterly corrupt," and the candidate of the Bowen ring of Charles-ton; Col. J. P. Reed, a "staunch Democrat" who had surprised his friends by joining the Republican party on the very eve of the last election and who was the candidate of Governor Chamberlain.

Many of the Democrats in the legislature did not forgive Reed his transgression in becoming a Republican, thus the Conservative backing was divided between Reed and Baker, a split which favored Whipper. At a caucus held on December 10, 1874, the evening before the vote was to be taken in a joint meeting of the House and Senate, Whipper appeared to have such a commanding lead (it was rumored that he had 80 votes, with 79 needed for election) that Governor Chamberlain himself appeared at the caucus to plead the cause of Colonel Reed. Although insisting he was there not as governor but as a "private citizen" and a "simple member of the Republican party," some of the legislators—mostly the blacks—reacted unfavorably to what they considered Chamberlain's attempt to dictate to them. Furthermore, the governor seemed to go out of his way to alienate the blacks by his abrasive and insinuating remarks about Whipper. There were some matters about his connection with the sinking fund commission that required explanation, said Chamberlain, which, considering the governor's own tarnished record with that very commission, made it a shaky argument to use against Whipper.

It is possible that Reed was the better-educated man, and thus perhaps more qualified for the judgeship, but Whipper was certainly not a stupid man, nor was he essentially a bad man. Something of a loner, he was not one of the "friends" referred to in the Woodruff diary; and, except for his admittedly dubious dealings with the sinking fund commission, he was not cited in any other connection in the *Report on Public Frauds*. He was frequently referred to by the most partisan of whites as a very able man and a competent lawyer. In fact, his most persistent sin seems to have been his fondness for betting large sums on horse races. He had been a staunch supporter of Chamberlain, both in the 1872 and the 1874 campaigns. Yet here was Chamberlain moving heaven and earth, appearing at a caucus where, as governor, he certainly did not belong, to block the election of a man that the black majority in the General Assembly clearly favored.

There was an obvious explanation for Chamberlain's sudden highhanded treatment of the Negroes who had elected him governor. The warm and flattering reactions which his inaugural address had received from the Democrats throughout the state had given him a whole new view of his potential position. Heretofore in General Assembly elections, the Conservatives, who had been few in number, had in effect thrown away their votes by putting forward other Conservative candidates who were scarcely in the running. But in the 1874 legislature there were more Conservatives, plus a sizable number of uncommitted Independents, all of whom showed signs of standing behind a governor whom they believed was sincerely dedicated to reform. If Chamberlain could solidify the Conservatives in the General Assembly (a total of thirty-seven) and the Independent Republicans (the twenty-three who had been elected from the Bolter's ticket) with some of the "better element" among the regular white Republicans, he would need only a comparatively small number of Negroes to forge a strong coalition and give himself a working majority in the legislature.

It must have been apparent to Chamberlain that Robert Brown Elliott was not a man he could call upon to deliver the necessary black votes to help build a coalition dominated by Conservative and Independent members. The governor, therefore, turned to the other strong, intelligent, well-educated, and influential colored politician in the state, making him his front man. Francis L. Cardozo had always enjoyed the best reputation of any Negro among the whites; he was not universally respected by the blacks because of certain tendencies which today might be called Uncle Tomism (strangely enough, the phrase was never used in the nineteenth century), but he did have enough of a following to accomplish what Chamberlain required of him, to swing a sufficient number of blacks to support Reed.

The coalition worked. When the vote for judge of the First Circuit was taken on December 11, 1874, the day following the caucus, Reed received 103 votes (all but three of the Conservatives voted for him) to Whipper's 40.

Elliott of course voted for Whipper, which was natural enough, since Whipper was his closest friend and had been his law partner. It is safe to say, however, that he probably would have voted for almost anyone to defeat the coalition. Elliott quickly understood that, if this alliance held firm, the blacks would lose their voting majority. Eventually, therefore, they would have to yield their power to a governor who gave signs of deserting them at the first opportunity in favor of the men whom Chamberlain considered to be South Carolina's "natural leaders."

By voting against the administration in this first test of strength, Elliott became *ipso facto* a "corruptionist"; he was also the principal villain and the favorite target of the *News and Courier:*

"There were only two parties in the contest," they wrote in the editorial of December 14, 1874, "a party of corrupt politicians with whom stealing is a habit and a necessity, and a party of true reformers . . . who will stand by Gov. Chamberlain as long as he walks on the line marked out in his inaugural." The vote for judge of the First Circuit was conclusive, said the *News and Courier*. "It may be taken for granted, therefore, that, in every measure which is clearly for the benefit of the State, Mr. Chamberlain can count on pretty nearly a two-thirds vote in each house, and that the minority, in every such case, will consist of the crew who are represented in the Senate by Swails and Whittemore, and in the House by Mr. Speaker Elliott, who is reported to have fouly cursed at Mr. Chamberlain on the floor of the house on Friday when the election of Mr. Reed was announced. Of course, Mr. Chamberlain was not present."

Plainly Elliott could not let this statement go unchallenged; he responded at once by calling the accusation a "vile fabrication" and the author of it a "willful falsifier." Vigorously scoring the *News and Courier* for their sweeping assertion that in every measure which was of benefit to the state Chamberlain could count on opposition from Elliott, he wrote, "It seems to me strange that the *News and Courier* should so speedily have come to such a conclusion, after having based its opposition to Mr. Chamberlain's election on the fact that an intimate friendship existed between Mr. Chamberlain, myself and others who seemed to be quite objectionable to the editor of that paper." In words which anyone reading between the lines could recognize as a warning to Chamberlain himself, Elliott continued, "In spite of the efforts of the *News and Courier* to sever that friendship I feel confident that it will long endure for it was neither born in a day, nor is it dependent on subserviency." (In other words, Elliott was subtly reminding the governor that it was his Negro constituency who had elected him, and not the Democratic friends who had suddenly taken him up and whom he seemed so eager to please.)

In answer to the charge that he, Elliott, had cursed at Chamberlain only because Chamberlain was not there to defend himself, Elliott wrote, "The editor mistakes me very much when he assumes that the presence of Mr. Chamberlain would prevent me from giving expression to my views upon any question. I supported Mr. Chamberlain when those who are now lavish in their praise renounced and traduced him. I trust that long after the *News and Courier* shall have ceased to find anything good or noble in him, I shall still be at his side supporting his every effort to give the people of the State good government." (Here again Elliott was warning the governor not be lulled into a belief that the Democrats would continue to support him, and reiterating that it was the black man who had put him in office and who would keep him in office.)

In this letter of December 15, 1874, and in the complex cross-currents that led to its writing, were the seeds of discord which would, within a year, bear bitter fruit.

12

Black Thursday

I N L A T E February 1875, the legislature of South Carolina
instituted an action to impeach State Treasurer Francis L. Cardozo on the grounds of misconduct and irregularity in office. The
charges against the treasurer, which concerned wrongfully funded
bonds and the diversion of the state's interest fund into improper
channels, were so technical that it is difficult to assess the true
merits of the accusation. It appears, however, that Cardozo's
transgressions—notwithstanding the many instances of his corruption cited in the Woodruff diary—were, in this case, marginal and
that the entire address (as it was called) against him was a power
play led by Elliott to realign and solidify the black majority of the
General Assembly. Cardozo was the leading Negro advocate of
Chamberlain. As such, it was essential from Elliott's point of view
to denounce him so that other blacks would not follow his lead and
join the coalition of Conservatives and Independents who were
supporting the governor.

It is possible, of course, to interpret the facts differently and
argue that Elliott acted from sheer vengeance and jealousy. Certainly elements of both may have been present either consciously
or unconsciously; it is impossible, however, to believe that his
actions were dictated primarily by such emotions. Elliott was a
pragmatic man. By that time it must have been clear to him that
any deal he may have made with Chamberlain about succeeding
him as governor in 1876 was vitiated. He may have suspected that

Cardozo, the current palace favorite, might inherit the royal mantle if Chamberlain chose to move on to the United States Senate. But what he really probably feared was that, if Chamberlain ceded his place as governor to anyone in 1876, it would be to a Democrat. Elliott knew that such an eventuality must be forestalled, not merely because it frustrated his own personal ambitions, but because he saw in Chamberlain's increasing affinity with the Democrats a threat to the entire Negro population of the state.

Chamberlain could, and probably did, tell himself that the only way to reform the state was to win the Conservatives to his cause. And Elliott could, and probably did, tell himself that the Conservatives toward whom Chamberlain was bending were the men pledged to degrade the Negro and return the white man's government to the state. But in South Carolina, where there were more blacks than whites, a white man's government could only be achieved by disenfranchising the Negro. It did not take a man of Elliott's extraordinary prescience to see that under a Democratic rule the blacks would lose not only their political power, but their vote as well. It did, however, take Elliott's subtle understanding to accept the fact that *even at the risk of appearing opposed to reform* he had to stop Daniel Chamberlain, either by turning him away from the Democrats or by turning the Democrats away from him.

Elliott's worst fears would have been realized had he known how assiduously Chamberlain was courting the white elite—particularly the Broad Street clique of Charleston—through their most powerful organ, the *News and Courier*. A correspondence between Chamberlain and Francis L. Dawson, the editor and part-owner of the *News and Courier,* had begun at the start of Chamberlain's administration and it grew ever warmer and more confidential as the months went by. In fact, there is one letter from Chamberlain to Dawson, written before he was even nominated for governor, which by its arch tone set the stage for the letters which were to follow: "Gentlemen," wrote Chamberlain on July 31, 1874, "I knew I was not in favor with the editor of the *News and Courier,* but I did not imagine you would go to the extent of refusing to sell me your paper. Seriously I find my N and C has not been sent in the past two weeks. I don't know how I stand in point of payment but if you will inform me I will pay up and renew. The *News and*

Courier is like surgery to me—painful but necessary. I wish I could add healthful." [1] He soon could.

Six months later, at the time of the Cardozo impeachment attempt, Chamberlain was on such an amiable basis with Dawson that he could with impunity write private and "doubly confidential" letters to him in which he did not hesitate to refer to his fellow Republicans as the "rabble" who were assailing Cardozo "because there is nothing this winter in the way of plunder in Columbia. My real judgment," he told Dawson, "is that with nine out of ten of those who are now hounding Cardozo, the motive is rage at him for not joining with them in devising ways and means for stealing. . . . Cardozo is the wisest and truest adviser I have. . . . I don't like to name names but I am surprised and grieved at the small number of them who mean reform in the Republican party. My inaugural chilled them . . . and nothing keeps them from attacking me as openly as they do Cardozo except the power of my office and the support which the Conservatives and the country at large give to me in all my efforts at reform." [2]

The *News and Courier* duly wrote in their next editorial, "The first shock to the political Chadbands * after the election was Governor Chamberlain's inaugural address. It chilled them. . . . Only their knowledge of Governor Chamberlain's strength in and out of the state prevented the chagrined corruptionists from framing articles of impeachment against him." [3]

All during the spring and summer of 1875, Chamberlain's star continued to rise among the Conservatives, and concurrently his correspondence with editor Francis Dawson of the "N and C" grew more fulsome. Chamberlain's every act and utterance was glowingly covered by the newspaper. For example, in May he was invited to attend a banquet celebrating the centennial of the German Fusiliers of Charleston, a military company dating from Revolutionary days which counted among its members the elite of Charleston society and, safe to say, absolutely no Republicans. Chamberlain was unable to go to Charleston for the occasion, but he was clearly so afraid that the German Fusiliers would misunderstand

---

* The word derives from the Reverend Chadband, a character in Dickens's *Bleak House*, described as a fat, greasy, unctuous clergyman engaged in blackmail, hence (according to *Webster's International Dictionary*, Unabridged, second edition, 1959) a sanctimonious hypocrite.

and think that he had declined because of the entirely Democratic guest list that his letter of regret bordered on the mawkish. It was not read at the banquet, as Chamberlain doubtless expected it would be, but it was published in full (as Chamberlain probably also expected) in the *News and Courier,* which referred to it as a "handsome letter." In fact, so handsome did they consider it, that the next day they ran an editorial, written by Dawson himself, headed "Savoir Faire," which was so extravagant in its praise of Chamberlain's habit of "saying and doing the right thing at the right time, and in the right way," that one might have thought the governor himself would have been slightly embarrassed. He was not in the least embarrassed, however; he was enchanted. "Thank you for your very kind notice, 'Savoir Faire,' " he wrote to Dawson. "I want to ask you for the favor of about six copies of each issue of May 5 and May 6 if perfectly convenient to you to send them. The real pleasure of the thing is to find so skillful and appreciative a critic as you prove to be. I can well retort Savoir Faire to you. . . . Let me serve you in any way that is right and proper —which is all of course which you would ask—*Cela va sans dire*—" [4]

Chamberlain appeared to worry very little about the reaction of his Negro constituency to his constant and increasingly fervid wooing of the Democrats, although he did in one of his letters to Dawson suggest that "we must not be *too good* friends." [5] Doubtless the governor depended on the faithful Cardozo to keep what he looked on as the "honest element" among the Negro legislators in line. Concerning the others—the so-called corruptionists— Chamberlain wrote to Dawson, "My evils have heretofore come from the *friendship* of bad men. Perhaps I shall fare better if I now have their hatred." [6]

In addition to this conduit to the most powerful Democratic newspaper in the state, the governor also had the rival Republican paper, the *Columbia Daily Union Herald,* under his thumb for the very good reason that he owned a controlling interest in it. This led to a political rarity never equaled before or since in South Carolina: Both the Republican and the Democratic press were saying the same thing. The unanimity was such that the *News and Courier* actually reprinted on its front page of February 23, 1875, an editorial from the *Daily Union Herald* of two days earlier which denounced the "corruptionists" who opposed Chamberlain. And then just to make things even more companionable, the *Daily Union Herald* in its editorial (reprinted in the *News and Courier*) went out of its way to praise the *News and Courier* for its fairness in reporting the reactions of the "Radical Chadbands."

Thus a formidable degree of power was arrayed against Elliott and the other blacks who foresaw, as he did, the grave consequences to their race in such an alliance and who tried to stem the tide and to get at Chamberlain through the Cardozo impeachment attempt. The fact that they were joined in this effort by many white men and a few blacks who genuinely *were* corruptionists has only served to obscure the true thrust of their effort.

The two newspapers urged all who loved their state to stand firmly with the governor (meaning, of course, with Cardozo) for "one more battle" after which they assured their readers, Democrats and Republicans alike, that the cohorts of corruption would be driven from the field.

Cardozo, who was to appear before the legislature on March 11, 1875, to answer the charge against him, sent a message through his lawyer, Sam Melton (Chamberlain's partner), asking for two more days to prepare his response. Elliott was among those who voted to grant him this postponement. Perhaps he felt it was the least he could do, for in some ways Elliott must have had little stomach to make this public fight against Cardozo. Although their friendship had undergone some ups and downs since they first met and clashed at the Constitutional Convention of 1868, their relations had been mostly cordial since the 1872 campaign. At that time the two men had worked together to prevent the nomination of Daniel Chamberlain for governor, and it had been Elliott who was instrumental in pushing through Cardozo's nomination as state treasurer. At the February reception honoring Elliott after his civil rights speech, Cardozo had acted as master of ceremonies. And more recently, Elliott, as Cardozo's lawyer, had successfully defended him in a mandamus suit instituted by Woodruff and some of the "friends" in a move to force the treasurer to pay state monies to the Republican Printing Company.

Now they were locked in a genuinely ugly conflict. On March 20, 1875, Cardozo gave an exhaustively prepared, convincing, if slightly defensive, account of his stewardship as treasurer, after

which the address to impeach him was defeated by a vote of 63 to
45. Elliott had spoken for two hours in favor of the address, and
of course voted for it, meaning against Cardozo.

Having failed in that attempt to thwart Chamberlain, Elliott
seemed willing to try anything to discredit the governor in the few
weeks remaining in that first session of the legislature. Some of his
actions were difficult to justify, even in the light of the large stakes
for which he was playing.

Both the upper and lower houses of the General Assembly had
passed, by large majorities, a bill legalizing payments of the float-
ing debt of the state, which included all the obligations incurred
by the two previous administrations. The measure became known
as the Bonanza Bill because of the obvious financial windfalls it
would produce for many members of the legislature. Governor
Chamberlain, who was earnestly trying to reduce state expendi-
tures, was convinced, doubtless correctly, that many of the claims
for payment covered by the Bonanza Bill were "tainted with il-
legality and fraud." He promptly vetoed the measure (as he had
previously vetoed eighteen other bills he considered not in the public interest), although, as it turned out in this instance, not
promptly enough. His veto message reached Elliott, as speaker of
the House, four days after the bill had been presented to him for
his signature. Accordingly, Elliott, knowing that he could not
muster the two-thirds majority necessary to override the governor's
veto, resorted to a petty parliamentary stratagem. He ruled that
the veto was void, basing his decision on a clause in the state
constitution which said that a governor's veto must reach the
legislature within three days of the governor's receipt of the bill.
The speaker's ruling, which required only a simple majority, was
sustained and the Bonanza Bill became law.

The day after his Bonanza Bill ruling, Elliott, somewhat foolishly, signed a warrant for the arrest of James Thompson, editor of
the *Columbia Daily Union Herald,* alleging contempt of the House
of Representatives. According to Elliott's charge, Thompson had
used "scandalous and malicious language tending to defame the
House of Representatives . . . and to excite against them the
hatred of the good people of South Carolina." What Thompson
had actually done was to disparage the Bonanza Bill and to refer to the "plunderers" (of whom he named seven, *not* including Elliott) as "animals howling in anguish and despair. No

pack of jackals scenting the carcass ever made night so hideous," said his editorial of March 18, 1875. Had he not counted on Chamberlain and Cardozo—the owners of his paper—to back him up, it is unlikely that Thompson would have written so crudely of his fellow Republicans. Still, he had not really committed an actionable crime and certainly not one which required his arrest.

When the "prisoner" was brought to the bar of the House, many members treated the entire scene with understandable ribaldry. Elliott did not. In an excessive show of self-righteousness, he implied that his fellow legislators had underrated the importance of the proceedings. Fortunately, cooler heads prevailed. Many members realized that the more attention they called to the charge against Thompson, the more fun the *Daily Union Herald* would have at their expense. The situation was best summed up by C. P. Leslie, one of the "plunderers" who was known for his wit. Capitalizing on all the various animal metaphors that were being bandied about the House chamber, the aging legislator from Barnwell pointed out that "those who meddled with editors were like those who tried to catch a porcupine—they would get nothing but a quill." [7] Thompson was released.

At the closing session of the legislature the following week Elliott seemed to have regained his composure and his sense of balance. He made what even the *News and Courier* referred to as a "well worded" final speech. He complimented the majority (Republicans) for being "tolerant in the just exercise of their power." He thanked the minority (Conservatives) for the uniform courtesy and kind consideration they had shown toward him on every occasion. "If the majority have refrained from arbitrary and wanton use of their powers," he told the Conservatives, "you have equally refrained from obstructing and impeding the public business." He commended both sides of the House for their patriotism and devotion to the common weal.[8] The members voted him an honorarium of one thousand dollars for his services as speaker, and the legislature adjourned amid protestations of good faith which had certainly not been much in evidence during its three-month session.

When the legislature reconvened in November 1875, a new spirit of cooperation seemed to prevail. The very first order of business to come before the General Assembly was the governor's veto of a supply bill left over from the last session; in the House this veto was *unanimously* sustained, causing widespread conjecture as to just what the anti-administration Radicals were up to in acquiescing to the governor without the slightest show of resistance. The most likely theory was that, knowing they did not have the votes to override a veto, they decided to be gracious in the face of inevitable defeat and at the same time score some good points as reformers. More dire, and as it turned out more accurate, was the suggestion that these Radicals were lulling the administration into a sense of false security as they gathered their forces for a definitive showdown with Chamberlain. But at the outset, at least, even Elliott got a favorable press for cooperating with the governor in his efforts to keep the tax levy down and for appointing several Conservatives to the very important Ways and Means Committee (where, as in the federal Congress, all financial bills originated). He also was praised for making an earnest effort to try to move legislation speedily through the House.

But, in fact, Elliott was counting on the supply bill and other tax bills to serve as a smoke screen to cover a crafty maneuver which he was initiating among the Republicans in the legislature. The state's eight circuit judges were due to be elected during this session of the General Assembly, and Radical forces, spearheaded by Speaker R. B. Elliott, were determined to give no quarter and to see that only regular Republicans were chosen to fill these judicial posts. With Chamberlain in the statehouse, the Radicals had lost influence with the executive branch. Therefore, to maintain their political strength, especially in an election year, they needed solid control over the judiciary.

On December 7, 1875, the *News and Courier* first broke the story that Whipper, who, it will be remembered, had been foiled by Chamberlain in his earlier bid to fill the unexpired term of the First Circuit judgeship, was again a leading candidate for that position. From the white Democratic point of view, this was an exceedingly sensitive post, since it covered the city (and county) of Charleston, which was more sacred to the Bourbon aristocracy than any other part of South Carolina. Furthermore, the judge who sat on the First Circuit would exercise dominance over the Broad Street clique. For an office of such significance and power to fall to a black was insupportable. The other prominent, and by no means unsullied, name on the list of Republican judicial aspirants was that of Franklin J. Moses, Jr., trying to make a comeback in public life as a candidate for the Third Circuit (Sumter) judgeship.

The Republicans had been secretly organizing for some weeks to secure a clean sweep of all eight circuits and they obviously thought time was of the essence in putting their plan into operation. They proposed to elect the judges well before the Christmas recess. Accordingly the state Senate met on Tuesday, December 14, and passed a resolution to hold the elections two days later on December 16. On that same Tuesday night, about fifty Republicans caucused in Elliott's office until the early hours of the morning, reiterating their promises to make no deals with Conservatives and to vote only for Republicans. On the following evening a supper party was given for the legislature by the nine Republican judicial candidates (setting each candidate back $50), at which further pressure was put on any man who had strayed into the Conservative-Independent-Republican coalition to return to the fold of regular Republicanism. Disaffection with the governor's constant courting of Democrats and anger at his frequent attempts to dictate to the legislature seemed to strengthen Republican party solidarity.

Caught unaware by the speed and resolution of the Republicans, Chamberlain could only play for time. As it happened, the governor was due to go to Greenville on Thursday, December 16, to deliver an address on the occasion of the awarding of the traditional Whittson Prizes for Excellence in Greek. Because of the importance of this erudite occasion, Chamberlain explained later, he appealed on the evening of Tuesday, December 14, to both his Conservative and Republican friends for a delay on the circuit judge vote. And since the House of Representatives had still to concur in the Senate's selection of Thursday, December 16, the governor also addressed a note to Speaker Elliott asking him on personal as well as public grounds to put off the election. Elliott came to Chamberlain's office the next morning (Wednesday, December 15) to say that, although he himself was committed to vote in favor of concurrence with the Senate date, he was certain that he could persuade others to postpone the election until at least after the governor's return from Greenville. Good to his word, Elliott on the same day presided over a vote in the House of Representatives *not to concur* with but to table the Senate resolution. The *News and Courier* regarded this action hopefully, as an indication that the strength of Whipper and Moses was not so great as had been feared and, reassured, Governor Chamberlain went off to give his oration at the scholarly convention in Greenville.

Afterward it was always alleged—and doubtless correctly—that Elliott deliberately arranged the Wednesday House vote as a red herring to get the governor out of town. In any case, on Thursday morning, December 16, 1875, a day which would be known for many years in South Carolina as Black Thursday, a well-organized majority in the House of Representatives promptly reversed their vote of twenty-four hours earlier and decided to select the judges that very day. Thereupon the legislators from both houses assembled and moved without delay to the judicial elections.

Virtually all the fury and excitement were concentrated in the First and Third circuits. As the candidate for the First Circuit, Whipper, running against the incumbent Judge Reed, led off the proceedings. Elliott made a strong—perhaps excessively so—seconding speech, insisting that Whipper was being stigmatized solely because of his complexion, praising his friend as a man of unimpeachable character, a man of learning, culture, refinement, and dignity, a man far more competent than the incumbent. Speaking, as he himself admitted, more plainly than was his custom, he concluded with words which were tantamount to a threat. He would measure the Republicanism of the members on the floor, said the speaker of the House, by the way they voted on this occasion. Whipper won with 83 votes out of the 138 cast. He was the first black to be elected to the Court of Common Pleas, as the overall body of circuit judges was called.

Thereupon Elliott did a bizarre turnabout. Despite all previous protestations to support only Republicans, despite having made a vote for Whipper a test of his fellow legislators' Republicanism, Robert Elliott calmly stood up and nominated the obviously superior *Democratic* candidate, incumbent Judge J. J. Maher, for the Second Circuit. Perhaps he permitted himself the luxury of voting his conviction only because he knew that, with the controversial Whipper safely elected, the bandwagon was rolling and the other circuits (including the Second) would go to the Republican candidates, which indeed proved to be true—Maher was defeated by a Republican nonentity named P. L. Wiggins.

It is difficult to reconcile Elliott's espousal of the Democrat Maher with his vote for Republican Franklin J. Moses, Jr., in the Third Circuit. Surely no one knew better than Elliott how unscrupulous the ex-governor really was and how ill-qualified for a judicial office. If Elliott were truly trying to follow the dictates of his conscience, this should certainly have been the moment for him to have voted accordingly.

In the end, the General Assembly, on that so-called Black Thursday, elected eight Republicans as circuit judges. Five of them were quite competent. But the public outcry which focused on Whipper and Moses (and to a lesser degree on Wiggins) was furious, and the reverberations of their election were far more profound than most of the legislators who put them into office— Elliott included—realized at the time. But Daniel Chamberlain immediately understood all too well the import of what had happened during his absence from the capital; he saw the election of Whipper and Moses as a catastrophic blow to his own future: "I look upon their election as a horrible disaster," he said on his return to Columbia. "This calamity is infinitely greater, in my judgment, than any which has yet fallen on this state, or I might add upon any part of the South." [9] (On the face of it, of course, the statement seemed absurd. Surely Moses as circuit judge for the county of Sumter was far less of a calamity for the state than Moses as governor had been.)

Asked by a reporter what he believed the effect of the election would be, Chamberlain said, "One immediate effect will obviously be the reorganization of the Democratic party within the state as the only means left for opposing . . . this terrible crevasse of misgovernment and public debauchery." [10] Here, of course, was the nub of the matter. Chamberlain feared he was going to lose his Conservative and Independent support because, as he rightly foresaw, the Conservatives and Independents were now going to seize upon the Moses-Whipper affair to mobilize the Democratic party and to run a Democratic candidate for governor. Already Chamberlain's faithful friend Dawson had pointed out in the *News and Courier* that the "three judges of the Black Band" would be the absolute masters of the low country containing ninety thousand voters, and from there they would rule the state. "Their plan is to Africanize the state and to put the white man under the splay foot of the negro and hold him there." There was only one solution for the white man, the editorial concluded: "They must pit discipline against discipline, organization against organization. The Democratic party must be so drilled and officered that not a vote shall be lost." [11]

The "Black Band" referred to in the editorial was a new phrase; its use was significant. The blacks were held entirely responsible for the election of Whipper and Moses. No white Republicans made any attempt whatsoever to justify the elections, and the *Daily Union Herald* wrote that there was not a single white Republican who did not admit that it was the Negroes who had rammed through the election of the two men whom the white Republicans claimed to find just as reprehensible as did the white Democrats. Thus, among the most disastrous results of the Whipper-Moses affair, was the fact that because of it the color line was now clearly drawn. No longer in the Democratic press was it the Negro-carpetbagger rule trying to rob the state, but the Black Band trying to Africanize the state.

All this was, of course, grist for the Democratic mill. "For a long time," wrote a contemporary observer, Dr. H. V. Redfield of the *Cincinnati Commercial,* "the whites have wanted sufficient excuse to rise up and overthrow the African government under which they live; and now they have it. . . . Before long you will hear of a 'great Democratic victory' in South Carolina." [12]

Faced then with a desperate situation, Chamberlain took a desperate step. He refused to sign the commissions of Whipper and Moses. Since their election was not a matter over which he had any veto power, he had to resort to a patently false technicality. His rationale was that, because the terms of the present incumbents in the Court of Common Pleas would not expire until after the election of the *next* General Assembly, therefore *this* session of the General Assembly did not have the right to elect their successors. The governor did, however, sign the commissions of the other six elected judges, thereby negating his entire premise. Boldly he faced this obvious inconsistency by stating that, "while in some cases presenting similar legal questions, it might not be required that the Governor decline to issue a commission, the circumstances of the present case [Whipper and Moses] compel me to this course."

The *News and Courier* was ecstatic over what they considered the governor's *"coup d'état."* He had not failed them; their belief in him as the savior of South Carolina was fully justified. He had carried the "war into Africa," he had stood at bay while the "Radical hounds" howled around him. His sole guide was the public duty. On December 23, 1875, they reported triumphantly that there was only one feeling in Charleston—a determination to stand by the governor and support him in what he had done.

But the *News and Courier* was wrong. There was another feeling, equally potent and fraught with more ominous consequences for the blacks. Because of the Whipper-Moses election, exactly what Chamberlain had feared and tried to forestall with his *"coup d'état"* had happened. The Democrats came alive. After eight years of referring to themselves as Conservatives, they were going to call themselves what they had always been—Democrats. They were going to stand together, but alone, brooking no alliance with Independents or with the "better class" Republicans. On the same Wednesday, December 23, that the *News and Courier* had proclaimed the people's determination to stand by the governor, Thomas Y. Simons of Charleston called for a meeting of the nearly dormant State Democratic Executive Committee with a view to reorganizing the party and putting together a Straightout Democratic ticket to run against Chamberlain and the Republicans in the fall of 1876.

The fire which the Straightouts (as they came to be called) flamed was ignited by the Whipper-Moses affair. But the kindling had been set for some time, as these members of the former ruling class watched with interest and with mounting hope events in Mississippi, the only other Southern state with a black majority.

Two years earlier the Mississippi White Liners—from whom the South Carolina Straightouts derived their inspiration—had pledged themselves to return the "white man to the white man's place and the black man to the black man's place, each according to the eternal fitness of things." [13] To accomplish this end, the control of the state government held by the Negroes and the Republicans had to be broken at any cost and by any means. Whites who persisted in their loyalty to the Republican party were to be silenced in one way or another, even by murder. Negroes were to be subjected to the most intense economic pressure. No white was to employ any black who had voted Republican, nor could his wife be hired. A black's only alternative was to join the Democratic party, where sooner or later he would be expected to vote away his political power.[14] If the White Liners failed to "persuade" the Negro by denying him employment, medical care, or any of a number of other essentials, they were prepared without scruple to resort to violence. When the plan was first put to the test in Mississippi in the September 1875 elections, the slogan was, "Carry the election, peaceably if we can, forcibly if we must." And carry the election they did—forcibly.

In South Carolina, as the Democrats began to organize during the winter and spring of 1876, the Straightouts were bent on following the Mississippi plan to the letter and they hoped to the same end. Opposed to the Straightouts, who represented the extreme—and in some cases fanatical—element of the Democratic party, were the more conservative Cooperationists, who believed that the only hope for the salvation of their state lay in returning Daniel Chamberlain to the statehouse, and that therefore the Democrats should not run a candidate against him. Their argument had many merits. Chamberlain had already shown his willingness—even eagerness—to bend toward the white Democratic point of view. He had proved his dedication to honest government, had in fact put into effect many sweeping reforms; only a balky, corrupt legislature had prevented him from accomplishing more. And, in addition to his obvious virtues, the plain fact was that Chamberlain was practically unbeatable. What chance did the Democrats have running against a Republican nominee in a state where the blacks had at least a thirty thousand voting majority?

They had a chance, the Straightouts countered, if enough blacks could either be won over to the Democratic party or—and this was considered more feasible—prevented from voting at all. The Mississippi plan had worked in Mississippi, which had an even larger black majority than South Carolina. Besides, Chamberlain had lost a great deal of support in his own party; he had many enemies who might cross over to the Democratic ranks just for the pleasure of voting against him.

Give Chamberlain a chance, pleaded the Cooperationists, led by Captain Francis W. Dawson, who ran a "support Chamberlain" editorial practically each day in his *News and Courier*. Do not rush to choose the desperate imperatives of violence which are implicit in the Mississippi plan without first testing Chamberlain's strength.

But, insisted the Straightouts, what strength has a governor who cannot control his own party enough to prevent the election of a Whipper and a Moses? Over and over again, as the conflict raged during the winter and spring of 1876, the Straightouts used Whipper and Moses to bolster their cause. Thus one might argue —and certainly some did—that, since Robert Brown Elliott was generally held accountable for the election of at least Whipper, it was he who had handed the most dangerous enemies of his race their strongest weapon.

Could Elliott not see that? Could he not have foretold it before he made a vote for Whipper a "test of each member's Republicanism"? The answer is that even if he had foreseen the consequences of his highhanded tactics, he probably would not have altered them. Elliott did not look upon the Straightouts, but rather upon Daniel Chamberlain, as the most dangerous enemy of his race. Although the Straightouts were pledged—covertly—to eliminating Negro rights, Elliott was certain they would be beaten at the polls. His reasoning was quite logical. No man could become a Straightout without becoming a Democrat; almost all Negroes loathed the very word *Democrat;* therefore almost none would be persuaded to join the party which now openly bore that name. And without the Negro vote, the Straightout Democrats could not possibly win.

Chamberlain, as a Republican, was pledged—overtly—to protect Negro rights, but Elliott was certain he would betray that pledge or at best honor it with only token recognition. His mistrust of the governor had become an obsession. At all costs, he sought to discredit him.

One might wonder at this point exactly what Elliott really did want; how did he wish the course of events to flow in South Carolina? Did he, for example, want the Straightout Democrats to nominate a candidate for governor? Probably he did, because in that case the Cooperationists would all desert Chamberlain and flock to a Democratic standard-bearer.

Did he then see the state becoming "Africanized" with himself as the logical candidate for governor? Probably he did not. Much as he once may have coveted the governorship, he would have realized by 1876 that a black man in the statehouse would not be tolerated by the ever-strengthening white-minority in the state, and might even lead to bloodshed. Moreover, he must have sensed that the climate throughout the entire country was changing. The tide, even among Northern Republicans, was turning back toward a white man's government, as sympathy for the black man ebbed. Certainly this was not a time to seek higher offices or more offices for his race. But it was a time to hold firmly to those positions which they had already achieved.

Did Elliott then believe that another white man should be the Republican governor of the state? Doubtless he did. Doubtless his ideal candidate would have been a man as dedicated to reform as Chamberlain, a man who commanded a decent respect among the whites, but who at the same time *had* a decent respect for his large Negro constituency. Above all, Elliott wanted the blacks to continue to control the legislature. In sum, he wanted for the blacks what he believed was their due—full representation in the affairs of state.

During the conflict-filled months of the new year, 1876, it was difficult for a politician to articulate such a simple objective without having an ulterior motive attached to it. Thus Elliott was often misunderstood; and being misunderstood made him rage and respond intemperately, sometimes foolishly. It must have been a wretched time for him. His short fuse led him to fight with his friends and finally even to turn on Whipper. Yet perhaps in this instance he acted not entirely out of anger, but rather out of his own quixotic sense of the fitness of things.

Not unexpectedly, Whipper had not taken kindly to Chamberlain's patently unconstitutional refusal to sign his commission. Although it took him some time to respond, when finally on January 20, 1876, Whipper rose on the floor of the House to a question of privilege, he treated the members to a lengthy diatribe in which he answered point by point every charge against him, excoriating Chamberlain and the *News and Courier* in the process. He did a splendid job of it, making much of the "strangely united" Democratic newspaper and Republican governor, scoring Chamberlain repeatedly as a man unfit by his own immorality and hypocrisy to cast the vile aspersions he had on the legislature's choice of judge for the First Circuit.

On balance one might assume that Elliott would have been delighted with Whipper's performance, which so vehemently expressed his own sentiments. And perhaps he was; but when Whipper had his entire speech "spread upon" the journal of the

House, Elliott was furious, particularly since it had been done without his knowledge on a day when he was absent from the House of Representatives because he was arguing a case in the state Supreme Court. Elliott was an excellent parliamentarian; he knew beyond question that Whipper's harangue against the governor of the state had no place in the official record of the House proceedings. Decidedly, said Elliott, he would not have permitted the speech to go into the journal had he been in the House that day, for as speaker it was his duty to pass on and correct all entries in the House journal. Furthermore, Elliott expressed his parliamentary displeasure to Whipper in the presence of the clerk of the House and several other persons in a way which vexed Whipper.

When a resolution was offered in the House to have Whipper's remarks expunged from the record, Elliott spoke in favor of it, peeling his sometime closest friend alive, stopping just short of calling him a fool because he knew that if he used that word he could properly be accused of having nominated a fool for a high judicial post. Even so, the *News and Courier* carefully noted the epithets he did use—"ingrate," "falsifier," "malingerer," and "knave"—but they were so pleased with Elliott's denunciation of Whipper that they said they almost forgave the speaker "for his mistake in supporting a 'knave' for the bench." [15]

One might have anticipated that Elliott's quarrel with Whipper, which so endeared him to the *News and Courier,* might also have led to some sort of rapprochement between Elliott and Chamberlain and between Elliott and Cardozo. Such, however, was not the case. Elliott continued to flail away at these two antagonists for whom he felt an abiding and highly motivated enmity. The Whipper contretemps had been a noisy public skirmish; the evidence is that the two contestants emerged from it with their friendship perhaps frayed but not entirely ruptured. Against Chamberlain and Cardozo, it was a fight to the kill.

On April 11, 1876, the continual internecine battles and the constantly shifting political alliances reached a climax when, in a wild, free-swinging conclave, the Republicans met to elect delegates to the national presidential convention to be held in June in Cincinnati.

Chamberlain's loyalty to the Republican party had been questioned outside the state as well as in. At the national level, his most prominent critic was Senator Oliver P. Morton of Indiana, who was one of the leading candidates for the presidential nomination. A large part of Morton's strength came from Southern Republicans, so that in February of 1876, when he accused Chamberlain of having become "entirely identified with the Democrats," he was obviously acting from self-interest.* [16] Morton wanted to keep Chamberlain and his friends, who he knew would not support him, away from the Cincinnati convention; he favored other carpetbaggers and blacks from South Carolina who he believed were more disposed toward his candidacy. To accomplish this, Morton dispatched a loyal backer—none other than South Carolina's Senator John J. Patterson—to Columbia to join with other anti-Chamberlain forces who were gathering at the Radical convention to elect delegates to Cincinnati. Thus another ironic coalition was formed with Elliott, in his role as president of the Republican State Executive Committee (and also as president— without portfolio—of the Stop Chamberlain club), in the middle. On one side was Elliott's onetime bitterest enemy, Patterson, who had literally robbed Elliott of his chance to become a United States senator; on the other was another old antagonist, Judge Robert B. Carpenter, who, it may be remembered, had run against the Radicals in 1870 as the candidate for governor of the Union Reform party and with whom Elliott had had numerous political skirmishes.

So it was now the Patterson-Elliott-Carpenter Ring.† Although the alliance was new, its members employed an old tactic which had come to be a standard operating procedure at Radical conventions. They strove to keep those delegates who were opposed to their interests—and in this case favoring Chamberlain's—from being seated. Elliott at least had the imagination to implement this objective with a different strategem. When the potential delegates assembled in the chamber of the House of Representatives at eleven o'clock on the morning of April 11, 1876, he announced that all persons were to go to the executive office committee room

* Chamberlain answered Morton's accusation in a long self-righteous letter printed in the *New York Herald* in which he said, among far too many other things, that "to cry 'Democrat' at me at this time is to support Moses and Whipper."

† A comprehensive listing of the many different combinations which constituted "rings" cited by the South Carolina Democratic press during the Reconstruction would probably number at least fifty.

to sign the roll and get their tickets of admission. Wisely, the twenty or thirty Chamberlain delegates refused to leave the House chamber for this purpose, knowing that if they did so they would not be readmitted.

At one o'clock Elliott announced that the roll would be called. Chamberlain then rose to inquire what names would be included and, of course, was told that the men who had not left the House chamber to get their tickets were not on the roll and would have to wait until after the convention had organized to be admitted. Cardozo protested the point vigorously and Judge E. W. Mackey, a strong Chamberlain man, did so even more furiously: "We are met here today face to face and eye to eye with the banded robbers who have plundered the state," shouted Mackey. Various anti-Chamberlain men converged on Mackey. Elliott himself confronted him and demanded who he meant by the "banded robbers." "You are one of them," Mackey screamed. "You are a liar," Elliott shouted back, and drew his pistol. Mackey also drew his. Tables were overturned, chairs were brandished, one over Chamberlain's head; he sat unmoved. Patterson made for the door and Grace Elliott, who happened to be in the hall, added to the wild confusion by screaming hysterically. The convention was off to a typical start.[17]

Through three days of bickering the Patterson-Elliott-Carpenter forces held firm and it began to look as if Chamberlain, the governor of the state, would not even be a delegate to his party's national convention. However, it was not until the night of April 13 that the state convention got down to the real business of electing delegates-at-large. Elliott was the first man nominated; he was elected almost unanimously. Then Senator Patterson was nominated, then Governor Chamberlain, whose nomination, according to a *New York Times* reporter, was greeted with such "shouts of derisive laughter" that if a vote had been taken he "would not have received twenty-five votes."[18] The convention had been in session for fourteen hours that day. It was three o'clock in the morning when Judge Carpenter rose, ostensibly to speak to the nomination of Patterson but in fact to confront Chamberlain directly with having been a traitor to his party.

Since his foray in the 1870 campaign, Carpenter had stayed out of politics, confining himself to his duties as judge of the Third Circuit (to which he had recently been re-elected). Why he chose this time to re-enter the arena is not clear, unless he had ambitions for the governorship. From all indications he was a quiet-spoken, fair-minded, capable, if not very exciting man. Although he tried to keep his attack against Chamberlain free of the ugly personal hatred which had characterized many of the other speeches, his assault was no less biting: "It has been stated by Governor Chamberlain or rather by his organ or organs, day after day, that the issue is between Governor Chamberlain and honesty and the Republican party and a den of thieves," said Carpenter. "I deny that this is the issue. I say that the issue is whether he has kept fealty with the band of men who by their suffrage put him in office. . . . I state without fear of contradiction that from the day he entered the office of Chief Magistrate of the state he has turned his back upon the men who fought for him and with him and sought only to advance himself at the cost of his allegiance to his party. (Cheers.)" [19]

Implicit in Carpenter's accusation, and later explicitly stated in a letter to the *News and Courier,* was his conviction, supported, he said, by "the most ample and conclusive proof," that the governor had not only deserted the friends who had elected him, but had "persistently with personal taunt and executive lash tried to drive and keep them in the wrong with a view to their destruction and his exaltation." [20]

Carpenter's points were on the whole very well made, but he was hardly the man to be making them, having himself, as an avowed Republican, been the candidate of a party composed largely of Democrats, which was formed expressly to knock the Radical Republicans out of office.

With obvious relish, Chamberlain took full advantage of his adversary's vulnerability. He felt calm, said the governor, "as calm and cool as a May morning, and as ready to meet the charges that have been brought against me as I shall be to meet the sweet kisses of my wife and children in the morning." He was then "reminded" of the only other occasion on which he had had the pleasure of "measuring swords" with Carpenter. It was in 1870, when "a strong vigorous hand was clutched at the throat of the Republican party," and when he (Chamberlain) was commissioned by that party to go to a meeting at Chester to see if he could loosen that death grip. "I went to Chester," said the governor. "I met there the chosen leader of the Democracy of South

Carolina, the man who now assails me with the charge of want of fealty to the Republican party." Here the governor was interrupted with a cry of "That's it, give it to the traitor of 1870!" [21] From that point on, as Chamberlain, an experienced, persuasive, and clever orator, warmed to his theme, the convention began to shift in his favor. When he finished speaking and when the vote was taken between Chamberlain and Patterson for the second delegate-at-large, Chamberlain won 70 to 40. It was then six o'clock in the morning and, in quick succession, Lieutenant Governor Gleaves, who was not a Chamberlain man, defeated Cardozo, who was, for the next delegate spot. Cardozo tried again for the fourth position and was defeated—this time by Patterson. Of the ten delegates previously chosen from the five congressional districts, seven were black and inclined toward Elliott's sphere so that, although Chamberlain had managed to get himself a trip to Cincinnati, he had almost no support among the gentlemen who were traveling with him to the national convention.

In contrast to the rowdy Republican conclave, the Democrats, when they convened on May 4, 1876, to elect delegates to *their* national presidential nominating convention (scheduled to take place in St. Louis on June 27), held a decorous session with no name calling, little personal acrimony, and certainly no drawn pistols. This relative harmony prevailed because there was really no fundamental difference in objective among the delegates: All were united in their passionate desire for one thing and one thing only—the return to a white man's government in their state. The only disagreement among them was how to accomplish this, whether by the clear-cut, decisive initiative advocated by the Straightouts or by the more moderate gradualist approach favored by the Cooperationists.

In yet another irony, the Straightout position was articulated and most strongly espoused by General M. C. Butler, the man who had been Judge Carpenter's running mate on the Union Reform ticket in 1870. At that time it would have been almost heresy to utter the word *Democrat,* for Butler and the Union Reformers of 1870 had insisted upon the pretense that their party was nonpartisan. Now in 1876 Butler stood before his fellow delegates at the convention and asked, "Why is it unwise to say that we are Democrats, to state the principles upon which we stand? Are we not Democrats today? Were we not so yesterday? Will we not be so tomorrow? If so, why not say so to the world?" Butler demanded that, with no further equivocation, they decide to nominate for governor a "true conservative moderate son of South Carolina—a native.[22] In this proposition he was strongly seconded by Martin C. Gary, a zealot and ardent advocate of the Mississippi plan who was to become the architect of the state's ultimate "redemption."

But the Cooperationists, whose strength was enhanced by the presence at the convention of a more blunt but temperate group of farmers who had not had a place in the elite antebellum councils of the Democratic party, argued successfully that zeal should not outrun discretion and that "the pear should not be plucked until it was ripe." Their concept that "negative action was really positive action" led the majority of the delegates to decide to await developments and to hold the policy of the party in abeyance until the plans of the Republicans were fully revealed.[23] A resolution was therefore adopted to empower the State Executive Committee to call another convention of the Democratic party to nominate state officers whenever in their judgment it was deemed necessary.

In the sense that a Straightout ticket had not been nominated, the convention was a victory for the Cooperationists. But, as such, the victory was short-lived. On July 4, 1876, in the sleepy, virtually abandoned little town of Hamburg on the Carolina side of the Savannah River, there occurred a bloody incident which some Democrats believed changed the course of their lives almost as much as an event which had taken place in Philadelphia on the same date one hundred years earlier had changed the course of history.

13

To Live and Die in Dixie

THE STATE militia in Hamburg, South Carolina, had about eighty men on its rolls, all black. Its captain, Doc Adams, was also black. On July 4 the company went out to drill on one of the public streets, a little-traveled thoroughfare overgrown with grass in many portions. While the company was drilling, two young white men, Thomas Butler and Henry Getzen, approached in a carriage and, when they were face to face, demanded that the company yield to let them pass. Doc Adams halted the company but did not order it to break ranks while he went forward and remonstrated with the two young men, pointing out that there was plenty of room on either side of the company for their carriage to pass. Butler and Getzen, however, refused to drive their buggy to the right or left of the militia column, but insisted upon going through the middle, causing some of the militiamen to dig in and state "insolently" that they would not move and the carriage could stay there all night. Their commander, Adams, however, wisely decided against forcing the issue; he ordered his troops to open ranks and let the buggy pass through. That should, of course, have been the end of a petty and wholly one-sided incident. It was not.

On the following day, the two young men appeared before black trial justice Prince Rivers to take out a warrant against Adams and one or two other officers of the militia. Their case was continued until July 8, by which time a powerful, prominent

Straightouter and determined activist, General M. C. Butler, had entered the case as counsel for Butler (no relation) and Getzen —or, rather, ostensibly as their counsel. General Butler's real purpose was to use the trivial occurrence of July 4 as a means of destroying the militia company, whose presence gave a sense of security to the local blacks, and thereby to initiate a program of terror and violence in the county.

To implement his design, General Butler had assembled some hundred or so armed white men, members of various rifle clubs, who converged on Hamburg, mounted and in squads of ten or fifteen, on July 8 at four o'clock when the hearing before Trial Justice Rivers was due to begin. Adams, upon learning of the presence of these white forces, refused to appear at the inquiry and instead took refuge with about twenty-five of his company in the red-brick building which the militia used as an armory. By this time Butler had dropped all pretense of appearing in the interest of the two youths; he demanded that Captain Adams surrender to him the arms of his militia company. Adams refused, stating that Butler had not "the shadow of a right" to make such a demand. Butler then notified Adams that he was going to have the arms in fifteen minutes. Adams spunkily replied that in that case Butler would have to take them by force. Butler's men, quickly augmented by many more armed whites who were awaiting his call just across the river in Augusta, Georgia, surrounded the armory and opened fire. Adams, trying to husband his very short supply of ammunition, kept his men under cover until some of the attacking force came into close range; his men then fired a shot which killed one of the whites. Butler's men retaliated by bringing an old cannon—a six-pounder—across the bridge from Augusta, placing it within fifty feet of the armory, and bombarding the building. At this point the trapped blacks began trying to escape. One was killed while running from the armory; all the others were captured by the numerically superior white forces and kept under guard for six hours. Finally, at two o'clock in the morning, five of the defenseless blacks were called out and shot in cold blood in the presence of their white captors. The other blacks broke loose; one was killed as he ran, four others were severely wounded.* The bodies of the dead (and in one horrible instance of the dying) were mutilated as well.

* This account is based on information supplied to Chamberlain by Attorney General William Stone, whom the governor dispatched at once to

"Such was the affair at Hamburg," wrote Governor Chamberlain, as he responded with revulsion to the naked brutality of the massacre in a letter to Senator T. J. Robertson in Washington. "If you can find words to characterize its atrocity and barbarism, the triviality of the causes, the murderous and inhuman spirit which marked it in all its stages, your power of language exceeds mine. . . . What hopes can we have when such a cruel, bloodthirsty spirit waits in our midst for its hour of gratification? Is our race so wantonly cruel?" [1]

The *News and Courier* was equally condemnatory: "We find little if any excuse for the conflict itself," they wrote on July 10, "and absolutely none for the cowardly killing of the seven negro militiamen who were shot down like rabbits long after they had surrendered." Still the *News and Courier* could not bring itself to regard the events at Hamburg as anything more than a "local disturbance." Editor Dawson would not admit that the real meaning behind the senseless slaughter was that Butler and his Straightouts were beginning to put into action the nefarious Mississippi plan.

Chamberlain saw this obvious implication at once and perceived it even more distinctly when, on July 12, four days after the Hamburg incident, the Democratic Executive Committee "deemed it necessary" to call another convention of the party to meet on August 15. Clearly this indicated that the Straightouts had gained the upper hand, that they were going to follow up their decisive action at Hamburg by seizing the initiative and forcing the Democrats to nominate a full slate of state officers without waiting for the Republicans to show their cards at their convention, which was not scheduled until September.

At the same time Robert Elliott took an initiative of his own. He called a meeting (to be held on July 20 and 21) of all black politicians in the state to protest the Hamburg murders. Out of this Convention of Colored People, from which whites were totally excluded, came a stirring document—"An Address to the People of the United States"—of which Elliott was the acknowledged author. The "Address" was described by a contemporary newspaper reporter and ardent Straightouter, Alfred B. Williams, as "skillfully temperate, plausibly appealing." Issued in pamphlet

Hamburg to find out what had actually occurred, and it is borne out by similar reports in the *News and Courier* and by stories carried in most of the Democratic papers of the state.

form, it was circulated widely as a campaign document, according to Williams, and "probably gained many Republican votes at the North." [2]

Elliott's document was indeed a lucid, dispassionate recital of the facts concerning the massacre and the underlying hatred which had led to it. He pointed out that, since such outbreaks invariably occurred on the eve of elections and in counties which had Republican majorities, he and the fifty-nine blacks who signed the "Address" were forced to the "irresistible conclusion" that the events at Hamburg had their origins in a "settled and well defined purpose to influence and control the forthcoming political election."

The signators therefore called upon the people of the United States to "place upon this wanton and inhuman butchery the indelible stigma of public abhorrence," and upon the "business men and property holders of the state to bend their energies toward the removal of this deadly nightshade of mob law and violence." Specifically, they exhorted the governor to "invoke every constitutional agency and legal method . . . to maintain the supremacy of the law, to vindicate the rights of the citizen to whom protection is due." And finally, looking to the highest authority, they asked the president of the United States to aid the chief executive of their state in enforcing the constitutional guarantees by affording national protection to the citizens of the United States domiciled in South Carolina.[3]

This last amounted to an open demand that the governor ask the president for federal troops, and Chamberlain quickly complied. On July 22, 1876, he wrote to Grant asking that troops be made available for duty in South Carolina. Perhaps he would have requested federal support even without the strong recommendation of the Negro leaders, for, by his every action and word, Chamberlain demonstrated that he was genuinely heartsick and appalled by the Hamburg massacre and by the sinister implications it posed for the black population of the state.

But Chamberlain was nothing if not a politician. He knew that the Hamburg affair all but vitiated the Cooperationists and that without them he had no chance of being the candidate for governor of both the Democratic and Republican parties. He knew too that if he were to become even the Republican candidate, he had some important fence mending to do among the blacks with whom he had been playing rather high, wide, and handsome over the past eighteen months in his eagerness to win the favor of the white Democrats. It would be unfair to suggest that Chamberlain's letter to Grant, in which he specifically asked the federal government to "exert itself vigorously to repress violence in the state during the present political campaign," [4] was written solely to regain his standing with the black majority in South Carolina. On the other hand, it is realistic to attribute some political overtones to the governor's ardent championship of the Negro and to his inclusion of Elliott's "Address to the People of the United States" in the communication to the president.

On August 16, 1876, the Democratic state convention nominated Wade Hampton as their candidate for governor, and along with him a full slate of candidates for every state office. Up to the last minute, Captain Dawson, through the *News and Courier,* had ceaselessly urged that the Democrats not follow this course but wait for the Republican convention so that they, the Democrats, might "pitch their battle with a full and thorough knowledge of the enemy's position." Dawson had continued to back Chamberlain, even justifying the governor's message to Grant as "not in the usual sense a 'call for troops' [but] rather a natural inquiry of a public officer who at a critical time desires to know what outside aid he can rely on." [5] But on August 17, Dawson gamely accepted his own personal defeat and the Straightout victory. The newspaper at once endorsed Hampton, headlined the "wild enthusiasm" which his nomination had elicited, and in its editorial of that date referred with contempt to the "heated and unnecessary letters of Chamberlain about the Hamburg affair." Thus ended the not-so-strange-bedfellow relationship between Francis Dawson and Daniel Chamberlain.

Wade Hampton, although not a brilliant man, was a brilliant choice to unite the two opposing Democratic factions and arouse them to fight for their desperately desired objective—the return of white supremacy to South Carolina. He was an aristocrat, the grandson and namesake of a revered Revolutionary War hero. A successful planter and renowned horseman, he had been a brigadier general (later major general) of the cavalry under J. E. B. Stuart and was the highest-ranking officer from South Carolina in the Confederate Army. He was a moderate who regarded the Negro fondly, but always as a menial. In the words of a twentieth-century historian, he "possessed the failings of a country squire—narrow education and sincere bigotry." [6] In short, Wade Hampton was himself the perfect symbol of white supremacy.

From the moment of his nomination, the Democrats were galvanized into almost frenetic action. The feeling of helplessness that had long kept the whites inert suddenly vanished. "It was as if an electric shock had reached every center, nook and corner and the white people of every age and station and roused them on the instant from a long stupor of despair to fierce united action," wrote a contemporary observer. [7]

On August 26 the Democrats staged a huge, noisy political rally and torchlight parade on the Citadel Green in Charleston. Such a raucous demonstration, unheard of in this decorous, gracious city, caused the *News and Courier* to comment rather sheepishly the next day (in a story headed "To Live and Die in Dixie") that Charleston, not being accustomed to manifesting her political feelings in popular displays, had perhaps not done as well as Tammany Hall would have. Still, the thousands of torches (ordered by wire from New York City), the music, the fifty-odd wagons carrying lighted "transparencies," the five hundred mounted men made a pageant "at once striking and unique."

Conspicuous among the throngs were the various rifle clubs. Although their rifles, which would later be much in evidence (and in use), were not flaunted on this occasion, one or two red shirts, soon to become the uniform of the "redeemers," were. In the ten days since Hampton's nomination, dozens of new clubs had been organized (usually referring to themselves euphemistically as baseball clubs). The presence of the quasi-military, and quite illegal, units at this spirited rally was a grim reminder that enthusiasm alone would not be sufficient. The November elections could not be won even if every Democrat in South Carolina voted, unless the black majority of thirty thousand could either be "persuaded" to cross over to the Democratic side or prevented from voting altogether.

The newly achieved unity of the Democrats was not quite paralleled by the Republicans when they met on September 14, 1876, for their nominating convention, although the party had, to a large extent, closed ranks behind Daniel Chamberlain. The reasons for the governor's improved position within his own party were paradoxical. Because he had reacted with appropriate indignation and firmness to the outrage at Hamburg, he had lost favor with the Democrats. And because he had lost favor with the Democrats, he had regained favor with the Republicans—at least with many of them; not, however, with Robert Brown Elliott.

Senator J. J. Patterson, lately of the Patterson-Elliott Ring, was the first to return to the Chamberlain fold, saying with candor that now that the Democrats were no longer praising the governor he again felt he could be trusted and would therefore support him. But Elliott let it be noised about that not only was he not going to support Chamberlain, but that he had in his possession some "startling documentary evidence" against him. Therefore, the dramatic peak of an otherwise quiet convention was anticipated on the third day when Elliott rose to speak. The excitement in the convention hall was "tumultuous and almost unmanageable," as those who had been waiting in the lobby pressed forward to hear Elliott's revelations. But almost as soon as he began, it was clear that Elliott's speech was going to fall far short of expectations. He had been advised by friends of Chamberlain's, he said, for the good of the party, not to make known what he had intended to say about the governor. He had urged a secret session, without success. He had also been warned that Governor Chamberlain had seventy-six votes that would stand by him even if he were guilty of grand larceny. "Great God!" said Elliott, "is that the position of members who talk of love of party?" (Later Elliott would have difficulty in establishing that he had not on this occasion ever actually accused Chamberlain of being guilty of grand larceny.)

Even though it was probably too late to change the views of the convention, Elliott proclaimed it his duty to give the reasons why he felt Chamberlain could not be trusted. He did not specifically say not trusted by the blacks, but his reasons made it clear that that was what he meant. First he read a letter Chamberlain, as attorney general, had written in 1870 to Niles G. Parker. At the time two Negroes, Cardozo and Martin Delany, were considering becoming candidates for the United States Senate (Elliott's try did not come until two years later). "About the United States Senatorship, I don't know what to say," wrote Chamberlain to Parker. "I am well satisfied with my present office but my position is just this: If my friends wish me to be a candidate to keep the party from going over to negroism I shall, if it is to defeat such a calamity, consent to run." [8]

The letter provided Elliott with his most damaging charge. His other examples of Chamberlain's lack of trustworthiness included a rehash of the Whipper-Moses affair in which Elliott said the governor had allowed his passions to influence him into overstepping his authority and, finally, a denunciation of Chamberlain for having appointed only whites to represent South Carolina on the national Centennial Board of Commissioners.

All in all, the much-touted speech was not one of Elliott's finest efforts; he was hampered, the *News and Courier* suggested with surprising sympathy, "caught between two fires—his desire to let out all he knew and his fear lest in the event of Chamberlain's nomination his disclosures might prove damaging to his beloved party." [9]

One cannot help wondering just what those disclosures would have been. It is improbable that Elliott at that juncture could have found any new evidence of fraud or corruption when all of Chamberlain's involvements with the various Railroad, Bond, and Sinking Fund rings had already been thoroughly explored—and exploited. Thus it seems more likely that what he proposed to reveal was something more personal—something known to him only. This then gives rise to the conjecture that he might have planned to lay bare the deal that Chamberlain may have made with him in 1874. At that time, it will be remembered, Elliott gave up his seat in the House of Representatives to return to South Carolina and help Chamberlain win election as governor, perhaps in exchange for some promise of subsequent higher office for himself. While it is doubtful that Chamberlain and Elliott would have committed the substance of such an understanding to paper, thus providing Elliott with his "startling documentary evidence," it is still possible that some tangible record of their arrangement existed—at least enough to embarrass Chamberlain.

One might also wonder why, if Elliott actually did have any such documentary proof that Chamberlain may have intended to seek the governorship in 1876 only as a stepping stone to the United States Senate, he had so easily been persuaded to suppress it. Perhaps once again Chamberlain had offered him an incentive to do so.

Chamberlain answered Elliott's watered-down attack as skillfully as he had answered the assaults against him in the earlier April convention, only this time he did not have his back against the wall. His nomination was all but assured (as Elliott himself had recognized) even before the convention began. "Honest John" Patterson capped a certain thing by reminding the delegates that no other man but Chamberlain would have the ear of the authorities in Washington in case federal protection in the forthcoming election was required. The vote was then taken and Chamberlain won 88 to 36 (1 of the 36 votes being cast for Elliott).

Having achieved such a solid victory, Chamberlain must certainly have been in a strong enough position to dictate the men he wanted to run on the ticket with him—the men he thought most likely to help him win a difficult election against a united and determined Democratic party. Emphatically Elliott would not have fallen into this category, as far as Chamberlain was concerned. Yet Patterson, who had been the one chosen to nominate Chamberlain for governor, again rose to nominate Elliott for the office of attorney general. Chamberlain had by that time left the convention hall. Elliott's name was greeted by a roar of applause; it was proposed to nominate him by acclamation, but the rules prevented this; he won by a vote of 115 to 1, amid wild cheering. Perhaps Elliott's popularity among the blacks was so great that Chamberlain could not have blocked his nomination, much as he must have wanted to. Perhaps he did not dare to try. Perhaps it was the price he had agreed to pay to keep Elliott's "startling documentary evidence" under wraps.

Chamberlain's own account of it is at variance with this last possibility; it also seems slightly at variance with the whole truth. In a letter to his good friend William Lloyd Garrison, which was written almost a year after the fact, Chamberlain said that he knew he had made a grave mistake in not refusing to run with R. B. Elliott, whose "bare presence on the ticket justly gave offense to some honest men of both parties." Elliott had opposed him brutally, continued Chamberlain; but, unable to defeat him, he had determined to "foist himself" on the ticket to cover his defeat. "I saw at once the bearing, in part, of this, and I took the resolution unknown to any friends to walk into the Convention and throw up my nomination and avow that I did it because I would not run on a ticket with Elliott. I knew it would result in putting him off the ticket. I had actually risen in my office to go into the hall for this purpose when I was met at the door by a dozen or more of my most devoted colored supporters who came to congratulate me on *the surrender of Elliott in seeking to stand on a ticket with me!* I was disarmed of my purpose and relinquished it. It was a mistake. Whether it affected the result which has now come I do not know. But I ought to have made Elliott's withdrawal the condition of my acceptance. This incident is now known only to *you and me.*" [10]

The weak point in this letter is that, if Chamberlain had really been resolved to keep Elliott off the slate (and one could hardly blame him if he had been), why did he not make his determination known to Patterson, who nominated Elliott, and, more importantly, to his many ardent supporters, virtually all of whom must have voted for Elliott, since only one of the convention delegates did not?

One thing is manifest, however. When Chamberlain and Elliott walked arm in arm down the aisle of the convention hall after Elliott's nomination, the Democrats were handed a dividend which they might otherwise not have had and on which they harped relentlessly throughout the campaign.* "A more iniquitous and infamous nomination was never made," wrote the *News and Courier* of Elliott. "Able, audacious, unscrupulous, he is open as a candidate for Attorney General to every objection that lay against Whipper as a candidate for judge. The election of such a man would be a horrible calamity. It casts a deeper gloom over the whole ticket, and brings every candidate upon it down to Elliott's level." [11] It is hardly necessary to add that from that point on it was the Chamberlain-Elliott Ring!

Chamberlain put the best face he possibly could on Elliott's nomination, defending his "admitted ability for the position, his long record of political service to the party and a desire to conciliate an element of the party which had been defeated in my nomination." [12] Chamberlain also pointed out that Elliott had declared his "full and cordial acceptance" both of the party's

---

* Another old antagonist of Elliott's, James Thompson, editor of the *Daily Union Herald,* left Elliott's name off the Republican ticket, which he ran in bold face on his editorial page of September 18, swearing that he would resign as editor rather than include his name. The following day Elliott's name was duly printed along with the others and Thompson continued to be editor of the newspaper.

nominee for governor and of its platform of reform. And for his part, Elliott did indeed seem to have submerged his antipathy to Chamberlain as he settled down to his duties not only as a candidate but as president of the Republican State Executive Committee, which put him in charge of the entire course of the campaign (in those days also called a canvass).

The Democratic campaign, which was going full force by the time of Chamberlain's nomination, was based on a two-pronged strategy. The ostentatious main even was a triumphant tour of the state by Wade Hampton, designed to arouse the whites and perhaps to convert a few blacks to the democracy—a change-over known as "cross Jordan." Meanwhile, in the background, men like M. C. Butler and his companion Martin Gary, an even more ardent Mississippi plan advocate, were organizing their program of force and terrorism which was to destroy Negro domination of the state.

General Hampton's progress through South Carolina began on September 2, 1876; accompanied by hundreds of mounted Red Shirts, it was a delirious success. For the first time in ten years, the white Democrats had something thrilling to cheer about, and they turned out by the tens of thousands at every depot in every city, village, and hamlet to acclaim their beloved hero. The old wartime "rebel yell" and the new "Hurray for Hampton" cry of the Red Shirts rang out from Greenville to Charleston.

Hampton was not an eloquent or even a particularly effective speaker, but it did not matter. He had only to evoke in his listeners memories of the past and call upon them to redeem their grand old state to its place of honor in the Republic, to be greeted with the wildest, most unrestrained enthusiasm. In every speech, however, he made a special point of addressing himself to the Negroes. Reminding them that he had been the first white man in the state, back in 1865, to advocate a qualified Negro suffrage, he pledged himself to assure the Negroes that "not one single right enjoyed by the colored people today shall be taken away from them. They shall be equals under the law of any man in South Carolina." [13]

But promises, however sincerely meant, were not enough, and Hampton, carefully walking the high road, turned his head away from the low road and the sterner methods that were being applied to neutralize the thirty thousand Negro majority in his state. Rifle clubs had, of course, been in existence since 1867, but by the summer of 1876 they had multiplied to an estimated 287 different organizations. With an average of 50 men in each company, this meant that approximately 14,500 were under arms, which number probably represented the majority of the white male population within the ordinary limits of age for military duty. The stepped-up activities of the well-drilled rifle clubs were threefold. Early in the canvass—in fact, before the Republican Convention, when Chamberlain was still campaigning for the nomination—they began what they euphemistically referred to as "divided meetings."

At Edgefield, Chamberlain faced such a confrontation when he addressed a Republican meeting on August 12, 1876. As he mounted the stand with Judge Mackey and Richard Cain, who were appearing with him, M. C. Butler and Martin Gary, backed by an estimated six hundred Red Shirts, elbowed their way onto the rostrum and, amid rebel yells, while their guard stood with pistols drawn, demanded to be heard as they denounced, harassed and threatened the Republican speakers. Similar occurrences followed when Chamberlain attempted to speak at Newbury, Abbeyville, Barnwell, and Lancaster during August. The first of these disturbances at Edgefield had been such a "success," from the Red Shirts' point of view, that thereafter the Mississippi plan was often referred to in South Carolina as the Edgefield plan.

After Chamberlain's nomination in September, A. G. Haskell, chairman of the State Democratic Executive Committee, in accordance with the "high road" principles of Hampton, wrote a letter to Chamberlain formally inviting him to appear at the scheduled Democratic mass meetings, in the interest of promoting "peaceful and untrammelled discussion that the people may become enlightened on the issues of the day."

Elliott, as Haskell's opposite number on the Republican side, responded to the letter politely and affirmatively with a proposal that Chamberlain and Hampton agree to meet in ten places—five in the low country where the blacks had the largest majority and five in the up country where the black majority was smaller. Elliott carefully spelled out all details of how he would like the meetings to be conducted, but expressed his willingness to accept any modifications in the interest of achieving the ends desired by both sides. It was all very circumspect and decorous. Negotiations went on through several exchanges of letters and culminated in a face-to-face meeting of Elliott and Haskell at which the actual locations of the ten meetings were agreed upon. Then the Democrats began to back down, which probably did not surprise Elliott. Clearly the "low road" advocates had prevailed in the Hampton camp. Why should the Democrats, with their far more extensive military strength, yield to equal time and polite discussion between candidates when they could with much greater effect—to wit, Edgefield—render the Republican candidates helpless by forcibly breaking up their meetings?

Martin Gary had written an elaborate "Plan of the Campaign of 1876" which was distributed to counties throughout the state. "We must attend every Radical meeting . . . in as large numbers as we can get together, and well armed," read his Rule 13; "as soon as their *leaders* or speakers begin to speak and make false statements tell them *then* and *there* that they are liars, thieves and rascals and are only trying to mislead the ignorant negroes." Rule 14 continued, "In speeches to negroes you must remember that argument has no effect on them. They can only be influenced by their *fears,* superstition or cupidity. . . . Treat them so as to show them you are the superior race and that their natural position is that of subordination to the white man." [14]

By promoting such "divided meetings," the Democrats made conditions too hazardous for Chamberlain and the other members of the ticket to continue their intended canvass of the state. And even when they did brave it to a meeting, they encountered small crowds because quiet, peaceful Republicans were afraid to come out to political gatherings and expose themselves to such treatment. Meanwhile, the mounted Red Shirts from the various rifle clubs rode by day and by night, shouting their rebel yell, menacing the blacks, threatening that if they did not vote the Democratic ticket they would all be killed. At the same time property owners and merchants applied all possible economic pressures, refusing to hire blacks who backed Chamberlain, refusing to lend money on liens or to give credit at stores to any Negroes except those who had "crossed Jordan" or pretended they had—quite a difference, as it turned out.

By early October the outrages committed against terrorized blacks and the numerous outright murders had multiplied to crisis proportions. After another bloody riot at Ellenton in Aiken County (about twenty miles southeast of Hamburg), Chamberlain declared that it had become "impracticable to enforce, by ordinary process of judicial proceedings, the laws of the state." The black militia, by then demoralized and undermined, was absolutely no match for the highly organized bodies of armed whites who dominated in many localities. Against them "a constable with a colored posse would be massacred in an attempt to execute the law," said Chamberlain. Accordingly, on October 7, 1876, the governor ordered the rifle clubs to disband and all members to disperse peacefully to their homes within three days. Failure to do so would force him to call for federal troops.

The Democrats responded with a "Proclamation to the People of the United States" in which they asserted that "in this period of profound peace" Chamberlain's "false and libelous charge, his tyrannical, unwarranted usurpation of power" was undertaken solely to prevent the "otherwise certain defeat of himself and his corrupt party." [15]

Chamberlain's position vis à vis the rifle clubs was somewhat compromised by the fact that during his days of courting favor with the Democrats, he had openly recognized the clubs, often "breaking bread" with them, as the *News and Courier* was quick to point out.[16] He had ridden into Charleston only a few months earlier escorted by the South Carolina Rifle Club, and had on one occasion publicly presented a "silken banner" to another such organization.

So, as had been expected, the rifle clubs ignored the governor's order; thereupon he appealed directly to the president. On October 17 Grant, recognizing a state of insurrection and domestic violence in South Carolina, issued a proclamation and commanded "all persons engaged in said unlawful and insurrectionary proceedings to disperse and retire peaceably to their respective abodes." The Democratic Executive Committee responded, "We cannot retire peaceably to our abodes because we are in our homes in peace, disturbed only by the political agitations created by the governor and his minions." The president, through General Sherman, then ordered all available forces in the military division of the Atlantic to report to Columbia to reinforce the eight United States companies already on duty in South Carolina.

The federal troops arrived a bare three weeks before election day, were equitably distributed throughout the state, and from all reports did an excellent and evenhanded job of quieting fears and maintaining order. Hampton had sent telegrams urging his people to submit quietly to martial law, which they resignedly did. Elliott, as chairman of the Republican State Committee, likewise urged his people to "endure to the end as you have heretofore done in peaceable silence the threats of the democracy, and look forward patiently to that restoration of human reason and truth which will speedily follow your certain success in the approaching election." [17]

On Tuesday, November 7, in an atmosphere of intense excitement and with at least an outward semblance of orderliness, whites and blacks, Democrats and Republicans went to the polls to vote not only for Hampton and Chamberlain and their slates of state officers, but also for Samuel J. Tilden and Rutherford B. Hayes, the Democratic and Republican nominees for the presidency of the United States. The election of 1876 was memorable both nationally and in South Carolina for many reasons, but chiefly for the fact that it took five months to decide who had actually won it.

14

A Giant Step Backward

SOUTH CAROLINA was one of only three Southern states which was still under Republican rule in 1876—the others were Louisiana and Florida—so throughout the country more than usual interest was focused on what would happen there on November 7. As the presidential returns began to come in, what happened in South Carolina became a matter not just of interest, but of crucial national importance.

At first it appeared that the Democratic candidate, Samuel J. Tilden, had won decisively over his Republican rival, Rutherford B. Hayes. By Wednesday morning, November 8, the *News and Courier* proclaimed "Tilden Our President"; in the story under that headline they printed a telegram to state Democratic chairman A. C. Haskell from the chairman of the National Democratic Committee, "I feel safe in saying your redemption is at hand." Returns at the state level were still too scattered to permit even the overconfident *News and Courier* to quite predict Wade Hampton's victory as governor, although they said that all signs pointed in that direction. To others the same signs also pointed in the opposite direction; it depended entirely on who was reading them.

By the next day a note of caution had crept into the reporting by the Democratic press—there was a "bare possibility," they wrote, of Hayes's election. And indeed it was very bare; for, by then (November 9), it was clear that, of the 185 electoral votes needed to win the presidency, Tilden, the Democrat, had won 184 of them. But by then it was also clear that the returns from the three Southern states still in Republican hands were all going to be contested. Tilden needed but one vote to win; Rutherford B. Hayes needed nineteen—the exact total of combined electoral votes of Louisiana, Florida, and South Carolina. When this became evident, national politicians, both Republican and Democrat, as well as writers for the Northern newspapers and weeklies began converging upon Columbia to see how the vote count was going to come out.

There was no doubt whatsoever that frauds and intimidations by both parties had occurred at each and every polling place in South Carolina; nor was there any question that the Democrats far exceeded the Republicans in the violent and illicit means they employed—even the most partisan of Democratic observers not only admitted that, but often actually boasted of it. Part of the Edgefield-Mississippi pre-election plan, as set forth by Martin Gary, called for the Democrats to "pretend" (Gary's actual word) that a large number of Negroes had "crossed Jordan," hoping that, as a consequence, a sizable number of blacks would actually do so on election day. All evidence indicated that this did not in fact occur; the Negroes who were permitted to vote—and a great many were forcibly prevented from so doing—remained loyal to the Republican party. But the Democrats had other means to swell their rolls. They realized that they could make little impact in the low country where the Negro majorities were strongest. Therefore they knew they had to win and win big in the up country. Two counties there were key to their strategy and became vital points of issue in the chaos which followed election day. In Edgefield and Laurens, both in the northwest part of the state, the Democrats went far afield to stuff the ballot boxes; they brought youths under eighteen to the polling places to vote Democratic and, most blatantly, they imported hordes of whites across the border from Georgia to vote for Wade Hampton.

With these tactics the Democrats overreached themselves. The returns from Edgefield and Laurens were widely at variance with previous voting patterns in those counties and, more significantly, ran quite counter to the latest census figures. For example, in Edgefield, where hundreds of Negroes were physically barred by the Red Shirts from voting, Hampton was alleged to have won by a sizable majority. Yet the total vote cast in 1876 greatly exceeded the vote cast in 1874 in Edgefield and also exceeded the census figure for white males over twenty-one in the county. An equivalent percentage of manifest fraud was also true in Laurens.

The unenviable duty of certifying the returns as received from the various county managers, in order to proclaim the winners at the state and national level, fell to the State Board of Canvassers. This ad hoc body was required by law to meet on the fifth day after election and to conclude its deliberations within ten days. The board claimed it had judicial powers (according to the law passed on March 1, 1870) to "go behind the returns," to hear protests and to then rule on the legality of the presidential electors and on all state officers and legislators. In the case of protests concerning the governor and lieutenant governor, however, the decision was to be left to a majority vote of the General Assembly. Since the Board of Canvassers had the final determination as to who was elected to the General Assembly and who was not, this was tantamount to giving them the final say about the governorship as well.

Because the Board of Canvassers was made up of five Republican state officers—three of whom, Cardozo, Haynes, and Dunn, were themselves candidates for election—the Democrats challenged their right to rule on protests and argued that their only function was to report on the "face of the returns." In order to reduce the Board of Canvassers to mere *pro forma* status, the Democrats took their case to the state Supreme Court, where they believed they would receive a sympathetic hearing, since two of the three members of the court were announced Hampton men. The chief justice was Franklin J. Moses, Sr., who obviously did not look kindly on Chamberlain for his refusal in the Whipper-Moses affair to sign his son's commission as judge. Associate Justice Willard, considered by the Democrats to be a carpetbagger of the "better kind," also had a personal dislike of Chamberlain. The third member was a black, J. J. Wright, characterized by the Democrats as drunk, dissolute, and weak, but actually, or perhaps even so, a man of ability and legal acumen. However, in this controversy he was distinctly a minority voice.

Robert Brown Elliott and David H. Corbin, a white attorney of good reputation, argued the case vigorously for the Board of Canvassers before the Supreme Court, while James Connor (who had just run against Elliott as the Democratic candidate for attorney general) and five other "attorneys of distinction" represented the Democrats. The motions were argued on November 16, and on November 17 the court issued an intermediate order to the Board of Canvassers which hedged the question by requiring the board to perform its purely ministerial function of forwarding to the court, without reference to the protests, the returns as received from the county managers. After noting these figures, the court would then decide whether the Board of Canvassers had a right to consider the protest. As the *New York Times* reported, this order in effect said that "the Supreme Court before it would decide on an abstract question of law, wanted to know what facts (whose election) would be affected by its decision." [1]

The Board of Canvassers duly complied. "The face of the returns"—including the protested returns from Edgefield and Laurens—indicated that two Democrats had been elected members of the federal Congress, that Republicans Elliott, Cardozo, and Haynes had won their respective offices, that the Democrats had prevailed by a majority of one in the General Assembly, *but* that the Republican electors for president and vice-president had also won. This statement placed the Democrats in a very difficult predicament. On the one hand it meant that Hampton would of course be chosen governor by the General Assembly; on the other, it dealt a serious blow to Democratic candidate Tilden's chance of becoming president.

To solve their problem so they could win both ways, the Democrats therefore asked the state Supreme Court for two orders, "one for each horn of the dilemma," quipped the *New York Times*. The first order was to demand that the Board of Canvassers certify as correct the vote for the General Assembly, the second order to demand that the board forward all official documents to the state Supreme Court in order that the court itself could then "go behind the returns" and determine who had won the presidential election.

The meaning behind these two orders which the Democrats asked the court to issue in the form of a peremptory mandamus was perfectly plain: 1) since we have won the General Assembly, let it go at that and do not go behind the returns; 2) since we have lost the presidential electors, do go behind the returns and see if we can find a way to change the outcome.

Although it was clear that the court, being so favorably disposed to the Democrats, would comply with their request, decorum de-

manded that they first make at least a show of judicial delibera-
tion. They therefore delayed issuing the two orders until the following day, November 22, which was the last day of the Board
of Canvassers' legal existence. They delayed too long, however.
The Board of Canvassers met at ten o'clock on the morning of
November 22 and, on the advice of their lawyers, Elliott and Corbin, fulfilled what they considered their legal function by "going
behind the returns" themselves. As a result they threw out the
palpably fraudulent returns from Edgefield and Laurens and refused to certify the members to the General Assembly from these
two counties. This action gave the General Assembly a Republican
majority and assured the election of Governor Chamberlain. Having thus completed their duties, the Board of Canvassers adjourned
at one o'clock that afternoon *sine die*. By the time the writ of
peremptory mandamus from the state Supreme Court reached them
later that afternoon, they were no longer a legal entity.

The Supreme Court was furious and at once ordered the five
members of the Board of Canvassers clapped into jail for contempt. They remained behind bars for seven days while both Democrats and Republicans claimed victory. However, on November
26, President Grant sent word to General Thomas H. Ruger, then
commanding the United States troops in South Carolina, stating
that Chamberlain was now governor and ordering the troops to
"sustain him in his authority against violence."

Elliott, of course, had been clearly elected even on the "face of
the returns" and was duly certified by the secretary of state as attorney general of the state of South Carolina.

On Tuesday, November 28, the day constitutionally fixed for
the convening of the legislature, excitement and suspense were high
in the city of Columbia. As the hour of noon approached, an immense crowd thronged about the capitol, waiting to see what the
Democrats would do to make good their boast that they would take
possession of the state House of Representatives and thus control
the General Assembly. Few people milling about the capitol
grounds knew that during the previous night Chamberlain had ordered General Ruger to move a company of infantry into the statehouse; federal troops were already stationed throughout the building; sentinels were posted in the corridors at each entrance to the
House and Senate chambers.

Promptly at twelve o'clock, the Democratic members-elect began a stately procession from South Carolina Hall at the corner of Main and Sumter streets to the capitol grounds, marching two by two, with the eight members from Edgefield and Laurens leading the column and with Wade Hampton and A. C. Haskell bringing up the rear. The Democrats entered the statehouse, but at the first door leading to the House of Representatives they were stopped by John B. Dennis, acting sergeant-at-arms. Backed by federal troops, he demanded to see each man's certificate of election. Naturally the Edgefield and Laurens men, who were the first ones addressed, were unable to comply and were refused admission. Thereupon the entire body about-faced, marched briskly out of the statehouse and back to Carolina Hall. Upon reassembling there, the fifty-seven Democratic members-elect who held certificates, and the eight who did not, declared themselves to be the legal House of Representatives of the state of South Carolina and elected General William H. Wallace as their speaker.

Meanwhile, at the statehouse, the fifty-nine Republican members proceeded to organize *themselves* as the legal House of Representatives of the state and to elect E. W. M. Mackey as their speaker. Since they were in actual possession of the official House chamber, they appeared to have a slight edge over the Democratic team. But not for long. The Democrats of the Wallace House allowed a day to elapse to let the dust settle and perhaps to lull their opponents into a sense of false security before they made a fresh assault on the statehouse, determined to storm their way into the House of Representatives chamber. Whether because the troops had received new orders (there had been a considerable negative reaction at the North against the use of federal troops to supervise the organization of a state legislature), or whether the doorkeepers were confused or, as the Democrats claimed, overpowered, the Wallace House gained admission to the chamber with comparative ease. It was eleven-thirty on the morning of November 30, Thanksgiving Day; the Mackey House was in recess. Wallace mounted to the speaker's desk, his clerk moved to the clerk's chair, the members took seats on the right-hand side of the chamber, and proceeded to business—or made a show of so doing.

In a few minutes members of the Mackey House returned from their recess. Their jaws dropped when they saw the speaker's desk occupied and half the chamber full of Democrats, but they did not lose their presence of mind. Mackey, "breathing hard, his dark eyes behind his big gold-rimmed spectacles glittering in his sallow face," walked quickly up the two or three steps to the speaker's desk and asked General Wallace, "Will you please vacate this seat?" [2] Wallace replied in the negative and read a brief prepared statement. Mackey then ordered his sergeant-at-arms to bring another chair and place it beside Wallace. The Republican clerk, Jones, pushed a chair in beside the Democratic clerk; the Republican members moved to the unoccupied seats at the left of the chamber. Both speakers rapped for order, and with commendable aplomb, especially considering that there was scarcely a man on either side who did not carry a pistol, the two Houses of Representatives went into session at the same time and in the same place.

It was an amazing scene; each speaker recognized only members of his own "House"; motions were made simultaneously, each side trying to be heard over the voices of the members on the other side, while trying to catch the gist of what their opponents were saying.

Because neither faction dared to call a recess and risk losing possession of the chamber, the famous Dual House stayed in session for four days and four nights. Food was brought in to the beleaguered statesmen by camp followers of both persuasions; blankets and pillows were obtained and, even though practically every man was armed to the teeth, some additional guns and ammunition were smuggled into the chamber. But these were never used. As the comedy aspects of this bizarre situation began more and more to strike the participants, a sense of camaraderie developed between opposing members of the two houses. Besides exchanging food and drink, the politicians started swapping jokes. Threats began to sound more comic than bellicose and were more often than not received with shouts of laughter from both sides. And when, in the early morning hours, the blacks began to sing, many of the assemblage, including some of the more stiff-necked of South Carolina's "best," joined in. It was a situation analogous to the Christmas or New Year's truce in a war when, for a few minutes or hours, combatants on a battlefield share a common feeling of good will before going back to shooting at each other. In South Carolina the contestants would soon go back, figuratively speaking, to shooting at each other and it would be a very long time before blacks and whites, as equals, would again share a common joke and a feeling of good fellowship.

The farce lasted from November 30 to December 4, when the Democrats, while still proclaiming themselves the officially constituted House of Representatives of South Carolina, suddenly vacated the House chamber and returned to Carolina Hall to continue their deliberations. Their withdrawal, they insisted, in no way contravened their absolute belief in their legality as the state legislative body, but was occasioned only by their desire to avoid bloodshed in the face of a threat contained in an anonymous letter sent to Wade Hampton the day before. The letter, they claimed, revealed a plan of Chamberlain's to bring a gang of a hundred Negro "roughs" known as the Hunkidories into the statehouse; these men were to be created special deputies by the governor, armed, and ordered by him physically to eject the members from Edgefield and Laurens. Any show of resistance by the Democrats would be answered by the intervention of federal troops. Although the anonymous letter itself was probably a fact, the threats it contained appeared to be without substantial basis. However, the Democrats were prudent to clear out when they did, since the situation of the Dual House could not have remained under control much longer.

With the Wallace House out of the way, the fifty-nine Republican members of the Mackey House immediately moved into joint session with the Senate (which had been completely without conflict, since it had a clear Republican majority) and proclaimed Chamberlain governor. By throwing out the votes from Edgefield and Laurens, the combined legislature ruled that Chamberlain had won with 86,620 votes to Hampton's 85,521. Three days later, on December 7, Chamberlain was inaugurated. One week after that, the Wallace House, having adjudged Hampton the winner by 92,261 to 91,127 for Chamberlain (including the Edgefield and Laurens votes) also inaugurated *him* as governor.

With all this drama being enacted in the House of Representatives, Elliott must have wished he were still speaker so that it could have been the Elliott House instead of the Mackey House (especially since E. W. M. Mackey was not one of his favorite Republicans). However, sitting in the attorney general's office next to the governor himself, Elliott was, if not at the very center of the excitement, certainly very much in the mainstream of the fast-moving events taking place during that fateful December of 1876. And by that time, drawn together by the terrible odds they were facing, he and Chamberlain had at last developed a viable working relationship.

One paragraph of Chamberlain's inaugural address had stirred particular controversy—as if any more controversy was needed in the state at that time: "The gentleman who was my opponent for this office in the late election," said Chamberlain in his speech, "has recently declared, as I am credibly informed, that he held not only the peace of the city and state, but my life in his hand. I do not doubt the truth of his statement," concluded Chamberlain. "My life can be easily taken." Wade Hampton pronounced the statement "infamously false"; he had never said anything of the sort.[3] However, the person who had "credibly informed" Chamberlain was Robert B. Elliott.

In response to Hampton's denial, Chamberlain requested that Elliott write a letter stating, as nearly as he could recall, everything that had taken place in the conversation between himself and Wade Hampton. It had occurred, wrote Elliott, on "Thursday the 30th ult"; Elliott had been standing near the door of the House of Representatives (probably watching the Dual House in action) when "General Hampton approached me and enquired if I were Mr. Elliott. I replied in the affirmative; whereupon he expressed a desire to confer with me for a moment." The two men, opposites physically, socially, and mentally (brains were never considered Hampton's long suit), having in common only their good manners, repaired to a small room to talk of the conditions in their state. General Hampton spoke of his ceaseless efforts to maintain order and of his hope for a peaceful solution to a difficult situation. "I joined him in the expression of such hopes," wrote Elliott, "and said that the efforts of the leading men on our side had been employed in like endeavors to maintain the peace."

After defining his position fully, Elliott continued, Hampton remarked that he considered Chamberlain to be responsible for the present state of affairs. He then said, as Elliott wrote Chamberlain, that he considered it "the duty as well as in the interest of leading colored men like myself to refuse our support and countenance to you, for, said he, 'I can protect the people of this State, black and white alike, while Chamberlain cannot protect either.' Continuing, he said further, '*Governor Chamberlain cannot protect his own life. I have had to protect him from the just indignation of the people, and if I were now to take my hands off the brakes for an hour, his life would not be safe.' "* [4]

Elliott ended his letter saying that his recollection of the above was strengthened by the fact that one Thomas Settle, a judge, had detailed to him a similar conversation that he had had with Hampton in which the same words Elliott had italicized were used verbatim. Judge Settle confirmed this in a letter to Chamberlain.

Parenthetically, it is worth noting the manner in which the white supremacist historian John S. Reynolds dealt with this episode when he wrote about it some twenty-seven years later: "When there arose a question of fact in relation to a charge made against Hampton by Chamberlain, the latter called Elliott as a witness whose words should settle it. Daniel H. Chamberlain, in order to impeach Wade Hampton, called as his own witness a man who had been false to every trust, who was fairly reeking with corruption, whose personal conduct was disreputable, and who had taken to wife a strumpet!" [5]

Commenting on this absurdity, W. E. B. DuBois, the Negro historian, later wrote that when "Reynolds runs out of accusations in attacking the character of a leading Negro statesman, he turns around and with adducing a single line of proof, calls his wife a strumpet." [6]

Immediately after Wade Hampton's inauguration as governor by the Democrats, he demanded that Chamberlain deliver up to him "the Great Seal of the State together with the possession of the Statehouse." Chamberlain refused: "I do not recognize in you any right to make the foregoing demand," he wrote to Hampton, "and I hereby refuse compliance therewith." [7]

While South Carolina was thus faced with the unparalleled situation of having two chief executives, the United States of America faced the even more extraordinary circumstance of having no president-elect.

Despite Democratic candidate Tilden's popular majority of two hundred fifty thousand, he still needed one more electoral vote to win the presidency, whereas Hayes still needed the combined electoral votes of Florida, Louisiana, and South Carolina to win. In all of these Republican states the boards of canvassers were under heavy pressure from visiting delegations of Republican politicians to certify the electoral majorities for Hayes. (South Carolina's Board of Canvassers needed no particular pressure; it will be remembered that they had certified on the face of the returns that even *with* the Edgefield and Laurens vote, which gave the governorship to Hampton, Hayes had won the presidential electoral vote.) By the end of November, the Republican boards of canvassers of all three states had determined that Hayes was the victor. In each state, however, there were Democrats (such as Hampton) who, considering themselves the winners, sent in their own returns certifying Tilden.

Matters thus stood at an impasse. The Constitution provides that in the case of such contested elections, the votes should be opened and counted by the legislative branch. But in the Forty-fourth federal Congress, where the House of Representatives was strongly controlled by Democrats and the Senate equally strongly by Republicans, the two bodies could not come to terms on any fair method of counting the votes and settling the dispute. After many weeks of frustrating debate, the stalemate was finally broken by the passage, on January 25, 1877, of an Electoral Count Act. This bill provided for the creation of an Electoral Commission to be composed of five senators, five representatives, and five justices of the Supreme Court who would rule on the returns and make the final determination as to who was to be the next president of the United States.

It was accepted that the Senate would choose three Republicans and two Democrats and the House three Democrats and two Republicans for the Electoral Commission. Four Supreme Court judges, two Republican and two Democratic, were to select the fifth judge, who would be the fifteenth member of the commission and the key man, since he would cast the decisive vote.

The one Indepedent on the Supreme Court was Justice David Davis, and it was agreed by both parties that he would be a satisfactory fifteenth man. However, on the evening that the Electoral Count Act was voted on in Congress, Judge Davis suddenly announced that he was retiring from the Supreme Court, having that very day been elected by the legislature of the state of Illinois to the Senate of the United States.* That made him unavailable for

---

* Independents were obviously a scarce commodity at the time. The Illinois legislature turned to Davis after having been deadlocked for several weeks with neither party able to muster a majority.

duty on the commission and left only the four remaining justices of the Supreme Court—all of whom were Republicans. But the Electoral Count Act had passed and there was no turning back for the Democrats. They were somewhat mollified, however, when Justice Joseph P. Bradley was chosen, since, although a Republican, his decisions had seemed decidedly favorable toward Southern interests; for example, he had written the opinion against the constitutionality of the Ku Klux Act.

The Electoral Commission did not cast its first vote until February 8, 1877. In the meantime, confusion and bitterness dominated the political scene throughout the nation. In South Carolina conflict over the rightful possession of the statehouse continued. The *News and Courier,* which had by mid-December begun to refer to the Democratic Wallace House as the Constitutional House and the Republican Mackey House as the Bayonnet House, daily ran stories on its front page describing the activities of the two rival bodies in highly partisan terms. Chamberlain, once the recipient of an equal bias in his favor from that newspaper, was now bitterly denounced: "Is Chamberlain Insane?" asked the headline of a December 21 story. Certainly he was not. He was simply harassed and beleaguered almost beyond endurance.

For example, he could not collect the taxes he needed to maintain his government, for he was enjoined by the state Supreme Court from using public funds on deposit in the banks until his anomalous position as governor was clarified.* To this end Chamberlain initiated a ploy which he hoped would legally establish his right to the statehouse. He issued a pardon from the state penitentiary—the prerogative only of a governor—to an inmate named Peter Smith. When T. W. Parmelee, the superintendent of the penitentiary, refused to release the prisoner, Elliott as attorney general of the state (also as one of Chamberlain's chief strategists), along with United States attorney, David H. Corbin, petitioned in behalf of the prisoner for a writ of habeas corpus.

The case was heard before Judge Carpenter of the Third Circuit in the last days of December 1876.† The defense counsel opened

---

* Hampton meanwhile had put into effect a voluntary tax levy which the leading taxpayers immediately paid to him. By March 1877, he had collected $120,000.

† Carpenter, it will be remembered, had been a strong ally of Elliott's (the Patterson-Elliott-Carpenter Ring) in opposing Chamberlain and attempting in April 1876 to prevent him from being elected a delegate to the

by stating that the pardon of Peter Smith as signed by D. H. Chamberlain was "of no force or validity" because D. H. Chamberlain was neither in fact nor in law the governor of South Carolina and Wade Hampton was.[8] All the familiar arguments were then used by both sides; the face of the returns, the certificates of election, the legitimacy of throwing out the Edgefield and Laurens members—all factors which bore on the basic question of whether the Mackey House or the Wallace House had the legal right to inaugurate the governor.

In strict constitutional fact neither had that right, and when Elliott made his plea the thrust of his defense of Chamberlain was somewhat different. It was not possible, he maintained, to invalidate Chamberlain's claim without "sweeping away every vestige" of General Wade Hampton's claim. "If it should be held neither Hampton nor Chamberlain was properly inaugurated, this court cannot avoid the conclusion that there is no interregnum and that Chamberlain holds over, awaiting his successor," Elliott said. Then forestalling the expected rebuttal, he continued, "It is said that Chamberlain, in submitting to inauguration again, destroyed his status as it existed up to that time. If the office were different it might be, but here the offices are the same and it is only a question of whether he holds [office] now under his old status or the new." [9]

Such was Elliott's argument and such was the view that prevailed when on January 29, 1877, Judge Carpenter rendered his decision. He found that neither Chamberlain nor Hampton had been legally installed as governor of South Carolina and that, "as there has been no legal qualification of his successor, D. H. Chamberlain is lawfully in possession of the executive office and entitled to discharge the functions of same." [10] Peter Smith, almost a forgotten man in the case, was duly released.

The Republicans had but little time to savor this triumph. Ten days after Carpenter's decision (which the Democrats of course appealed), Wade Hampton pardoned a prisoner of his own. On February 9, Tilda Norris of Laurens County was ordered released from the state penitentiary. Superintendent Parmelee again refused to release the prisoner; her attorney petitioned for a writ of habeas corpus, and the entire scene was enacted all over again.

presidential nominating convention at Cincinnati. Now Elliott and Chamberlain were allies in a sense against Carpenter, whose antagonism to Chamberlain was well known.

Once more Elliott appeared, only in this instance he was on the opposite side. Although still in defense of Chamberlain, this time he was against freeing the prisoner. For reasons which are not clear, the case bypassed the Circuit Court and went directly to the state Supreme Court, where the Democrats had heretofore had a distinct advantage because two of the three judges were favorably disposed toward them. But when the Tilda Norris case came before the Supreme Court, Chief Justice Moses lay near death, so the final judgment could be arrived at only by agreement of the remaining two justices—Willard, who was outspokenly pro-Hampton, and Wright, who was black and pro-Republican.

When all the same arguments had been heard again (and by many of the same people), Judge Willard made the expected decision. On February 27, 1877, which was a Tuesday, he had an order written releasing Tilda Norris from the penitentiary, thus recognizing Hampton's right as governor to pardon her. With the words "I concur in the above," Judge Wright signed the order but asked that the actual filing of it be suspended until Friday (March 2) and that word of it not be made public until that day.

Both the Republican and Democratic press agreed that Wright acted under duress. The Republican *Daily Union Herald* claimed that he signed the order because he was in fear of Democratic reprisals against his life and the lives of his family if he did not do so.[11] The *News and Courier* claimed that he delayed making the order public because he feared Republican reprisals against his life and the lives of his family when the fact of his having signed the order became known.[12] The *Daily Union Herald* reported that by Wednesday, when Wright became convinced that his fears had been played upon by the Democrats, he sent for one friend (identified elsewhere as R. B. Elliott) and told him that he regretted having signed the order and that he intended to retract his signature and write an opinion denying the validity of the pardon granted to Tilda Norris.[13] The *News and Courier,* on the other hand, claimed that Wright was being subjected to a well-organized "system of espionage, persuasion, intimidation and cajoling" by Republican leaders.[14] It was also reported that he was being kept continually drunk—not a difficult feat, apparently. The most widespread rumor was that the lengthy new opinion which Wright attached to his statement, invalidating his original concurring signature, was the work of Robert Elliott.

Since the opinion closely paralleled Elliott's own briefs in the two habeas corpus cases, since it accorded more with his form and diction than with Wright's own "abrupt style and original etymology," and since Elliott had apparently been in around-the-clock attendance on Wright during the critical few days, the rumor was doubtless true.[15]

In any event, whosoever work it was, neither the opinion nor Wright's about-face did much to strengthen Chamberlain's situation. On March 2, Judge Willard, having waited as long as he had agreed to, caused the original order, as signed by himself and Wright, to be placed upon the record of the court and ordered Tilda Norris to be released forthwith.

In Washington, on the same day, a more devastating blow was dealt to Chamberlain, and indeed to all Southern Republicans, although at first glance it may have appeared to be a victory for their cause. On March 2 the Electoral Commission formally declared the Republican nominee, Rutherford B. Hayes, the next president of the United States. Behind this declaration lay a tangled web of partisanship and intrigue which led to what would be known in history as the Compromise of 1877.

The first of the three contested Southern states which the Electoral Commission had considered was Florida, and on the eve of their first vote, extreme tension prevailed in Washington as both parties waited to see how the fifteenth man—Judge Bradley— would cast his ballot.

An in-the-know Democrat who had read Bradley's opinion on the Florida case the night before he gave it, said that it was "in favor of counting the votes of the Democratic electors for the state of Florida," which automatically meant that Tilden, who needed but one more electoral vote, would be the next president.[16] However, when the commission met on February 8, Bradley had apparently changed his mind and his opinion; in the last sentence he pronounced himself in favor of the Republican electors in Florida, and the commission vote of eight to seven upheld this decision. If this strictly partisan voting pattern held in the commission's votes on Louisiana and South Carolina—and both parties had every reason to think it would—Tilden would never get his one vote and Hayes would get the nineteen necessary to elect him.

The frustrated and furious Northern Democrats at once started a filibuster in the House of Representatives, hoping to slow down and eventually prevent the completion of the Electoral Commission's count. To succeed in their purpose, they needed full cooperation from the Southern Democrats, but gradually it became apparent that they were not going to get it. The Southern Democrats had other ideas. They saw some advantages to their own interests —which were, after all, quite different from those of the Northern Democrats—in playing ball, albeit discreetly, with the Republicans.

A series of complex maneuvers thus began between certain Southern Democrats and certain highly placed Republicans. The result, summarized in much simplified terms, was that the Southerners expressed their willingness not to block Hayes's election by joining the Northerners in the filibuster if the Republicans would promise four major concessions: first, to remove federal troops from the South; second, to appoint more Southern Democrats to federal offices; third, to channel federal funds and private Northern capital into the rebuilding of the South; fourth, to let the Southern whites handle the Negro problem.

This then was the accord—the Compromise of 1877—never explicitly stated, but implicitly and widely understood, which led to the formal declaration two days before the inaugural date of Rutherford B. Hayes as the nineteenth president of the United States.

On April 3 President Hayes made good on the first of the compromises. He informed Chamberlain that all federal troops would be ordered out of South Carolina one week hence, on April 10.

Chamberlain had just come back from Washington, where both he and Wade Hampton—separately—had conferred with Hayes; he knew that the removal of troops was going to be ordered, but still he hung on. An Associated Press dispatch from Washington, dated April 8, reported that there were "new complications in the South Carolina affair" because Chamberlain and his advisers continued to assert his claim as governor. On Monday, April 9, Chamberlain was closeted for most of the day with Elliott, Cardozo, and the other state officers: John R. Tolbert, superintendent of education; James Kennedy, adjutant and inspector general; Thomas C. Dunn, comptroller general; and H. E. Hayne, secretary of state.

On the following day these men wrote Chamberlain a letter which was published in both the Democratic and Republican press. Since Elliott's name appeared first among the six signers, it was understood, according to tradition, that he was the author of the fateful letter which finally counseled Chamberlain to resign:

> While we are no less inspired with admiration for the dignified and resolute manner in which you have consistently maintained your claim . . . than we are solemnly impressed with the validity of your title to the office, we are unanimous in the belief that to prolong the contest . . . will be to incur the responsibility of keeping alive partisan prejudices which are in the last degree detrimental to the best interest of the people of the State. . . . We are agreed therefore in counselling you to discontinue the struggle for the occupancy of the gubernatorial chair, convinced as we are that in view of the disastrous odds to which its maintenance has been subjected by the action of the National Administration, your retirement will involve no surrender of principle, nor its motive be misapprehended by the great body of that political party to which, in common with ourselves, you are attached, and whose success in the past in this State has been ennobled by your intelligent and unselfish service.[17]

This letter was written and received on the day the troops were formally withdrawn. The complete loss of federal support plus the well-reasoned counsel of his advisors left Chamberlain with little choice but to capitulate. On that same day he renounced his office. In an "Address to the Republicans of South Carolina" he bitterly excoriated Hayes: "Today—April 10, 1877—by order of the President whom your votes alone rescued from overwhelming defeat, the Government of the United States abandons you, deliberately withdraws from you its support, . . . and by the withdrawal of troops now protecting the State from domestic violence, abandons the lawful Government of the State to a struggle with insurrectionary forces too powerful to be resisted." [18]

The *News and Courier,* commenting editorially on Chamberlain's understandably harsh valedictory, wrote that "instead of dying decently, he savagely turned upon the Administration, and fiercely arraigns that policy of justice and law which the whole country approves and praises." [19]

And the tragedy was that a large majority in the country really did approve and praise Hayes's policy of conciliation. The Compromise of 1877 could never have been reached if the white population of the United States, North and South, Republican and

Democrat, had not been willing to abandon the Negroes and been ready to sweep the question of their civil and political equality neatly under the rug. After their "two hundred and forty-three years of suffering, anguish and degradation," the blacks had had eleven years of freedom since the Emancipation Proclamation and nine years since the Reconstruction acts to demonstrate their fitness as independent, responsible citizens. The whites believed that the blacks had not proved themselves and were glad of the opportunity to seize upon the shortcomings of the Reconstruction as evidence of the inferiority of the Negroes as a race. By 1877 the country was weary of the Southern question, sick of the race problem. We tried, the whites told themselves—*they* failed. The pattern was thus established.

Elliott and the other five state officers did not resign with Chamberlain because one aspect of their situation was different from his. They had been elected to their offices, even counting the votes from Edgefield and Laurens, which made them a good deal more difficult to get rid of, a fact which clearly gave Elliott a grim satisfaction and a determination to compel his enemies to force him out of office. To prove that James Conner, not Robert Elliott, had been elected attorney general of the state, the Democrats brought an action "in the nature of *quo warranto*." This legal phrase, little in use today, meant an action "addressed to preventing a continued exercise of authority unlawfully asserted." [20]

When the case first came before the state Supreme Court in mid-January, Elliott, the defendant, asked for twenty days to prepare his answer, and subsequently kept moving to have that time extended so that the case was still pending on April 11, when D. H. Chamberlain gave over the Great Seal of the State of South Carolina to Wade Hampton. One of the new governor's first official acts was to swear in James Conner as attorney general of the state. At once Hampton had his private secretary (and godson), Wade H. Manning, write to Elliott asking him to turn over the records and papers of his office to Mr. Conner. The tone of the letter was politely threatening. The private secretary begged to inform Mr. Elliott that "in the event of your refusing to take this course, he [Hampton] sees nothing in your present position entitling you to the use of the rooms and custody of the records of the office referred to and that he cannot consent to it. His responsibility for the proper discharge of the administration will require him to prevent such an obstruction to the conduct of government." [21]

Elliott's response was a masterpiece of injured innocence. The troops were gone, Chamberlain had ceded his office, the entire Republican structure in the state was crumbling; Elliott must have known his days in public life were numbered. Yet he put up such a bold front in his answer to Hampton that one would have thought the suggestion that he even consider giving up his office was—to use his own word—an "absurdity."

All five state officers had received similar letters from Hampton's private secretary. Cardozo and Dunn answered their own; Elliott included Tolbert and Kennedy in his response, which was written on official "Executive Department, Office of Attorney General" stationery. After briskly reviewing his and his co-signers' legal elections and the legal steps by which they had entered upon the duties of their offices, he pointed to the proceedings of the *quo warranto* instituted "by those to whom we had respectively been opposed as candidates for election to test the validity of our titles to such office." Since no determination of this matter had yet been reached, he could see no reason in law or in fact which would justify them in complying with the governor's wishes. "We are in no sense *claimants* for the various offices which we fill," he pointed out. "We are lawful possessors, and are in Court, not to seek to have our titles granted, but to maintain them against those who, as plaintiffs, are asking that we should be ousted. . . . It would be a legal absurdity for us to voluntarily shift position with our contestants, and would result, logically, in a complete abandonment of our rights." He therefore respectfully declined to accede to Hampton's request.

"We are not insensible to the fact that it is physically competent for the Governor to carry his wishes into effect by excluding us from access to our offices and their records," he wrote in his final paragraph; and concluded, "Whilst we shall make no resistance to such a process as that, should he determine to institute it, we trust that the same sense of 'responsibility for the proper discharge of the administration' which he pleads in advance as justification for the covert threat of force, will inspire him to pause before taking a step that will obviously trench upon rights guaranteed by that Constitution which he has sworn to obey." [22]

His tenacious, well-reasoned prose notwithstanding, Elliott knew that Hampton would indeed resort to force if necessary. The evening after he sent his letter, the *News and Courier* reported triumphantly that he and the other men had removed their private papers to their own residences.

The following day Hampton had their rooms sealed off, denying access to both the Republican incumbents and the Democratic claimants until the *quo warranto* should be settled. The Democrats meanwhile set up temporary offices in another part of the statehouse.

On Tuesday, May 1, 1877, at eleven o'clock in the morning, the Supreme Court of South Carolina heard the case of the *State ex rel James Connor, Plaintiff* v. *R. B. Elliott, Defendant, Action in the Nature of Quo Warranto.*[23] The sitting judges were still Willard and Wright, Wright having by then completely caved in to the overwhelming power of the Hampton forces. Considering the foregone conclusion of the case, the arguments on both sides were surprisingly lengthy.

The Democrats once again turned to their favorite county—Edgefield—where they contended that a "perversion of the ballot boxes" showed that Elliott had been defeated by an even greater number of votes than the original count had indicated. Dozens of managers of election boxes in Edgefield County were called to bear out the state's claim of "irregularities" in counting the ballots. Elliott's attorney, Thomas S. Cavender, brought his own set of managers to sustain his counterclaim that blacks who would have voted for Elliott were threatened at the polls and prevented from voting at all. But his was a futile exercise, as all the parties concerned must have realized. The Democrats contrived to "prove" that Elliott lost by enough votes in Edgefield County to wipe out his statewide majority (which admittedly had been small), and thereby to declare James Conner the victor.[24]

The final disposition of the *Conner* v. *Elliott Quo Warranto* read, "And now on this first day of May A.D. 1877 comes the Defendant [Elliott] and withdraws his answer herein and consents that Plaintiff have the judgment prayed for; and the said Supreme Court so orders. Whereupon it is considered and adjudged by the said Court that the Defendant be ousted from the office of Attorney General of the State of South Carolina and the Plaintiff is entitled to hold, use, exercise and enjoy the said office, and that he be let into the possession thereof." [25] Similar orders were entered against the other five state officers.

With the defeat of these last Republican holdouts, the Reconstruction came to an end in South Carolina, as it virtually already had in all the other Southern states. The noble endeavor, undertaken to assure the freedmen of their rightful place as citizens of the United States, was concluded. Only the Fourteenth and Fifteenth amendments remained as permanent monuments to that nine-year effort. To the Southern whites the collapse of Reconstruction meant the end of their "Tragic Era"; to the Southern blacks it meant the beginning of theirs. For America's more than four million Negroes the giant step backward, which so many of them had valiantly fought to prevent, had finally been taken.

15

In the Midst of His Years

D URING the next two years Elliott struggled to make his
living as a lawyer, concentrating his efforts in his Orangeburg firm, Elliott, Stewart, and Straker. Elliott's two young partners and warm friends, T. McCants Stewart and Daniel A. Straker,
were both excellent lawyers; neither had been much involved in
the affairs of state (Straker was barred from holding elective office
as a native Barbadian), but each had been active in the Republican party and, unlike Elliott, had been strongly pro-Chamber-
lain. With three such men of exceptional intellect and ability, there
was every reason why their law firm should have done well. But
the climate in which Negro attorneys in South Carolina could
prosper—could even exist—was gone. This is not to say that automatically, with the failure of Reconstruction, the blacks lost all
their civil and political rights. That came about gradually.

The Democrats, having gotten rid of the Negroes in the executive arm of the state government, speedily moved to the judiciary
to impeach and remove J. J. Wright from the Supreme Court on a
charge of drunkenness. Then, on one pretext or another, they
forced resignations of enough Republican legislators to gain control of both branches of the General Assembly. Their next order
of business was to initiate the giant investigation of public frauds,
the findings of which have been frequently alluded to. The investigation produced volumes of self-righteous propaganda for the

Democrats and, more firmly than ever (if that is possible), stigmatized the Republican party in the public mind as venal, incompetent, and degraded. Despite the hundreds of witnesses who were called and the reams of testimony collected against the Radical Republicans during Reconstruction, only twenty-five of them were indicted; of this number, only three were convicted: two blacks, Francis L. Cardozo and Robert Smalls, and one white, L. Cass Carpenter. These men were later pardoned and never served any part of their jail sentences.

Elliott was called before the investigating committee only once; he was not charged with any specific misdemeanor, but was referred to throughout the *Report on Public Frauds* in the most disparaging terms as an unscrupulous corruptionist.

Elliott probably bore the frankly vindictive tactics of the Democratic legislators toward their Republican predecessors more stoically than he did the kindly, patronizing *noblesse oblige* of Wade Hampton. Despite Hampton's basic doctrine of white supremacy and black inferiority, the governor tried, within the boundaries of these beliefs, to carry out a policy of conciliation toward the blacks. He did appoint a number of Negroes (mostly Democrats) to public office, although always to minor public office, being careful, as the *News and Courier* suggested, to "avoid putting colored persons in positions where they would, or could be, peculiarly offensive." [1] Hampton had promised in his campaign to protect the blacks and to continue to secure for them their rights, and he made a staunch effort to carry out this worthy, if essentially negative, pledge. But he was hampered and eventually disarmed of his purpose by the Negrophobes in his party—white supremacists like Martin Gary and M. C. Butler who wanted nothing less than the denial of the Negroes' constitutional right to vote. Various strategems were speedily put into practice to accomplish this disfranchisement.

By the time of the 1878 bi-election, many voting precincts which had large Republican majorities had been simply abolished. Blacks and the comparatively few remaining white Republicans had to walk as much as twenty miles to vote. Even more devastating was a new voting device adopted by the South Carolina legislature in what was known as the Eight Box Law. At every polling place there were as many boxes as there were officers to be elected; the voter was compelled, unassisted, to place a separate ballot in each appropriate box. As calculated, a vast number of unlettered or unsophisticated Negroes made the inevitable mistakes which invalidated their ballots.

Within a few years after Reconstruction, the blacks, according to Elliott, were "but citizens in name and not in fact." [2] Even then the militant white supremacists were not satisfied; they would not feel secure until they could disfranchise the Negro population as thoroughly as possible without openly defying the laws of the federal government. Ultimately, in 1895, South Carolina held a convention to write a new constitution which embodied a series of rigid voting requirements. The poll tax, which Elliott had once successfully staved off, was to be stringently enforced; suffrage was denied to anyone who did not pay tax on at least $300 worth of property. Literacy tests far more severe than any that Elliott had so vigorously objected to in 1868 were adopted. Voters were required to read and write out large sections of the state constitution. (However, ample provisions were made to waive these requirements for the many white citizens who could not comply with them.) By the late 1890s, the desired effect was achieved; the Negro was completely eliminated from public life in South Carolina.

Robert Elliott could not have foreseen, or at least would not have admitted to himself, that complete political extinction lay ahead for his race in the South from the moment Reconstruction terminated. He felt bound to try to hold the sagging Republican party together in South Carolina, if only to give it some slight leverage with the national organization. Although the Republicans did not put up a slate of candidates in 1878, they did hold a convention and continued to do so for the next few election years. But more and more the state party's activities became *pro forma* and their conventions empty gestures.

Meanwhile the law firm of Elliott, Stewart, and Straker had been forced to close its doors, so that by the fall of 1879 Elliott was in desperate financial straits. No doubt his plight was known to many in Columbia; some perhaps delighted in his misfortune as others sympathized. Luckily one of the sympathizers was a man who could do something tangible for Elliott. Early in September 1879, Ellery M. Brayton, the white collector of taxes in Columbia, wrote a letter to John Sherman, the secretary of the treasury, describing Elliott's circumstances and asking if he could be appointed to a post in Washington.*

"I appreciate all you say about General R. B. Elliott," wrote John Sherman in answer to Brayton's letter. "Cannot you give him some suitable employment in your office? It is not practicable to appoint him here at present, nor should he leave your state. I should be much pleased to approve any appointment you may be able to give him. Please advise Mr. Elliott of this request." [3] With such an endorsement from the top man, even bureaucratic machinery moved quickly. Within the month Elliott was hired by the Treasury Department to be a special inspector of customs based in Charleston. His salary was $144 per month. Having been a prominent statesman, close to the seat of power, Elliott now became a minor public servant in a relatively obscure post. For a man of such intense pride, he did not seem to have been greatly depressed by this comedown; on the contrary, Elliott appeared to really enjoy himself in his new job. His numerous letters to his immediate superior in Washington, A. K. Tingle, to whom he reported regularly on his activities, reflected his engagement with his duties.

His work consisted of inspecting various southeastern seaboard ports to ascertain that the proper duty on imported items was being collected and to assure that adequate security measures against smugglers were in force. The latter afforded him an opportunity to play adventurously at cops and robbers and to gratify a love of the sea and of boats which probably dated back to his days in the British Navy. Reporting to Tingle on the matter of smuggling around Charleston harbor, he wrote that on November 29 he had procured a boat and for four days had "proceeded to make a quiet but careful examination and inspection of the rivers, inlets and other entrances to Charleston." He was fully satisfied, he said, that there was but little chance for the landing of smuggled goods on the north side of the harbor. But on the south side the case was quite different because of inlets at Folly Beach and at Edisto where large vessels could "stand off in deep water," while a smaller craft, "a sloop or schooner in waiting, could run out and, under cover, receive goods liable for duty," then make its way through a series of backwaters—and Elliott carefully designated

* Unfortunately, Brayton's actual letter is not preserved, but the answer from Sherman makes its contents self-evident.

the depth of each river and inlet—to run smuggled "segars" [sic], for instance, into Charleston harbor.

The only way to prevent such practices, Elliott was convinced, was to have one or two "launches drawing not more than five feet of water" employed in patrolling the rivers and inlets South of Charleston." The revenue cutter then on duty was useless, he pointed out; for, besides being of too great draught, the vessel was so conspicuous that "she serves rather as a beacon light for smugglers." Whereas one of the small launches "could always nicely stow herself up any of these entrances and observe everything going on." [4] Had his advice been followed—and there is no indication that it was—it is a safe bet that Elliott would have found many excuses to be aboard the small launch himself, happily patrolling the waters around Charleston harbor and St. Helena Sound.

While perhaps reveling in the freedom of his new position, Elliott never put politics out of his mind. He had been on the job barely two months when, while on a "trip of observation and secret inspection" in Wilmington, North Carolina, he began some heavy canvassing for his superior, Treasury Secretary Sherman, who was an avowed candidate for the presidency in the forthcoming national election.

John Sherman, the younger brother of William Tecumseh, had had a long and distinguished career in public life. He had been a representative from Ohio from 1855 until 1861, and a senator until 1876, when President Hayes appointed him to his cabinet. A man of unquestioned integrity and financial acumen, he had greatly strengthened the Treasury during his four years as secretary; the unparalleled prosperity that he had helped to create in the country was such as to almost assure a Republican victory in 1880. As a result of his success, Sherman believed that the party, and particularly the business community, owed him a chance at the highest office. On Reconstruction matters he had been somewhat more moderate than the intense Sumner or the fiery Thaddeus Stevens, but nonetheless dedicated to the interests of the freedmen. Because he had always voted staunchly with the Radicals, he also felt he merited the support of the black members of his party from the Southern states.

It is difficult to say with certainty whether or not Sherman and Elliott knew each other personally when Elliott first became a

Treasury inspector. The tone of Sherman's response to Collector Brayton about finding Elliott a position suggested more than a slight acquaintanceship. But the letter Elliott wrote Sherman from Wilmington, North Carolina, which opened "My Dear Sir" and began with an apology for addressing him personally, indicated a quite distant relationship. In any case, after Elliott's letter, their friendship certainly ripened.

While Elliott was in North Carolina he had delivered the annual address at the Colored Industrial and Agricultural Fair at Raleigh and had afterward, as he reported to Sherman, met with a large number of leading blacks from many parts of the state to discuss their dissatisfaction with the way they were being ignored in Washington and denied federal appointments. On the matter of the presidency, Elliott wrote Sherman, "I entered the conference finding the general sentiment for Grant first [the former president was making the first try in the history of the Republic for a third term] and the second choice divided between Mr. [James G.] Blaine and yourself. I have the pleasure to say without extending this letter by entering into details, that I left it with the unanimous sentiment expressed that you are now their first and only choice." An organization was being formed, said Elliott, to educate the masses and bring the leaders into line. "Everything looks cheering and hopeful," he concluded. "I feel satisfied that with such a work as we shall put in during the present winter, North and South Carolina cannot be wrested from you by any other candidate." [5]

That letter was written on November 21, 1879, and, during the next few months, Elliott must have been busy trying to make good on his optimistic appraisal by persuading the blacks to vote for Sherman rather than for Grant, whom most of them still regarded as their savior, although perhaps only out of force of habit. Elliott's own shift of allegiance was not, as his detractors would insist, to polish the apple for his boss and improve his own situation in the Treasury Department. He favored Sherman over Grant because, at the same time that Sherman was denouncing the Bourbons for having used "midnight murder and masquerade" to perpetrate the shameful election frauds of 1876, Grant, returning from a twenty-six-month world tour, was taking an extraordinarily conciliatory attitude toward these same Southern whites.[6] Ironically, Grant was warm in his praise of Hayes's Southern policy, even though it had displaced the Negroes from power and was leading to their disfranchisement. Still more ironic was the fact that, as a result, numerous newspapers in the South (as well as some previously unfriendly ones in the North) endorsed Grant's third-term attempt, believing that only he could end sectional unrest. For Elliott the clincher must have been when even the ex-vice-president of the Confederacy, Alexander H. Stephens, his strong antagonist in the civil rights debate of 1874, came out for Grant. Grant's apparent courting of favor from Southern whites was in Elliott's mind the exact equivalent of Daniel Chamberlain's efforts to ingratiate himself with the South Carolina Democrats. Both represented the betrayal of the Negro by a Republican statesman. So, even if Elliott had been a storekeeper with no connection to the Treasury Department, he would have switched from Grant to either Blaine or Sherman. But since he was a Treasury agent, his espousal of Sherman was logical and also briefly rewarding, for it permitted Elliott once more—and for the last time—to play a role of some importance in the political arena.

When the Republican National Convention met in Chicago on June 1, 1880, Elliott was on hand not only as a delegate from South Carolina, but as a floor manager for Sherman in charge of wooing and winning black delegates. As each Southern Negro would arrive, Elliott and one or two other Treasury agents (among them Rapier of Alabama, who had also served in the House of Representatives) would greet the newcomer, see that he had proper lodging, food, and entertainment, and stay with him as much as possible to shield him from any but Sherman influences. Ample funds were provided for this "hospitality"; the *New York Times,* which was strongly pro-Grant, was very snide indeed about these efforts in behalf of Sherman, whom they considered at best an also-ran. The *Times* singled out Elliott for particularly caustic comment: "In the South Carolina delegation, which has always been counted in the Grant column, and to which it legitimately belongs, there is an intimation that ex-Congressman Elliott, a black man of great influence will, for the sake of a petty office, betray his race and his party by voting for John Sherman. Happily, however, he will not be able to carry any other men from the South Carolina delegation with him." [7] In this last the *Times* turned out to be more or less correct. Elliott did manage to persuade a few of the South Carolina delegates to follow him (Whipper, for one) but he actually had far greater success with the North Carolina contingent.

In addition to his managerial duties, Elliott also addressed the entire convention. Just after Sherman had been nominated by his fellow Ohioan, James A. Garfield, Elliott rose and by "unanimous consent" began a speech extolling the virtues of his candidate. He went far over his allotted time, but because he was generally regarded as the representative of the Negroes at the convention, the delegates did not interrupt him. The *New York Times* again, in its highly partisan comments, pointed to the fact that Elliott in his fulsome praise of the secretary had not mentioned his own position as a Treasury agent, nor did he allude to the fact that he had spent the last few months in that position furthering the ambitions of "his master." [8]

In any case, none of Elliott's activities in any capacity were of avail. Sherman went into the convention in third place behind Grant and Blaine and came out of it in fourth place. The Blaine-Sherman forces combined had managed to prevent Grant's nomination, and, as a result, to deadlocking the convention. After thirty-five ballots, the delegates turned to a compromise candidate, James Garfield (who had nominated Sherman), and on the thirty-sixth ballot he received the nomination. From Elliott's point of view the outcome was not a bad one. If it could not be Sherman, the next best thing was Sherman's friend Garfield. There was every reason to believe that the nominee recognized the failure of Hayes's Southern policy, and that he would try to correct it by faithfully observing the Fifteenth Amendment and seeing to it that all blacks had the opportunity to vote and to vote as they pleased.

The mess of pottage for which Elliott was accused of having, in effect, sold his birthright amounted to nothing more than a promotion—probably quite routine—from customs inspector to special agent at an increase in salary of $36 per month. However, coincident with his insignificant rise in station, Elliott seems to have run into a string of bad luck. First, "business of a domestic nature" made it necessary for him to leave Washington (where he had been briefly assigned after the Republican Convention) and proceed South. Next, he respectfully asked for leave for two weeks to permit him to visit his wife, who was "absent from her home under the care of a medical adviser." [9] After that there were financial problems: He was indebted to Messers J. H. Squier, Bankers of Washington City (as it was then referred to), for the sum of two hundred dollars. Would Mr. Tingle please hold one hundred dollars out of his salary for the months of August and September and pay that money directly to Squiers?

Most serious of all, although perhaps not recognized as such at the time, was an attack of malarial fever which he caught during an inspection trip to Apalachicola, Florida. A letter from his doctor in Charleston written to A. K. Tingle on August 27, 1880, described Elliott as having returned from Florida critically ill with "Williams Remittant Fever," and Elliott himself wrote to Tingle on September 14, "I have been very ill indeed with malarial fever contracted in Florida. Today is my first day out of bed since my return here on the 26th. My physician thinks I will be all right again in about a week's time." Unfortunately, that was but the first of many bouts with the fever.

Nor were his financial problems solved. While he was lying in bed, a complaint that ex-Governor Scott had filed three years earlier against Grace Elliott for a decree of foreclosure and sale of the premises on Taylor Street in Columbia came to trial. The judge ruled that the property should be sold by a master in bankruptcy "at public outcry" on October 4, 1880. The Elliotts had long since moved from Taylor Street, but apparently they had never repaid Robert Scott for the mortgage he held on the property. But by this time, clearly, Elliott had no money. The house was sold, after having been conspicuously advertised; Scott's claim was settled.

In the spring came yet another embarrassment when a Charleston man named Louis Dunneman wrote to the secretary of the Treasury (by that time John Sherman had been replaced by William Windom) complaining that Robert Elliott had failed to repay a debt to him. Furthermore, Dunneman charged that Elliott had borrowed money from him on the pretext that he needed it "for government purposes." In response, Elliott acknowledged with no reservations that the amount of money Mr. Dunneman claimed was due him was absolutely correct, but denied most positively that he had obtained the loan for government purposes. What he had told Mr. Dunneman was that he needed cash to pay his way to Florida, where he had been ordered by the Treasury to do an inspection job. Then, as now, the federal government in its wisdom did not advance money for official trips and, as a result, minor employees like Elliott were often without ready cash to pay for trips. As justification for not having repaid Mr. Dunneman, Elliott cited very large expenses entailed by his wife's illness, which compelled him to "keep her at a long distance from home for many months under surgical treatment." However, he assured his superiors he was at the moment "perfecting arrangements to meet Mr. Dunneman's claim to the uttermost farthing." [10] (This was a rare instance of Elliott's use of a British term.)

Despite all his personal problems—including a second bout of malarial fever in April 1880—Elliott still had the spunk to put up spirited fights for others. He wrote to John Sherman directly, for example, asking for a job as day inspector for one L. L. Guffin, a reliable white Republican of South Carolina who had "suffered very much on account of his opinions" and who had been one of the few men who stood faithfully beside Sherman at the Republican Convention. He recommended to his supervisor, Tingle, that the pay of the bargemen in Charleston be increased from $35 to $40 per month, pointing out that they had once received $60 per month and, from that high, had gone steadily downward until they reached $30; after which they went up to $35 only because their employers found that that was the going rate in Savannah, Charleston's rival city in all matters.

Shortly after his own appointment, Elliott had started wheels moving to secure jobs for R. H. Gleaves, who had been lieutenant governor of the state at the end of Reconstruction, and for his friend and law partner, D. A. Straker. Both men were hired as special inspectors in Charleston; Elliott was technically their superior when he became special agent, and as such he guarded their rights and interests (especially Straker's) assiduously, probably irritating his superiors in Washington by his constant intercessions in their behalf.

The most prestigious occasion for Elliott during 1881 came in January when he led a delegation of black leaders to Ohio to wait upon President-Elect Garfield to discuss with him the pressing needs of their race. Straker and Samuel Lee, who had been speaker of the House, were the South Carolina men in the delegation, which also included representatives from Texas, Georgia, Florida, Virginia, and North Carolina. As the spokesman for the group, Elliott was the one to address the president-elect. Although his speech seemed unduly stiff and formal for the occasion, which was simply a meeting at Garfield's home in Mentor, just outside of Cleveland, it was nonetheless arresting. Throughout, Elliott stressed that in the Southern states the rights of the *majority* were being "illegally and wantonly subverted" by the "imperious will of an unscrupulous *minority*." * The words had a strange ring; for, in the four

* Author's emphasis.

short years since the end of Reconstruction, the public had already ceased to think of the Southern Negroes as a majority, so effectively and so determinedly had they been forced into a minority role. But Elliott was not deluded; over and over he made pointed use of the terms, reminding Garfield that it was the majority who remained loyal to the country of which they were citizens, and to the Republican party, which had saved the nation; it was the majority who would "preserve the results accomplished by the late war." Had he but realized it, Elliott was stating a truth about the Negro's loyalty to his country, a loyalty which would remain constant for the next century. Through the years, in the South, the black man, who has had little reason to have faith in our form of government, has nonetheless remained loyal to the Republic and has tried to improve his status by working through the legal procedures of the system, while the white man has repeatedly in the twentieth century, as he did in the nineteenth, continued to take the law of the land into his own hands whenever it suited his purposes.

Because Elliott's own belief in the inherent value of the legal procedures of the system was paramount, he was particularly passionate when he spoke to Garfield of the way it was being subverted at the South. Not only was the Negro virtually disenfranchised, but it was becoming impossible for him to get a fair trial in the state courts. Blacks—the majority—no longer served as jurors; they had been eliminated as judges and as trial justices—eliminated in fact from the entire legal structure. White juries were composed of men who not only sympathized with the violators of the law, but who were oftentimes the violators themselves. Furthermore, Elliott pointed out that, even in the federal courts, wrongs against the blacks were permitted to pass unchallenged, while the "perpetrators of them go unwhipped of justice."

As a result of this condition, and because of the unfair treatment that blacks received at the hands of those who constituted the class of employers, Elliott warned that a spirit of unrest among his race was prompting many of them "to seek relief in strange and uncongenial parts of the country."

The other thrust of Elliott's charge to the president-elect concerned the inability of the Southern state governments to meet the educational demands of their citizens. Recognizing as he did the vital truth that "our children can only be rendered permanently effective by a general diffusion of education among our people," he urged the creation of a national system of education for the masses which would put control under the federal government instead of leaving the "enlightenment of the youth of the country solely dependent upon the changeful policies of political parties or the inadequate resources of state governments." [11]

Garfield, who knew Elliott personally, having served with him in the House of Representatives, responded emphatically, if somewhat patronizingly, to this point. Without speaking directly to questions of disenfranchisement or lawlessness in the South, he used a slightly trite analogy of the piers and stone abutments "sunk beneath the water and out of sight" which held up the "gaudy structure of a bridge" to illustrate the fact that education was the true foundation not only of all life's riches, but of its very essentials. It was true that Garfield did, during his short term in office, try to keep the principal of universal education in the forefront of his thoughts and actions; but such an objective, however lofty, was long range and did not ameliorate the immediate and growing problems facing the Southern majority.

The *New York Times,* unmindful of the disdainful manner in which they had described Elliott's activities at the Republican National Convention a few months earlier, reported on his and his fellow delegates' visit to Garfield with the utmost sympathy and approval. Not only Garfield, but "all who had met Elliott and the other colored gentlemen from the South, had been impressed with their unusual good sense, sagacity and patriotism," as well as with the earnestness and fairness of their demands.

For Robert Elliott this was to be the last such encounter—the last time his name would appear in the national press until his obituary was printed three and a half years later. A strong man who fought unceasingly and courageously for simple justice, his impact in the final years of his life was blunted, not through any failure on his part to raise his voice, but because he was in the end denied a platform from which to speak and be heard.

With no advance warning whatsoever, on May 20, 1881, Elliott was ordered to "transfer his station" from Charleston to New Orleans. On the face of it, this may have looked like a step upward, for New Orleans must certainly have been considered a more important port than Charleston (to everyone but Charlestonians). But even if it could be counted a promotion, Elliott did not view it as such. He received the news with obvious dismay, and at once wrote to A. K. Tingle to "respectfully request that if it is not inconsistent with your own feelings, you would grant me the opportunity to confer with you in person before ordering the transfer to be made." [12]

Plainly, Elliott did not want to be uprooted, partly, of course, for domestic reasons. Even though the Elliotts had not been able to afford to keep their expensive house on Lady Street in Columbia and had had to sell it in 1879, Elliott frequently spoke in his letters to the Treasury Department of going from Charleston to Columbia "to visit my family," so apparently he and his wife had kept some sort of residence in that city which both of them must have looked on as home. But more important than any purely personal consideration was his reluctance to leave his power base in South Carolina. And it was doubtless for precisely this reason that he was being ordered to New Orleans—to get him out of the state where he was known and revered by the blacks and where he could continue to exhort them to fight for their rights. The country had begun to find the endless "Southern problem" monotonous. In Washington, the administration, responding to this ennui, was not eager to have black leaders like Robert Brown Elliott in positions where they could stir up protests that would remind white citizens of a situation which almost all of them preferred to forget. So, despite Elliott's objections, and without even being given time to put his affairs in order, he was shifted to Louisiana, where he knew no one and had no following.

There were few of the old Radicals left in South Carolina to take up the slack of his departure. Francis L. Cardozo, who might or might not have done so if he had remained, had gone to Washington as a clerk in the auditing department of the Treasury. He later became the principal of a Negro high school in that city and fared better than most blacks after Reconstruction. Robert De Large had died of consumption before the end of Reconstruction. Alonzo Ransier, who had been both a United States representative and the lieutenant governor of the state of South Carolina, ended his days as a street cleaner in Charleston. He died in August 1882. Joseph Rainey, who had served longer in the Congress than any of the other blacks, was an internal revenue agent in Charleston until 1881, when he resigned and moved to Washington to try his luck in the brokerage business. He failed completely and returned to South Carolina with no resources and in broken health, to die in 1887 in Georgetown, the place of his birth.

Richard Cain had probably the most successful post-Reconstruction career. He left South Carolina in 1880 (after completing his term in the United States House of Representatives in 1879), having been elected bishop of the African Methodist Episcopal Church and assigned to Louisiana and Texas. In that capacity he helped found Paul Quinn College in Waco, Texas, and became its second president. He died in Washington in 1887.

Only two of the prominent black politicians remained in South Carolina: Robert Smalls and William Whipper, who, as it happened, were the bitterest of rivals. Because both lived in Beaufort, where Negroes outnumbered whites twenty to one (by far the largest black majority in the state), both remained in public life much longer than the other Negro statesmen. Whipper continued to practice law in Beaufort with a fair degree of success and ultimately made up in some small measure for having been denied his post as judge of the First Circuit by becoming a probate judge in his home county, an office he occupied for ten years. He was also vice-chairman of the almost defunct Republican State Executive Committee until 1889.

In a sense Robert Smalls inherited the mantle of Robert Brown Elliott as the most influential Negro in South Carolina. He had never played so dynamic a role as Elliott in the state, partly because he was a man of more limited intellectual capabilities (born a slave, he had received only a haphazard education in his adult years). But he was an extremely popular figure among the lowcountry blacks, and long after Reconstruction his faithful constituency continued to send him to the Congress of the United States, where he served until 1887.

Both Whipper and Smalls were delegates to the 1895 South Carolina Constitutional Convention. Along with three other blacks from Beaufort and one from Georgetown, they were the only Negroes—and the only Republicans—to attend. For Whipper and Smalls, who had been delegates to the 1868 Convention at which the great doctrine of universal manhood suffrage had been enunciated with such high hopes, it must have been painful indeed to sit by helplessly (their vigorous protests were of course in vain) while 154 white Democratic delegates officially adopted a program of voting restrictions, deliberately (and unconstitutionally, it would seem) designed to eliminate the Southern Negro as a voting citizen.

Smalls was the only one of the famous black Radicals to survive the turn of the century. A portly, courteous gentleman who is still remembered by some of that town's older residents, he was a customs inspector in Beaufort until his death in 1915.* One of Beaufort's public schools is named for him.

The three Reconstruction governors had all departed South Carolina by the time Elliott left for Louisiana in June 1881. Robert K. Scott disappeared promptly in 1877 to escape possible prosecution by the Democratic Committee on Public Frauds. He returned to Henry County, Ohio, and went into the real estate business. On Christmas Day 1880 he killed a young drug clerk, Walker L. Drury, whom Scott believed was responsible for leading his son to drink. (With his own weakness for alcohol, Scott need hardly have looked far for the person responsible for making his son a drunk.) The ex-governor pleaded accidental homicide and was acquitted after a lengthy trial. He lived his few remaining years in his native Ohio.

Franklin J. Moses was already hopelessly bankrupt by the end of his term as governor in 1874. With alleged liabilities of $92,000, his property was all sold at auction. In 1878 his wife divorced him (members of his family changed their names), and Moses went to New York, presumably in the company of a prostitute. He appeared unannounced one day at the offices of the *New York Sun* and offered to assist in the exposure of his former accomplices by selling to the newspaper accounts of corruption and graft in South Carolina.[13] From that time on his life went steadily downhill. He spent various terms in jail for passing bad checks and for other forms of swindle; he had also become a drug addict. He found his way eventually to Winthrop, Massachusetts, where, with his still-ingratiating manner, he managed a few good years as the town moderator and editor of a small local weekly paper. He finally died of asphyxiation in a sordid boardinghouse room.

In contrast to the misery suffered by his two predecessors, Daniel H. Chamberlain prospered. As soon as he was ousted from the governorship by Wade Hampton in 1877, he repaired to

* Rainey, Ransier, Whipper, and Smalls all have known grandchildren living today.

New York, where within a few months he became senior partner of the law firm of Chamberlain, Carter, and Eaton. Furious at President Hayes for his entire Southern policy and, in particular, for having removed the federal troops from South Carolina, Chamberlain soon extended his anger at the Republican president to the entire Republican party, chiding its leaders not only for having ended the Reconstruction, but even more for having started it in the first place. Fixing the blame particularly on Thaddeus Stevens and Oliver P. Morton for "putting the white Southerner under the heel of the black Southerner" (a phrase which was beginning to symbolize the Reconstruction in many minds), Chamberlain denounced their entire concept of reconstruction as a "frightful experiment which could never have given a real statesman any hope of success." [14] As he loosed his wrath on the Republicans, Chamberlain also became an outspoken apologist for the Southern Democrats: "My sympathy and judgment are with the Democratic party," he said; and, to prove it, he returned on several occasions to South Carolina where he was warmly received by the whites who welcomed him as one who had seen the light.[15]

Nothing could have justified Robert Elliott's mistrust of Chamberlain more than this complete reversal of his political affiliations, to say nothing of ideologies. But it is doubtful if even Elliott had fully understood the depth of Chamberlain's antipathy toward the Negro race. "The negro has been helped as no race has ever been helped before," Chamberlain wrote in 1890, only twenty-seven years after the Negro had been released from slavery. "He was set free by others, not by his own efforts. He was enfranchised by no efforts of his own. He had full opportunity to build up and protect his liberties. The whole power of the United States was at his call for eight years, and what was the result of it all? Am I wrong when I say the result was that the negro showed only weakness and unfitness for the task laid upon him?" [16]

Even more deplorable was Chamberlain's attitude toward the education a Negro should receive: "Primarily, and in nine hundred and ninety-nine cases out of one thousand, he does not need, in any proper sense of the words, literary, scientific or what we call higher education. . . . Give him, or rather stimulate him to provide for himself education suited to his condition; to wit, abundant training in the three R's; and after that, skill in handicraft, in simple manual labor of all kinds, which it is his lot to do—a lot fixed not by us, but by powers above us." [17] Such were the thoughts of a man whom the vast majority of Negroes in South Carolina had (with some notable exceptions) believed in and had twice elected to their state's highest office. Chamberlain died of cancer on April 13, 1907.

A disspirited and disgruntled Robert Elliott arrived in New Orleans on June 10, 1881. He had not wanted to come, had "not anticipated a transfer so far from my home." [18] (He was at least given ten days' leave to return to South Carolina, set his domestic affairs in order and move his wife to New Orleans.) To make matters worse, Louisiana, as Elliott knew even before he moved there, was a state in which the Republican party was torn by factionalism revolving around loyalty to or mistrust of William Pitt Kellogg, the highly controversial ex-governor who was then serving in the United States Senate and was thus in undisputed charge of all federal patronage. Elliott's boss in New Orleans, Special Agent D. A. Nevin, was a strong Kellogg man. Elliott, whether because he disliked Nevin personally or Kellogg by reputation, soon allied himself with the anti-Kellogg forces.

Having chosen the impolitic side of the fence, Elliott went on the warpath, apparently determined to demonstrate in his reports to Washington how just was the anti-Kellogg cause and how "confused the state of affairs" was in the Louisiana Customs District. Conditions on the levees of New Orleans were far from satisfactory; the bonded warehouses were deteriorating, security was lax, manifests were improperly filed. In two locations the collectors of port had recently died. In one station the port was in charge of an acting collector, an unfortunate man who was of advanced age and demoralized by "too frequent use of strong drink."

Gone was Elliott's verve, the sense of adventure which had characterized his early reports as a customs inspector. In South Carolina he had gone out of his way to praise and commend. In Louisiana everything and everyone was wrong. The wonder was that he lasted as long as he did. On April 29, 1882, eleven months after his transfer to New Orleans, Elliott acknowledged a letter from L. G. Martin, supervising special agent (fortunately the faithful A. K. Tingle was spared having to perform this duty), informing him that his services as special agent of the Treasury were discontinued and asking him to return to the government any public property in his possession. Elliott responded that he had two books, "one (1) copy 'Instructions to Special Agents' and one (1) copy 'List of Common Carriers, bonded for the transportation of Appraised and Unappraised Dutiable Merchandise.' The two articles above mentioned comprise all the public property in my possession." [19] It seems little enough to have accumulated after fourteen years of public life.

Elliott was now completely cast adrift. It was too late to turn back. He had no financial resources and no longer any cogent reason to move back to South Carolina. He had somehow to make his way in New Orleans. Ever resourceful, he managed to join up with a lawyer named Thomas de S. Tucker, whom he had first met in Pensacola, Florida, and establish the firm of Elliott and Tucker with offices at 13 (later 8) St. Charles Street. But it was a precarious living. For two years he contrived to pick up a bare existence as an attorney in the police courts of the city. As his fortunes declined, he moved from one residence to another, while suffering recurring bouts of the fever he had first contracted in 1880.

By the summer of 1884, the odds had turned completely against him and time had run out. He died of a final attack of malarial fever on August 9. He was forty-two years old. "He leaves a wife to mourn his loss," read his death notice. Friends and acquaintances were respectfully invited to attend the funeral, which took place at the "late residence of the deceased at the corner of Villere and Le Sharpe Street." [20] He was interred in the St. Louis Cemetery Number 2, a unique graveyard in that all the dead were buried above ground in vaults resembling little windowless houses— unique, too, in that blacks and whites alike were laid to rest there. If there was a tablet to mark Elliott's vault, it has been eroded by time and is no longer visible.

His obituaries were much as might have been expected. Most newspapers simply copied from the *New Orleans Daily Picayune* dispatch, which spoke of Elliott as a "well known and remarkable colored man," recounted the accepted facts of his life and briefly detailed the highlights of his career.[21] The *News and Courier,* however, gave a great deal of space to Elliott's death, headlining their report, "Another of the South Carolina Thieves Gone to his Account." From a long list of the abusive columns which they had written about Elliott in the past, they chose the most scurrilous to reprint as his obituary.[22]

At the other extreme was the lengthy front-page summation in the *New York Globe* (newest and most widely read of the national Negro weeklies) headlined "Gen. R. B. Elliott, Statesman, Jurist and Orator." Written by Elliott's friend and partner, T. Mc-Cants Stewart, it was an intimate, affectionate portrait of the man, honest in its recognition of his faults, admiring of his many virtues, and reflecting great pride in his brilliant achievements.

This notice brought forth a response from the eminent black leader Frederick Douglass to the editor of the *Globe,* thanking him for a "tribute . . . natural, unstrained and beautiful and felt. . . . Living as I have in an atmosphere of doubt and disparagement of the abilities of the colored race, early told that ignorance and mental weakness were stamped by God upon the members of the race, Robert Brown Elliott was to me a most grateful surprise, and in fact a marvel," wrote Douglass. "Upon sight and hearing of this man I was chained to the spot with admiration and a feeling akin to wonder. . . . To all outward seeming he might have been an ordinary Negro, one who might have delved, as I have done, with spade and pickax or crowbar. Yet from under that dark brow there blazed an intellect and a soul that made him for high places among the ablest white men of the age. . . . We are not over rich in such men and we may well mourn when one such is fallen in the midst of his years. I with thousands who knew the abilities of young Elliott was waiting and hoping to see him emerge from the obscurity of his later years and stand in the halls of the national Congress and there lift the standard for his people with a power which no other man of his day could do." [23]

Elliott could not have hoped for a higher accolade and, since he was not a conspicuously modest man, he would probably have felt the encomiums were well deserved. He was, however, a realistic man; he would have recognized how vain was Frederick Douglass's hope that he, Elliott, would again stand in the halls of Congress.

By the end of his life Elliott had faced the bitter fact that he and the other Southern black leaders were in almost total eclipse. During the first two decades of Negro freedom, these gallant statesmen had battled to erase civil and political distinctions between blacks and whites, but they had failed of their purpose. They were powerless to stem the flood tide of racial prejudice which coursed through the United States in the later years of the nineteenth century and which would threaten to inundate it in the twentieth.

Elliott had once warned that the rights of man were not held by a "perpetual or irrevocable charter, but were subject to constant hazards." [24] Revolutions can and do go backward, he said, and he was all too aware that the revolution to which he had devoted his life had faltered. He died knowing that the "mighty future" he had envisaged for his race was far from becoming a mighty present. He could not have imagined how far.

Key Political Figures
in South Carolina, *1868–1877*

(in the order of their appearance)

ROBERT BROWN ELLIOTT: black, delegate to Constitutional Convention, member General Assembly, assistant adjutant general, speaker of the House, attorney general, United States congressman.

RICHARD H. (DADDY) CAIN: black, delegate to Constitutional Convention, member General Assembly, United States congressman.

ROBERT SMALLS: black, delegate to Constitutional Convention, member General Assembly, United States congressman.

BENJAMIN F. PERRY: white, provisional governor (1865), member General Assembly.

ROBERT D. DE LARGE: black, delegate to Constitutional Convention, member General Assembly, United States congressman.

ALONZO J. RANSIER: black, delegate to Constitutional Convention, member General Assembly, lieutenant governor, United States congressman.

JOSEPH H. RAINEY: black, delegate to Constitutional Convention, member General Assembly, United States congressman.

THOMAS J. ROBERTSON: white, delegate to Constitutional Convention, United States senator.

A. G. MACKEY: white, president of the Constitutional Convention.

JASPER J. WRIGHT: black, delegate to Constitutional Convention, member General Assembly, associate justice state Supreme Court.

WILLIAM J. WHIPPER: black, delegate to Constitutional Convention, member General Assembly.

FRANCIS L. CARDOZO: black, delegate to Constitutional Convention, secretary of state, state treasurer.

FRANKLIN J. MOSES, JR.: white, delegate to Constitutional Convention, speaker of the House, adjutant general, member General Assembly, governor.

DANIEL H. CHAMBERLAIN: white, delegate to Constitutional Convention, attorney general, member General Assembly, governor.

CHARLES P. LESLIE: white, delegate to Constitutional Convention, member General Assembly.

B. F. WHITTEMORE: white, delegate to Constitutional Convention, member General Assembly, United States congressman (expelled).

E. W. M. MACKEY: white, delegate to Constitutional Convention, member General Assembly, Republican speaker of the Dual House.

ROBERT K. SCOTT: white, governor.

JAMES L. ORR: white, pre-Reconstruction governor, member General Assembly.

DAVID H. CORBIN: white, member General Assembly, United States attorney for the South Carolina District.

FRANCIS A. SAWYER: white, United States senator.

JOHN B. HUBBARD: white, chief of constabulary force.

JOHN B. DENNIS: white, ordinance officer.

S. L. HOGE: white, United States congressman.

C. C. BOWEN: white, delegate to Constitutional Convention, member General Assembly, sheriff of Charleston County.

ROBERT B. CARPENTER: white, Union Reform (Democratic) candidate for governor, circuit judge.

M. C. BUTLER: white, Union Reform (Democratic) candidate for lieutenant governor.

J. B. KERSHAW: white, chairman Democratic State Committee.

MARTIN DELANY: black, political leader.

JOHN J. (HONEST JOHN) PATTERSON: white, railroad entrepreneur, United States senator.

NILES G. PARKER: white, delegate to Constitutional Convention, state treasurer.

SAMUEL J. LEE: black, delegate to Constitutional Convention, member General Assembly, speaker of the House.

REUBEN TOMLINSON: white, member General Assembly, Bolter candidate for governor.

R. H. GLEAVES: black, member General Assembly, lieutenant governor.

SAMUEL MELTON: white, attorney general.

JUNE MOBLEY: black, member General Assembly.

JOSEPHUS WOODRUFF: white, clerk of the Senate and diarist.

FRANCIS L. DAWSON: white, editor of the *News and Courier*.

A. G. HASKELL: white, chairman Democratic State Committee.

WADE HAMPTON: white, governor.

WILLIAM H. WALLACE: white, Democratic speaker of the Dual House.

Bibliography

Abbott, Martin. *The Freedman's Bureau in South Carolina, 1865–1872.* Chapel Hill: University of North Carolina Press, 1967.

Aiken County Courthouse Records.

Allen, Walter. *Governor Chamberlain's Administration in South Carolina: A Chapter of Reconstruction in the Southern States.* New York and London: G. P. Putnam, 1888.

Ames, Blanche. *Adelbert Ames: 1835–1933.* New York: Argosy-Antiquarian, 1964.

Ames, Mary. *From a New England Woman's Diary in Dixie in 1865.* 1906. Reprint. New York: New York Universities Press, 1969.

"Appeal to the Honorable the Senate of the United States in behalf of the Conservative People of South Carolina, against the adoption by Congress of the New Constitution proposed for South Carolina." Columbia, 1868.

Aptheker, Herbert. "The Negro in the Union Army." *Journal of Negro History,* April 1947.

————, ed. *From the Reconstruction Era to 1910: A Documentary History of the Negro People in the United States.* Vol. 2. New York: Citadel Press, 1964.

Avary, Myrta Lockett. *Dixie After the War.* New York: Doubleday, Page, 1906.

Bancroft, Frederic A. *A Sketch of the Negro in Politics, especially in Mississippi and South Carolina.* New York, 1885.

Ball, William Watts. *The State That Forgot.* Indianapolis: Bobbs-Merrill, 1932.

Bardolph, Richard. "Social Origins of Distinguished Negroes, 1770–1865." *Journal of Negro History,* July 1955.

Barnwell County. *Clerk of Court Sessions Journal* (1857–71).

Beale, Howard K. *The Critical Year: A Study of Andrew Johnson and Reconstruction.* 1930. Reprint. New York: Frederick Ungar, 1958.

Bennett, Lerone, Jr. *Before the Mayflower: A History of the Negro in America.* Chicago: Johnson, 1962; Baltimore: Penguin Books, 1966.

———. *Black Power U.S.A.: The Human Side of Reconstruction, 1867–77.* Chicago: Johnson, 1967.

Biographical Directory of the American Congress, 1774–1961. Washington, D.C.: United States Printing Office, 1961.

Black, Henry Campbell. *Black's Law Dictionary.* 4th ed. St. Paul: West, 1957.

Blaine, James G. *Twenty Years of Congress, 1861–1881.* 2 vols. Norwich, Conn.: Henry Bill, 1884.

Bleser, Carol K. Rothrock. *The Promised Land: The History of the South Carolina Land Commission, 1869–1890.* Columbia: University of South Carolina Press, 1965.

Boston, Massachusetts. *City Directory, 1865–68.*

Botume, Elizabeth Hyde. *First Days Amongst the Contrabands.* Boston: Lee & Shepard, 1893.

Bowers, Claude G. *The Tragic Era.* 1929. Reprint. Boston: Houghton Mifflin, 1957.

Brown, William Wells. *The Black Man: His antecedents, his genius and his achievements.* New York: Thomas Hamilton, 1863.

Bruce, J. E., Papers. Schomburg Collection of Negro History and Literature, New York Public Library, New York.

Bryant, Lawrence C. "Negro Legislators in South Carolina, 1868–1902." Mimeographed. Orangeburg: South Carolina State College, 1967.

Buck, Paul H. *The Road to Reunion, 1865–1900.* Boston: Little, Brown, 1937.

Buckmaster, Henrietta. *Let My People Go.* New York: Harper & Brothers, 1941.

Bullock, Henry Allen. *A History of Negro Education in the South From 1619 to the Present.* New York: Praeger, 1970.

Campbell, Sir George. *White and Black: The Outcome of a Visit to the United States.* New York: R. Worthington, 1879.

Cardozo, Francis L. *Address before the Grand Council of the Union Leagues at their Annual Meeting, July 27, 1870.* Columbia: J. W. Denny, 1870.

Carter, Hodding. *The Angry Scar: The Story of Reconstruction.* Garden City, New York: Doubleday, 1959.

Chamberlain, Daniel H. *The Facts and the Figures: The Practical and Truthful Record of the Republican Party of South Carolina.* Campaign Document. October 12, 1870. Harvard College Library, Cambridge, Massachusetts.

———. *The Financial Management of the Republican Administration of South Carolina*. Campaign Document. August 19, 1870. Harvard College Library, Cambridge, Massachusetts.

————. *Present Phases of our So-Called Negro Problem: Open Letter to the Right Honorable James Bryce, M.P. of England*. Charleston *News and Courier*, August 1, 1904. Reprint. Charleston, 1904.

————. Papers. *See* Governor's Papers.

————. "The Race Problem at the South." *The New Englander and Yale Review*, June 1890.

————. "Reconstruction and the Negro." *North American Review*, 1879.

————. "Reconstruction in South Carolina." *Atlantic Monthly*, April 1901.

Charleston, South Carolina. *City Directory, 1867–72*.

Charleston Illustrated. Charleston: Walker, Evans & Cogswell, 1882.

Christopher, Maurine. *America's Black Congressmen*. New York: Thomas Y. Crowell, 1971.

Columbia, South Carolina. *City Directory, 1870–77*.

Congressional Globe, 1870–1872. Washington, D.C.: United States Government Printing Office.

Congressional Record, 1873–77. Washington, D.C.: United States Government Printing Office.

Cromwell, John W. *The Negro in American History*. Washington, D.C.: American Negro Academy, 1914. Reprint. New York: Johnson, 1968.

Crosland, Edward, Papers. South Caroliniana Library, University of South Carolina, Columbia.

Cruden, Robert. *The Negro in Reconstruction*. Englewood Cliffs, New Jersey: Prentice-Hall, 1969.

Current, Richard N., ed. *Reconstruction in Retrospect*. Baton Rouge: Louisiana State University Press, 1969.

Daniels, John. *In Freedom's Birthplace: A Study of Boston Negroes*. Boston: Houghton Mifflin, 1914.

Dawson, Francis W., Papers. Duke University, Durham, North Carolina.

De Santas, Vincent P. "The Republican Party and the Southern Negro, 1877–1897." *Journal of Negro History*, April 1960.

Dibble, Samuel, Papers. Duke University, Durham, North Carolina.

Donald, David. *Charles Sumner and the Rights of Man*. New York: Alfred A. Knopf, 1970.

————. *The Politics of Reconstruction, 1863–1867*. Baton Rouge: Louisiana State University Press, 1965.

Douglass, Frederick, Papers. Library of Congress, Washington, D.C.

————. *Life and Times of Frederick Douglass: His Early Life as a slave, his escape from Bondage and his complete history*. Revised Edition, 1892. Reprint. London: Collier-MacMillan, 1962.

Drothing, Phillip T. *A Guide to Negro History in America.* Garden City, New York: Doubleday, 1968.
Duberman, Martin. *The Uncompleted Past.* New York: Random House, 1964.
DuBois, W. E. B. *Black Reconstruction in America, 1860–1880.* 1935. Reprint. Cleveland: World, 1964.
————. *The Souls of Black Folk.* 1903. In *Three Negro Classics.* New York: Avon Books, 1965.
Dunning, William Archibald. *Reconstruction Political and Economic, 1865–1877.* New York: Harper & Brothers, 1907.
Durden, Robert Franklin. *James Shepherd Pike: Republicanism and the American Negro, 1850–1882.* Durham, North Carolina: Duke University Press, 1957.
————. "The Prostrate State Revisited: James S. Pike and South Carolina Reconstruction." *Journal of Negro History,* April 1954.

Elliott, Robert Brown. "An Address to the People of the United States Adopted at a Conference of Colored Citizens Held at Columbia, S.C., July 20 and 21st, 1876." Columbia: Republican Printing Company, State Printers, 1876.
————. Broadside. N.d. (Speech delivered February 16, 1874.)
————. Civil Rights Speech. *Congressional Record,* Forty-third Congress, 1st Session, January 6, 1874.
————. Letter to his wife, Grace Elliott, probated as his will in 1884. Civil District Court, Parish of Orleans, State of Louisiana.
————. Letter to John Sherman. John Sherman Papers. Library of Congress, Washington, D.C.
————. Letter to Ulysses S. Grant. E.6. Box 17. Henry E. Huntington Library, San Marino, California.
————. Letterbook of the Adjutant and Inspector General, 1869–70. South Carolina Archives, Columbia.
————. Letters to Governors Robert K. Scott, Franklin J. Moses, Jr., Daniel H. Chamberlain, Wade Hampton. South Carolina Archives, Columbia.
————. Letters to the Treasury Dept., 1879–81. National Archives, Record Group 36, Box #225, Bureau of Customs, Special Agents' Reports and Communications, 1865–1915.
————. *Oration Delivered at the Celebration of the Tenth Anniversary of Emancipation in the District of Columbia.* Washington, D.C.: H. Polkinhorn, 1872.
————. *Oration delivered in Faneuil Hall, April 14, 1874, under the auspices of the Colored Citizens of Boston.* Boston: Published for the Committee of Arrangements by Charles L. Mitchell, 1874.
————. Speech against Amnesty. *Congressional Globe,* Forty-second Congress, 1st Session, March 14, 1871.
————. Speech in favor of the Enforcement (Ku Klux Klan) Act. *Congressional Globe.* Forty-second Congress, 1st Session, April 1, 1871.

————. *Speech of Col. R. B. Elliott at Anderson Court House, S.C.* The Campaign in the Third Congressional District. N.d., probably Sept. 1870.

———— *et al. v. Connor.* Manuscript. Complete transcript of reference to Supreme Court, with judgment and affadavits. South Carolina Archives, Columbia.

Fast, Howard. *Freedom Road.* New York: Duell, Sloan and Peirce, 1944.

Fleming, Walter L. *Documentary History of Reconstruction.* 2 vols. Cleveland: Arthur H. Clark, 1906.

————. *The Sequel to Appomatox: A Chronicle of the Reunion of the States.* New Haven: Yale University Press, 1920.

Franklin, John Hope. *From Slavery to Freedom: A History of Negro Americans.* 1947. Reprint. New York: Vintage Books, 1969.

————. *Reconstruction after the Civil War.* Chicago: University of Chicago Press, 1961.

Freund, Paul A.; Sutherland, Arthur E.; Howe, Mark De Wolfe; Brown, Ernest J. *Constitutional Law: Cases and Other Problems.* Boston: Little, Brown, 1954.

Garland, Hamlin. *Ulysses S. Grant, His Life and Character.* New York: Macmillan, 1920.

Garner, James W. *Reconstruction in Mississippi.* 1901. Reprint. Baton Rouge: Louisiana State University Press, 1968.

Governor's Papers. Robert K. Scott, 1868–1872; Franklin J. Moses, Jr., 1872–1874; Daniel H. Chamberlain, 1874–1876; Wade Hampton, 1876–1878. South Carolina Archives, Columbia.

Graydon, Nell S. *Tales of Columbia.* Columbia: R. L. Bryan, 1964.

Green, Constance McLaughlin. *The Secret City.* Princeton: Princeton University Press, 1967.

Hampton, Wade. Letterbook. South Carolina Archives, Columbia.

————. Papers. *See* Governor's Papers.

Hennig, Helen Kohn, ed. *Columbia: Capitol City of South Carolina, 1786–1936.* Columbia: State Printing, 1966.

Herbert, Hilary A. et al. *Why the Solid South? or, Reconstruction and its Results.* Baltimore, R. H. Woodward, 1890.

Higginson, Thomas Wentworth. *Army Life in a Black Regiment.* Michigan State University Press (no location given), 1960.

Hirshson, Stanley P. *Farewell to the Bloody Shirt: Northern Republicans and the Southern Negro, 1877–1893.* Bloomington: Indiana University Press, 1962.

Hollis, John Porter. *The Early Period of Reconstruction in South Carolina.* Johns Hopkins University Studies. Baltimore: Johns Hopkins University Press, 1905.

Hyman, Harold M. *Stanton: Life and Times of Lincoln's Secretary of War.* New York: Alfred A. Knopf, 1962.

Hyman, Harold M., ed. *The Radical Republicans and Reconstruction, 1861–1870.* Indianapolis and New York: Bobbs-Merrill, 1967.

Jarrell, Hampton M. *Wade Hampton and the Negro.* Columbia: University of South Carolina Press, 1949.
Johnson, Allen, and Malone, Dumas, eds. *Dictionary of American Biography.* New York: C. Scribner's Sons, 1928–58.
Johnson, James Weldon. *The Autobiography of an Ex-Colored Man.* 1927. In *Three Negro Classics.* 1927. Reprint. New York: Avon Books, 1965.
Julian, George W. *Political Recollections, 1840–1872.* Chicago: Jansen, McClurg, 1884.

King, Edward. *The Great South.* Hartford, 1875.
King, W. L. *The Newspaper Press of South Carolina.* Charleston, 1872.
Korngold, Ralph. *Thaddeus Stevens: A Being Darkly Wise and Rudely Great.* New York: Harcourt, Brace, 1955.
Ku Klux Conspiracy: Testimony taken by the Joint Select Committee to inquire into the condition of affairs in the late insurrectionary states. Vols. 3, 4, 5. Washington, D.C., 1872.
Kutler, Stanley I. *The Dred Scott Decision: Law or Politics?* Boston: Houghton Mifflin, 1967.

Langston, John M. *From a Virginia Plantation to the National Capitol.* Hartford, Conn.: American Publishing, 1894.
Leland, John A. *A Voice from South Carolina: Twelve chapters before Hampton. Two chapters after Hampton. With a journal of a reputed Ku-Klux.* Charleston: Walker, Evans & Cogswell, 1879.
Lewinson, Paul. *Race, Class, and Party: A History of Negro Suffrage and White Politics in the South.* 1932. Reprint. New York: Grosset & Dunlop, 1965.
Logan, Mary. *Reminiscences of the Civil War and Reconstruction.* George Worthington Adams, ed. Carbondale: Southern Illinois University Press, 1970.
Logan, Rayford W. *The Negro in American Life and Thought: The Nadir, 1877–1901.* New York: Dial Press, 1954.
Lynch, John R. *The Facts of Reconstruction.* New York: Neale, 1913.
————. *Some Historical Errors of James Ford Rhodes.* Boston and New York: Cornhill Publishing, 1922.
————. "Southern Question. Reply to Mr. Lamar. Speech in the House of Representatives. August 12, 1876." Washington, D.C., 1876.

Mackay Family Papers, 1822–1926. South Caroliniana Library, University of South Carolina, Columbia.
McKay, Robert, Scrapbook, 1865–1887. "South Carolina Redeemed." South Caroliniana Library, University of South Carolina, Columbia.

McClure, A. K. *Recollections of a Half Century.* Salem, Massachusetts: Salem Press, 1902.
————. *The South: Its Industrial, Financial and Political Condition.* Philadelphia: J. B. Lippincott, 1886.
McPherson, Edward. *The Political History of the United States of America during the Period of Reconstruction.* Washington, D.C.: Solomans & Chapman, 1875.
McPherson, James M. *The Negro's Civil War: How American Negroes Felt and Acted During the War for the Union.* New York: Vintage Books, 1965.
Massachusetts Historical Society. *Proceedings, 1907, 1908.* Boston: Published by the Society, 1908.
Meier, August. *Negro Thought in America, 1880–1915.* Ann Arbor: University of Michigan Press, 1966.
"Memorial from the Labor Convention to the Honorable Senate and House of Representatives of the State of South Carolina. November 26, 1869." Manuscript. South Carolina Archives, Columbia.
Military Records of the Civil War, Colored Troops. National Archives, Washington, D.C.
Mitchell, Edward P. *Memoirs of an Editor.* 1924.
Moseley, J. H. *60 Years in Congress and 28 Out.* New York: Vantage Press, 1960.
Moses, Franklin J., Jr., Papers. *See* Governor's Papers.
Morgan, James Morris. *Recollections of a Rebel Reefer.* Boston and New York, Houghton Mifflin, 1917.

National Cyclopedia of American Biography.
New Orleans, Louisiana. *City Directory,* 1880–84.
Norton, Charles Eliot, Papers. Houghton Library, Harvard University, Cambridge, Massachusetts.

Pearson, Elizabeth Ware, ed. *Letters from Port Royal.* Boston: W. B. Clarke, 1906.
Pike, James S. *The Prostrate State: South Carolina Under Negro Government.* 1874. Reprint. New York: Harper & Row, 1968.
Ploski, Harry A., and Brown, Roscoe C., eds. *The Negro Almanac.* New York: Bellwether, 1967.
Post, Louis F. "A Carpet-Bagger in South Carolina." *Journal of Negro History,* January 1925.
Pratt, Fletcher. *Stanton, Lincoln's Secretary of War.* New York: W. W. Norton, 1953.
Proceedings in the Ku Klux Trials of Columbia in the U.S. District Court, November term, 1871. Columbia: Republican Printing Co., State Printers, 1872.
*Proceedings of the Colored People's Convention of the State of South Carolina, held in Zion Church, Charleston, November, 1865. * Together with the Declaration of rights and wrongs; an address to the people; a petition to the legislature, and a memorial to Congress.* Charleston, 1865.

Proceedings of the Constitutional Convention of South Carolina, held at Charleston, S.C., beginning January 14th and ending March 17th, 1868. Including the Debates & Proceedings. Reprint. Arno Press and the *New York Times,* 1968.

Recent Election in South Carolina: Testimony Taken by the Select Committee on Recent Elections in South Carolina. U.S. House of Representatives. *Miscellaneous Documents.* Forty-fourth Congress, 2nd Session. Report 175. Washington, D.C.: Government Printing Office, 1877.

Reid, Whitelaw. *After the War.* London: Sampson, Low, Son & Marston, 1866.

Revels, Hiram R. "Autobiography." Manuscript. Carter C. Woodson Papers. Manuscript Division, Library of Congress, Washington, D.C.

(A) *Review of the Resolutions of the Press Conference.* Charleston: William G. Mazyck, 1870.

Reynolds, John S. *Reconstruction in South Carolina.* Columbia: The State Co., 1905.

Rhodes, James Ford. *History of the United States, 1850–1909.* Vol. 7, *1872–1877.* New York: Macmillan, 1928.

Richland County Courthouse Records. Deed Books E, G, and H.

Rollin, Frank A. *Life and Public Services of Martin R. Delany.* 1868. Reprint. New York: Kraus Reprint, 1969.

Rose, Willie Lee. *Rehearsal for Reconstruction: The Port Royal Experiment.* New York: Bobbs-Merrill, 1964.

St. Clair, Sadie Daniel. "The National Career of Blanche Kelso Bruce." Unpublished thesis. University of Michigan, 1947.

Scott, Robert K., Papers. *See* Governor's Papers.

Shapiro, Herbert. "The Ku Klux Klan During Reconstruction: The South Carolina Episode." *Journal of Negro History,* January 1964.

Sheppard, William Arthur. *Red Shirts Remembered: Southern Brigadiers of the Reconstruction Period.* Atlanta: Ruralist Press, 1940.

Sherman, John, Papers, Library of Congress, Washington, D.C.

Siebert, Wilbur H. *Underground Railroad from Slavery to Freedom.* New York: Macmillan, 1898.

Simkins, Francis B. "The Election of 1876 in South Carolina." *South Atlantic Quarterly,* July 1922.

———. "The Ku Klux Klan in South Carolina, 1868–1871." *Journal of Negro History,* October 1927.

———, and Woody, Robert Hilliard. *South Carolina During Reconstruction.* Chapel Hill: University of North Carolina Press, 1932.

Simmons, William J. *Men of Mark.* Cleveland: George M. Rewell, 1887.

Singletary, Otis A. *Negro Militia and Reconstruction.* 1957. Reprint. New York: McGraw-Hill, 1963.

Smith, Samuel D. *The Negro in Congress, 1870–1901.* Port Washington, New York: Kennikat Press, 1940. Reissued 1966 by arrangement with the University of North Carolina Press.

Snowden, Yates, Papers. South Caroliniana Library, University of South Carolina, Columbia.

South Carolina. *Biographical Dictionary of the Senate of the State of South Carolina, 1776–1964.*

———. *Evidence Taken by the Committee of Investigation of the Third Congressional District Under the Authority of the General Assembly of the State of South Carolina, Regular Session, 1868–69.* Columbia: John W. Denny, Printer to the State, 1870.

———. *Journal of the House of Representatives of the General Assembly of the State of South Carolina.* July 1868–March 1870, November 1874–March 1876.

———. *Journal of the Senate of the General Assembly of the State of South Carolina.* July 1868–March 1870, November 1874–March 1876.

———. *Legislative System,* 1877. South Carolina Archives, Columbia.

———. *Minutes of Supreme Court,* April 1870 to November 1885. South Carolina Archives, Columbia.

———. *Report on Public Frauds. Report of the Joint Investigating Committee on Public Frauds and Election of Hon. J. J. Patterson to the United States Senate made to the General Assembly of S. Carolina at the Regular Session, 1877–78.* Columbia: Calvo & Patton, State Printers, 1878.

———. *Reports & Resolutions of the General Assembly of the State of South Carolina.* July 1868–March 1870, November 1874–March 1876.

Stampp, Kenneth M. *The Era of Reconstruction, 1865–1877.* New York: Alfred A. Knopf, 1966.

———, and Litwack, Leon F., eds. *Reconstruction: An Anthology of Revisionist Writings.* Baton Rouge: Louisiana State University Press, 1969.

Sterling, Dorothy. *Captain of the Planter.* Garden City, New York: Doubleday, 1958.

Still, William. *The Underground Railroad.* Philadelphia: Porter and Coates, 1872.

Stone, Chuck. *Black Political Power in America.* New York: Dell, 1968.

Styles, Fitzhugh Lee. *Negroes and the Law.* Boston: Christopher Publishing House, 1937.

Sumner, Charles, Papers. Houghton Library, Harvard University, Cambridge, Massachusetts.

Taylor, A[lrutheus] A[mbush]. *The Negro in South Carolina During Reconstruction.* Washington, D.C.: The Association for the Study of Negro Life and History, 1924.

————. "Negro Congressmen a Generation After." *Journal of Negro History*, April 1922.
Thompson, Henry T. *Ousting the Carpetbagger from South Carolina.* Columbia: R. L. Bryan, 1926.
Tindall, George Brown. *South Carolina Negroes, 1877–1900.* Columbia: University of South Carolina Press, 1952.
Tourgee, Albion W. *A Fool's Errand.* John Hope Franklin, ed. Cambridge, Massachusetts: Belknap Press of the Harvard University Press, 1961.
Trelease, Allen W. *White Terror.* New York: Harper & Row, 1971.

Ullman, Victor. *Martin R. Delany: The Beginnings of Black Nationalism.* Boston: Beacon Press, 1971.

Voegeli, V. Jacques. *Free but Not Equal. The Midwest and the Negro During the Civil War.* Chicago and London: University of Chicago Press, 1967.

Walker, C. Irvine. "Carolina Rifle Club." Charleston, 1869.
Washington, Booker T. *Up From Slavery.* In *Three Negro Classics.* New York: Avon, 1965.
Werlich, Robert. *"Beast" Butler: The Incredible Career of Major General Benjamin Franklin Butler.* Washington, D.C.: Quaker Press, 1962.
Wharton, Vernon Lane. *The Negro in Mississippi, 1865–1890.* Chapel Hill: University of North Carolina Press, 1947.
Whyte, James H. *The Uncivil War: Washington During the Reconstruction, 1865–1878.* New York: Twayne Publishers, 1958.
Wiley, Bell Irvin. *Southern Negroes, 1861–1865.* New Haven: Yale University Press, 1938.
Williams, Alfred B. *Hampton and His Red Shirts: South Carolina's Deliverance in 1876* (1927). Charleston: Walker, Evans & Cogswell, n.d.
Williams, George W. *History of the Negro Race in America From 1619 to 1880,* Vol. 2. New York: G. P. Putnam's Sons, 1883.
Williamson, Joel R. *After Slavery: The Negro in South Carolina During Reconstruction, 1861–1877.* Chapel Hill: University of North Carolina Press, 1965.
Wish, Harvey, ed. *Reconstruction in the South, 1865–1877. Firsthand Accounts of the American Southland after the Civil War, by Southerners and Northerners.* New York: Farrar, Strauss & Giroux, The Noonday Press, 1965.
Woodruff, Josephus, Diary of. Manuscript copy. South Carolina Archives, University of South Carolina, Columbia.
Woodson, Carter G. *Free Negro Heads of Families in the U.S. in 1830, Together with a brief treatment of the free Negro.* Washington, D.C.: The Association for the Study of Negro Life and History, 1925.

————. *The Negro in Our History.* Washington, D.C.: Associated Publishers, 1922 and 1928.

————. *Negro Orators and their Orations.* Washington, D.C.: Associated Publishers, 1925.

————, Collection. Manuscript Division, Library of Congress, Washington, D.C.

Woodward, C. Vann. *The Burden of Southern History.* Baton Rouge: Louisiana State University Press, 1960 and 1968.

————. *Origins of the New South, 1877–1913.* Baton Rouge: Louisiana State University Press, 1951.

————. *Reunion and Reaction.* 1951. Reprint. Boston: Little, Brown, 1966.

————. *The Strange Career of Jim Crow.* London: Oxford University Press, 1957.

Woody, R. H. "Behind the Scenes in the Reconstruction Legislature of South Carolina: Diary of Josephus Woodruff." *Journal of Southern History,* February and May 1936.

————. "Franklin J. Moses, Jr. Scalawag Governor of South Carolina, 1872–74." *The North Carolina Historical Review,* April 1933.

————. *Republican Newspapers of South Carolina.* Southern Sketches #10 First Series. Charlottesville, Va.: Historical Publishing Co., 1936.

————. "South Carolina Election of 1870." *The North Carolina Historical Review,* April 1931.

————. See also Francis B. Simkins and R. H. Woody.

Work, Monroe H. *A Bibliography of the Negro in Africa and America.* New York: H. W. Wilson, 1928.

————, ed. "Materials from the Scrapbook of William A. Hayne." *Journal of Negro History,* July 1922.

————, ed. "Some Negro Members of Reconstruction Conventions and Legislatures and of Congress." *Journal of Negro History,* July 1929.

NEWSPAPERS AND PERIODICALS

Beaufort Republican
Boston Evening Transcript
Charleston Daily Courier
Charleston Mercury
Charleston Daily News
Charlestown [Massachusetts] *Chronicle*
Daily Union Herald (Columbia)
Daily Republican (Charleston)
Harper's Weekly (New York)
Missionary Record (Charleston)
Nation, The (New York)
National Republican (Washington)

New National Era (Washington)
New National Era and Citizen (Washington)
News and Courier (Charleston)
New York Globe
New York Herald
New York Times
New York Tribune
New York World
St. Louis Globe
South Carolina Leader (Charleston)
Times-Democrat (New Orleans)
Washington Star

Notes

CHAPTER 1   A MAN OF MYSTERY

1. Quoted but not attributed, John W. Cromwell, *The Negro in American History* (Washington, D.C.: American Negro Academy, 1914), p. 179.
2. *New York Globe,* August 16, 1884.
3. *National Cyclopedia of American Biography.*
4. Cromwell, p. 179.
5. The most complete study of Boston Negroes is *In Freedom's Birthplace* (Boston: Houghton Mifflin), by John Daniels. This book published in 1914 would almost certainly have included some mention of Elliott if he had indeed been a native Bostonian.
6. Records of St. Louis Cemetery, Folio 256, New Orleans, Louisiana.
7. Letter of Lord Caccia, Provost, Eton College, November, 10, 1969.
8. Military Records of the Civil War, Colored Troops, National Archives, Washington, D.C.
9. The source of Miss LeBaron's information was an item in the *New York Times* of January 5, 1874, quoting from a letter sent by a reader in Rushville, New York. However, the Ontario County Historical Society in Canandaigua, New York, can uncover no facts to substantiate the story.
10. *Charlestown Chronicle,* February 18, 1871.
11. October 17, 1874.
12. Richland County Courthouse Records, Deed Books E, G, and H.
13. James Morris Morgan, *Recollections of a Rebel Reefer* (Boston and New York: Houghton Mifflin, 1917), p. 331.

CHAPTER 2   ALL COLORS AND CONDITIONS

1. Francis Butler Simkins and Robert Hilliard Woody, *South Carolina During Reconstruction* (Chapel Hill: The University of North Carolina Press, 1932), p. 39.

2. Ibid., p. 41.

3. *South Carolina House Journal*, Extra Session, 1865, p. 15, as cited in Simkins and Woody, p. 49.

4. *South Carolina House Journal*, Extra Session, 1865, as cited in A. A. Taylor, *The Negro in South Carolina During Reconstruction* (Washington, D.C.: The Association for the Study of Negro Life and History, 1924), p. 45.

5. *Proceedings of the Colored People's Convention of the State of South Carolina, held in Zion Church, Charleston, November, 1865*, pp. 24–31, as cited in Simkins and Woody, p. 55.

6. Whitelaw Reid, *After the War* (London: Sampson, Low, Son & Marston, 1866), Appendix A.

7. Kenneth M. Stampp, *The Era of Reconstruction, 1865–1877*, (New York: Alfred A. Knopf, 1966), pp. 121–22.

8. *Charleston Daily Courier*, March 1, 1866.

9. Simkins and Woody, p. 74.

10. Ibid., pp. 76–77.

11. 1860 Census.

12. *Charleston Daily Courier*, January 13, 1868.

13. Robert Brown Elliott, *Oration Delivered at the Celebration of the Tenth Anniversary of Emancipation in the District of Columbia* (Washington, D.C.: H. Polkinhorn, 1872), April 16, 1872.

CHAPTER 3   THE GREAT DOCTRINE OF MANHOOD SUFFRAGE

1. January 15, 1868.

2. *New York Times*, January 27, 1868.

3. *Proceedings of the Constitutional Convention of South Carolina, held at Charleston, S. C., Beginning January 14th and ending March 17th, 1868. Including the Debates & Proceedings* (Reprint, Arno Press and the *New York Times*, 1968), p. 6.

4. *Charleston Mercury*, February 5, 1868.

5. Ibid., January 28, 1868.

6. Ibid., January 29, 1868.

7. Ibid., January 28, 1868.

8. Ibid., January 21, 1868.

9. Ibid., February 20, 1868.

10. Ibid.

11. January 20, 1868, as cited in Francis B. Simkins and Robert H. Woody, *South Carolina During Reconstruction* (Chapel Hill: University of North Carolina Press, 1932), p. 90.

12. February 6, 1868.

13. *Constitutional Convention*, pp. 221–27.

14. Ibid., p. 229.

15. Ibid., p. 231.

16. Ibid., pp. 102–3.

17. *Charleston Daily Courier*, February 4, 1868.

18. *Constitutional Convention,* p. 391.

19. Abbott, Martin, *The Freedman's Bureau in South Carolina, 1865–1872* (Chapel Hill: University of North Carolina Press, 1967), p. 52.

20. W. E. B. DuBois, *The Souls of Black Folks* (1903), p. 38, cited in Abbott, p. 65.

21. *Constitutional Convention,* p. 379.

22. Ibid., p. 401.

23. Carol K. Rothrock Bleser, *The Promised Land: The History of the South Carolina Land Commission, 1869–1890* (Columbia: University of South Carolina Press, 1965), p. 22.

24. *Constitutional Convention,* pp. 508–9.

25. *South Carolina Leader,* November 25, 1865.

26. *Constitutional Convention,* p. 686.

27. Ibid., pp. 694–95.

28. April 2, 1868.

29. *Constitutional Convention,* p. 703.

30. Ibid., p. 707.

31. Ibid., p. 713.

32. Ibid., p. 719.

33. Ibid., pp. 730–31.

34. Ibid., p. 725.

35. Ibid., p. 734.

36. Ibid., pp. 826–27.

37. Ibid., pp. 924–26.

38. Ibid., p. 800.

CHAPTER 4   GOD SAVE THE STATE OF SOUTH CAROLINA

1. C. Irvine Walker (pamphlet) "Carolina Rifle Club" (1869).

2. April 2, 1868.

3. *Sumter Watchman,* March 26, 1868, as cited in Francis B. Simkins and Robert H. Woody, *South Carolina During Reconstruction* (Chapel Hill: University of North Carolina Press, 1932), p. 107.

4. As reported in the *Charleston Daily Courier,* April 9, 1868.

5. Ibid.

6. John P. Hollis, *The Early Period of Reconstruction in South Carolina,* Johns Hopkins University Studies (Baltimore: Johns Hopkins University Press, 1905), p. 104.

7. John S. Reynolds, *Reconstruction in South Carolina* (Columbia: The State Co., 1905), p. 93.

8. Printed in Columbia, South Carolina, 1868.

9. Cited in Simkins and Woody, p. 109.

10. July 7, 1868.

11. Robert F. Durden, Introduction to James S. Pike, *The Prostrate State: South Carolina Under Negro Government* (1874; reprint, New York: Harper & Row, 1968).

12. Pike, p. 18.

13. Ibid., p. 19.

14. Claude Bowers, *The Tragic Era* (1929; reprint, Boston: Houghton Mifflin, 1957), pp. 354–55.

15. As quoted in the *Charleston Daily Courier*, July 10, 1865.

16. *The Tragic Era*, p. 354.

17. *Charleston Daily News*, August 17, 1868.

18. Ibid.

19. Ibid.

20. Alfred B. Williams, *Hampton and His Red Shirts: South Carolina's Deliverance in 1876* (Charleston: Walker, Evans & Cogswell, n.d.), p. 27.

21. Cited in George Brown Tindall, *South Carolina Negroes 1877–1900* (Columbia: University of South Carolina Press, 1952), p. 81.

22. Barnwell County, *Clerk of Court Sessions Journal, 1857–71*.

23. September 1, 1869.

24. "Memorial from the labor convention to the Honorable Senate and House of Representatives of the State of South Carolina. November 26, 1869." Manuscript.

25. *Daily Republican*, November 30, 1869.

26. Cited in Joel Williamson, *After Slavery: The Negro in South Carolina During Reconstruction 1861–1877* (Chapel Hill: University of North Carolina Press, 1965), p. 118.

CHAPTER 5   THEIR MURDEROUS WORK

1. *Congressional Globe*, Fortieth Congress, 3d Session, December 15, 1868, p. 84.

2. Ibid., p. 81.

3. Ibid., p. 83.

4. John S. Reynolds, *Reconstruction in South Carolina* (Columbia: The State Co., 1905), p. 132.

5. *Evidence Taken by the Committee of Investigation of the Third Congressional District Under the Authority of the General Assembly of the State of South Carolina, Regular Session, 1868–69* (Columbia: John W. Denny, Printer to the State, 1870), p. 103.

6. Ibid., p. 100.

7. Ibid., p. 340.

8. *Ku Klux Conspiracy: Testimony taken by the Joint Select Committee to inquire into the condition of affairs in the late insurrectionary states* (Washington, D.C., 1872). Talbert's testimony was republished from a previous congressional document in *Ku Klux Conspiracy*, pp. 1256–60.

9. As reprinted in the *New York Times*, October 22, 1878.

10. *Journal of the House of Representatives of the General Assembly of the State of South Carolina*, Tuesday, December 1, 1868, p. 46.

11. *Journal of the Senate of the General Assembly of the State of South Carolina*, Tuesday, March 16, 1869, p. 477.

12. C. Irvine Walker, "Carolina Rifle Club" (1869). Copy at the Charleston Library Society, Charleston, S.C.

13. Letterbook of the Adjutant and Inspector General, 1869–70 (South Carolina Archives, Columbia, S.C.).

14. Ibid.

15. Ibid.

16. Otis Singletary, *Negro Militia and Reconstruction* (1957; reprint, New York: McGraw-Hill, 1963), p. 35.

17. *Report of the Joint Investigating Committee on Public Frauds and Election of Hon. J. J. Patterson to the United States Senate made to the General Assembly of S. Carolina at the Regular Session, 1877–78* (Columbia: Calvo & Patton, State Printers, 1878), p. 703.

18. Robert B. Elliott to Governor Robert L. Scott, April 1, 1870. Robert L. Scott Papers, Box 44.

19. *Report on Public Frauds*, p. 727.

20. October 26, 1869.

21. As recorded in Aiken County and Richland County Deed Books.

22. *Report on Public Frauds*, p. 730.

23. Ibid., p. 733.

24. Ibid., p. 735.

25. Ibid., p. 677.

26. Letterbook of the Adjutant and Inspector General, 1869–70 (South Carolina Archives, Columbia, S.C.). N.B. Letters in this book are nineteenth-century equivalents of carbon copies and in many instances, including this one, were imperfect impressions. Often the original letters were found in the appropriate governor's letterboxes on file in the State Archives. In the case of this particular letter, no original was found in Governor Scott's file for obvious reasons.

27. *Report on Public Frauds*, p. 589.

CHAPTER 6   REPUBLICANISM FIRST, FOREMOST, AND ALWAYS

1. *A Review of the Resolution of the Press Conference, 1870*, Printed at Charleston, S.C. (1870). Copy at the Charleston Library Society.

2. *Charleston Daily Republican*, April 29, 1870.

3. Ibid., June 8, 1870.

4. Ibid., June 9, 1870.

5. Ibid., June 24, 1870.

6. Ibid., June 9, 1870.

7. *Sumter Watchman*, March 4, 1870, as cited in R. H. Woody "The South Carolina Election of 1870," *North Carolina Historical Review*, April 1931, p. 171.

8. June 15, 1870.

9. *Charleston Daily Courier*, June 18, 1870; author's emphasis.
10. Ibid., June 23, 1870.
11. Ibid., June 18, 1870.
12. Ibid.
13. Ibid.
14. Quoted in the *Charleston Daily Courier*, June 24, 1870.
15. Ibid.
16. Ibid., June 17, 1870.
17. *Charleston Daily Republican*, June 24, 1870.
18. Ibid.
19. Ibid.
20. Ibid., June 30, 1870.
21. *Charleston Daily Courier*, July 30, 1870.
22. February 6, 1869.
23. *Charleston Daily Courier*, August 18, 1870.
24. *Charleston Daily Republican*, August 19, 1870.
25. August 25, 1870.
26. *Charleston Daily Republican*, August 16, 1870; *Charleston Daily Courier*, August 17, 1870.
27. *Charleston Daily Republican*, August 16, 1870.
28. Ibid.
29. Woody, "Election of 1870," pp. 168–86.
30. *Address before the Grand Council of the Union Leagues at their Annual Meeting, July 27, 1870* (Columbia: J. W. Denny, 1870). Copy in Harvard College Library.
31. *Ku Klux Conspiracy: Testimony taken by the Joint Select Committee to inquire into the condition of affairs in the late insurrectionary states* (Washington, D.C.: 1872), p. 228.
32. "Election of 1870," p. 182.
33. November 5, 1870, as cited in Woody, *"Election of 1870,"* pp. 184–85.
34. *Columbia Daily Union*, July 15, 1874.

CHAPTER 7   IN THE CONGRESS OF THE UNITED STATES

1. February 17, 1871.
2. *New York World*, February 10, 1872, cited in James H. Whyte, *The Uncivil War: Washington During the Reconstruction, 1865–1878* (New York: Twayne Publishers, 1958).
3. *New National Era*, December 7, 1871.
4. *Congressional Record*, Forty-third Congress, 1st Session, p. 565.
5. From speech given February 19, 1874 at a reception in his honor as reported in the Columbia *Daily Union*, February 23, 1874.
6. *Congressional Globe*, Forty-second Congress, 1st Session, March 14, 1871.
7. March 16, 1871.
8. March 21, 1871.

9. Ibid.

10. *Ku Klux Conspiracy: Testimony taken by the Joint Select Committee to Inquire into the Condition of Affairs in the Late Insurrectionary States, South Carolina, 1872*, pp. 74–75.

11. Quoted in John S. Reynolds, *Reconstruction in South Carolina* (Columbia: The State Co., 1905), pp. 185–86.

12. *Congressional Globe*, Forty-second Congress, 1st Session, March 28, 1871.

13. Ibid., April 1, 1871.

14. *New York Tribune*, April 3, 1871.

15. *Congressional Globe*, Forty-second Congress, 1st Session, April 1, 1871.

16. Reynolds, pp. 199–200.

17. This letter served as Elliott's will which was probated in the Civil District Court, Parish of Orleans, State of Louisiana, September 5, 1884.

CHAPTER 8   HIGH CRIMES AND MISDEMEANORS

1. Cited in Hamlin Garland, *Ulysses S. Grant, His Life and Character* (New York: Macmillan, 1920), p. 412.

2. James Ford Rhodes, *History of the United States 1850–1909*, vol. 7, *1872–1877* (New York: Macmillan, 1928), p. 72.

3. Poland Committee report as cited in Rhodes, p. 75.

4. *Congressional Globe*, Forty-second Congress, 3rd Session, February 27, 1873.

5. Rhodes, p. 75.

6. John A. Leland, *Voice from South Carolina: Twelve chapters before Hampton. Two chapters after Hampton. With a journal of a reputed Ku-Klux* (Charleston: Walker, Evans & Cogswell, 1879), p. 185.

7. P. 704.

8. The material on the Blue Ridge Railroad stems mainly from Francis B. Simkins and Robert H. Woody, *South Carolina During Reconstruction* (Chapel Hill: University of North Carolina Press, 1932), pp. 208–22.

9. *Report of the Joint Investigation Committee on Public Frauds and Election of Hon. J. J. Patterson to the United States Senate made to the General Assembly of S. Carolina at the Regular Session, 1877–78* (Columbia: Calvo & Patton, State Printers, 1878), p. 643.

10. *Charleston News and Courier*, September 22, 1874.

11. Ibid., September 25, 1874.

12. John S. Reynolds, *Reconstruction in South Carolina* (Columbia: The State Co., 1905), p. 470; *Report on Public Frauds*, p. 583.

13. Reynolds, p. 471.

14. *Report on Public Frauds*, pp. 587–90.

15. Ibid., p. 590.

16. *New National Era*, April 25, 1872.

17. Ibid.; author's emphasis.

18. R. B. Elliott, *Oration Delivered at the Celebration of the Tenth Anniversary of Emancipation in the District of Columbia* (Washington, D.C.: H. Polkinhorn, 1872). (A copy of this pamphlet signed "With the compliments of Robert B. Elliott," was presented to the Harvard College Library by the Honorable Charles Sumner of Boston and of the Harvard Class of 1830, on August 13, 1872.)

19. David Donald, *Charles Sumner and the Rights of Man* (New York: Alfred A. Knopf, 1970), p. 527.

20. Ibid., p. 549.

21. Quoted in Donald, p. 552.

22. *New York Times,* June 6, 1872.

23. By permission of The Henry E. Huntington Library, San Marino, California.

CHAPTER 9   THE ALMIGHTY DOLLAR

1. *Charleston Daily News,* August 23, 1872.

2. John S. Reynolds, *Reconstruction in South Carolina* (Columbia: The State Co., 1905), p. 465.

3. *Charleston Daily News,* August 21, 1872.

4. Ibid.

5. Ibid., August 22, 1872.

6. Ibid., August 23, 1872.

7. Ibid.

8. Ibid., August 24, 1872.

9. Ibid.

10. August 24, 1872.

11. *Charleston Daily News,* August 24, 1872.

12. Ibid.

13. October 14, 1872.

14. Reynolds, *Reconstruction in South Carolina,* p. 226.

15. *Report of the Joint Investigating Committee on Public Frauds and Election of Hon. J. J. Patterson to the United States Senate made to the General Assembly of S. Carolina at the Regular Session, 1877– 78* (Columbia: Calvo & Patton, State Printers, 1878), p. 911.

16. Ibid., p. 917.

17. Ibid., p. 906.

18. Ibid., pp. 914–15.

19. Ibid., p. 908.

20. Governor Moses's Papers, South Carolina Archives.

21. *Report on Public Frauds,* p. 935.

22. Ibid., p. 937.

23. *Columbia Daily Union Herald,* December 10, 1872.

24. *Charleston Daily Courier,* December 12, 1872.

25. December 11, 1872.

26. Deed Book A, #178, Aiken County Courthouse Records.

27. *Washington Star,* March 4, 1873.

28. Mary Logan, *Reminiscences of the Civil War and Reconstruction*, edited by George Worthington Adams (Carbondale: Southern Illinois University Press, 1970), pp. 243–44.
29. James Morris Morgan, *Recollections of a Rebel Reefer* (Boston and New York: Houghton Mifflin, 1917), p. 331.

CHAPTER 10   A NATURAL GIFT FOR ORATORY

1. As quoted in David Donald, *Charles Sumner and the Rights of Man* (New York: Alfred A. Knopf, 1970), p. 580.
2. As quoted in the *New National Era and Citizen*, January 22, 1874.
3. As quoted in *Columbia Daily Union Herald*, February 23, 1874.
4. As quoted in *New National Era and Citizen*, January 22, 1874.
5. *Congressional Record*, Forty-third Congress, 1st Session, January 5, 1874.
6. Ibid., January 6, 1874.
7. Ibid., January 5, 1874.
8. Ibid., December 19, 1873.
9. Ibid., January 6, 1874.
10. Ibid., December 19, 1873.
11. Ibid., January 6, 1874.
12. Ibid., January 5, 1874.
13. Ibid., January 6, 1874.
14. *National Republican*, April 16, 1874.
15. *Congressional Record*, Forty-third Congress, 1st Session, January 7, 1874.
16. January 8, 1874.
17. As quoted in *New National Era and Citizen*, January 8, 1874.
18. January 10, 1874.
19. January 7, 8, 1874.
20. *Columbia Daily Union Herald*, February 17, 1874.
21. February 16, 1874.
22. From undated Broadside, South Caroliniana Library, also reprinted in part in *News and Courier*, February 18, 1874.
23. February 18, 1874.
24. February 21, 1874.
25. February 20, 1874.
26. *Columbia Daily Union Herald*, February 23, 1874.
27. February 21, 1874.
28. *Columbia Daily Union Herald*, February 21, 1874.
29. *Charleston News and Courier*, March 30, 1874.
30. March 28, 1874.
31. Quoted in Donald, *Charles Sumner and the Rights of Man*, p. 586.
32. R. B. Elliott, *Oration delivered in Faneuil Hall, April 14, 1874,*

under the auspices of the Colored Citizens of Boston (Boston: Published for the Committee of Arrangements by Charles L. Mitchell, 1874). (Copy in the Massachusetts Historical Society, Boston.)

33. April 15, 1874.

34. Frederick Douglass to Hon. R. B. Elliott, April 15, 1874, Frederick Douglass Papers, Library of Congress.

35. September 22, 1874.

CHAPTER 11   SEEDS OF DISCORD

1. As cited in R. H. Woody, "Franklin J. Moses, Jr., Scalawag Governor of South Carolina, 1872–74," *The North Carolina Historical Review*, April 1933, p. 123.

2. May 20, 1874.

3. May 21, 1874.

4. *Daily Republican*, June 24, 1870.

5. May 30, 1874.

6. *Columbia Daily Union Herald*, June 23, 1874.

7. Ibid., July 31, 1874; included the quote from the *New York Times*.

8. *Charleston News and Courier*, September 9, 1874.

9. *Columbia Daily Union Herald*, September 9, 1874.

10. November 25, 1874.

11. Woodruff manuscript, March 10, 1874. The manuscript of the Woodruff diary was found in the basement of the statehouse at Columbia by R. H. Woody who published two segments of it in the *Journal of Southern History* (February 1936, pp. 78–102, and May 1936, pp. 233–59). The entire manuscript is now in the state archives at Columbia. Entries quoted from the published Woody segments are so indicated. Others come from the original manuscript.

12. Cited by Woody, *Journal of Southern History*, February 1936, p. 93.

13. Woodruff manuscript, April 21, 1874.

14. Ibid., November 30, 1874.

15. Ibid., December 5, 1874.

16. Ibid., July 17, 1874.

17. Ibid., May 20, 1874.

18. Ibid., November 5, 1874.

19. Cited by Woody, *Journal of Southern History*, February 1936, p. 98.

20. Ibid.

21. Quoted in the *Columbia Daily Union Herald*, December 13, 1874.

CHAPTER 12 BLACK THURSDAY

1. Daniel Chamberlain to Editors, *News and Courier*, Francis W. Dawson Papers, Duke University, July 31, 1874.

2. Daniel Chamberlain to Francis W. Dawson, Dawson Papers, February 18, 1875.

3. February 20, 1875.

4. D. H. Chamberlain to F. W. Dawson, Dawson Papers, May 7, 1875.

5. Ibid., June 24, 1875.

6. Ibid., May 11, 1875.

7. *Columbia Daily Union Herald*, March 19, 1875.

8. *Charleston News and Courier*, March 29, 1875.

9. Ibid., December 20, 1875.

10. Ibid.

11. Ibid., December 18, 1875.

12. Quoted in Walter Allen, *Governor Chamberlain's Administration in South Carolina: A Chapter of Reconstruction in the Southern States* (New York and London: G. P. Putnam, 1888), p. 221.

13. Vernon Lane Wharton, *The Negro in Mississippi 1865–1890* (Chapel Hill: University of North Carolina Press, 1947), p. 184.

14. Ibid., p. 187.

15. February 7, 1876.

16. Quoted in Allen, *Governor Chamberlain's Administration*, p. 230.

17. *Charleston News and Courier*, April 12, 1876.

18. Quoted in Allen, *Governor Chamberlain's Administration*, p. 260.

19. *Charleston News and Courier*, April 12, 1876.

20. Ibid., April 19, 1876.

21. Ibid., April 14, 1876.

22. Ibid., May 8, 1876.

23. Ibid.

CHAPTER 13 TO LIVE AND DIE IN DIXIE

1. Quoted in Walter Allen, *Governor Chamberlain's Administration in South Carolina: A Chapter of Reconstruction in the Southern States* (New York and London: G. P. Putnam, 1888), p. 505.

2. Alfred B. Williams, *Hampton and His Red Shirts: South Carolina's Deliverance in 1876* (Charleston: Walker, Evans & Cogswell, n.d.), p. 52.

3. *Columbia Daily Union Herald*, July 29, 1876.

4. Quoted in Allen, *Governor Chamberlain's Administration*, p. 324.

5. Ibid., p. 326.
6. Francis B. Simkins, "The Election of 1876 in South Carolina," *South Atlantic Quarterly,* July 1922.
7. Williams, *Hampton and His Red Shirts,* p. 139.
8. *Charleston News and Courier,* September 16, 1876.
9. Ibid.
10. Quoted in Allen, *Governor Chamberlain's Administration,* p. 505.
11. September 16, 1876.
12. Allen, *Governor Chamberlain's Administration,* p. 371.
13. Hampton M. Jarrell, *Wade Hampton and the Negro* (Columbia: University of South Carolina Press, 1949), p. 73.
14. Francis B. Simkins and Robert H. Woody, *South Carolina During Reconstruction* (Chapel Hill: University of North Carolina Press, 1932), p. 564.
15. *Charleston News and Courier,* October 20, 1876.
16. October 9, 1876.
17. *Daily Union Herald,* October 28, 1876.

CHAPTER 14   A GIANT STEP BACKWARD

1. Quoted in Walter Allen, *Governor Chamberlain's Administration in South Carolina: A Chapter of Reconstruction in the Southern States* (New York and London: G. P. Putnam, 1888), p. 431.
2. Alfred B. Williams, *Hampton and His Red Shirts: South Carolina's Deliverance in 1876* (Charleston: Walker, Evans & Cogswell, n.d.), pp. 401–2. (At the time the author was a young reporter on the *Charleston Journal of Commerce,* assigned to cover events in Columbia.)
3. Allen, *Governor Chamberlain's Administration,* p. 449.
4. Robert B. Elliott to Daniel H. Chamberlain, December 9, 1876, as quoted in Allen, *Governor Chamberlain's Administration,* p. 449–50.
5. John S. Reynolds, *Reconstruction in South Carolina* (Columbia: The State Co., 1905), p. 510.
6. W. E. B. DuBois, *Black Reconstruction in America, 1860–1880* (Cleveland: World, 1964), p. 420.
7. Allen, *Governor Chamberlain's Administration,* pp. 454–55.
8. *Charleston News and Courier,* December 27, 1876.
9. Ibid., January 1, 1877.
10. Ibid., January 30, 1877.
11. *Daily Union Herald,* March 2, 1877.
12. *Charleston News and Courier,* March 2, 1877.
13. March 2, 1877.
14. March 2, 1877.
15. *Charleston News and Courier,* March 2, 1877.

16. Cited in C. Vann Woodward, *Reunion and Reaction* (Boston: Little, Brown, 1966), p. 155.

17. *Charleston News and Courier*, April 11, 1877.

18. Allen, *Governor Chamberlain's Administration*, p. 481.

19. April 11, 1877.

20. Henry Campbell Black, *Black's Law Dictionary* (4th ed. St. Paul: West, 1957).

21. Governor Hampton's Letterbook, South Carolina Archives.

22. R. B. Elliott to Wade Hampton, April 16, 1877, Governor Hampton's Papers, South Carolina Archives.

23. Minutes of Supreme Court, April 1870 to November 1885, South Carolina Archives.

24. A handwritten transcript of the proceedings in this case is in the South Carolina Archives.

25. Legislative System, 1877, South Carolina Archives.

Chapter 15   In the Midst of His Years

1. April 14, 1877, cited in George Brown Tindall, *South Carolina Negroes, 1877–1900* (Columbia: University of South Carolina Press, 1952), p. 22.

2. Quoted in Stanley P. Hirshson, *Farewell to the Bloody Shirt: Northern Republicans and the Southern Negro, 1877–1893* (Bloomington: Indiana University Press, 1962), p. 92.

3. National Archives, Record Group 56, Vol. A13.

4. National Archives, Record Group (N.A.R.G.) 36, Box 225, Bureau of Customs, Special Agents' Reports and Communications, 1865–1915.

5. Robert Elliott to John Sherman, November 21, 1879. John Sherman Papers, Box 190, Library of Congress, Manuscript Division.

6. Hirshson, *Farewell to the Bloody Shirt*, pp. 58–60.

7. May 30, 1880.

8. *New York Times*, June 6, 1880.

9. R. B. Elliott to John Sherman, July 2, 1880, N.A.R.G. 36, Box 225.

10. R. B. Elliott to H. F. French [Assistant Secretary of the Treasury], April 18, 1881, N.A.R.G. 36, Box 225.

11. *New York Times*, February 15, 1881.

12. R. B. Elliott to A. K. Tingle, May 26, 1881, N.A.R.G. 36, Box 225.

13. Edward P. Mitchell, *Memoirs of an Editor*, (1924), pp. 324–27.

14. Daniel H. Chamberlain, "Reconstruction in South Carolina," *Atlantic Monthly*, April 1901, reprinted in Richard N. Current, ed. *Reconstruction in Retrospect* (Baton Rouge: Louisiana State University Press, 1969), p. 77.

15. Daniel H. Chamberlain, "The Race Problem at the South," *The New Englander and Yale Review*, June 1890, pp. 507–8.

16. Ibid., pp. 512–13.

17. Current, *Reconstruction in Retrospect*, pp. 93–94.

18. R. B. Elliott to A. K. Tingle, May 31, 1881, N.A.R.G. 36, Box 225.

19. R. B. Elliott to L. G. Morton, April 29, 1882, N.A.R.G. 36, Box 225.

20. *New Orleans Times-Democrat*, April 10, 1884.

21. August 11, 1884.

22. August 13, 1884.

23. Frederick Douglass Papers, Library of Congress. Douglass wrote two versions of this letter, substantially alike except that the second version is somewhat shorter.

24. R. B. Elliott, *Oration Delivered at the Celebration of the Tenth Anniversary of Emancipation in the District of Columbia* (Washington, D.C.: H. Polkinhorn, 1872).

Index

319